FORMULA ONE
THE CIRCUITS
THEN AND NOW

Frank Hopkinson

FORMULA ONE
THE CIRCUITS
THEN AND NOW

Contents

6	Introduction
	Circuits
10	Aintree
16	Anderstorp Raceway
20	Circuit of the Americas, Austin
28	AVUS
36	Brands Hatch
42	Circuit de Charade
48	Dijon-Prenois
54	Donington Park
60	Goodwood Circuit
64	Hockenheimring
72	Circuit Enzo e Dino Ferrari, Imola
80	Indianapolis Motor Speedway
84	Autódromo José Carlos Pace, Interlagos
90	Circuito di Madrid, Jarama
96	Caesars Palace, Las Vegas
102	Long Beach
106	Autódromo Hermanos Rodríguez, Mexico City
112	Circuit de Monaco
132	Montjuïc Park, Barcelona
138	Circuit Gilles Villeneuve, Montréal
144	Autodromo Nazionale, Monza
156	Norisring
158	Nürburgring
166	Red Bull Ring
172	Circuit de Pau-Ville
176	Circuit Paul Ricard
180	Circuito di Pescara
186	Reims-Gueux
194	Rouen-les-Essarts
200	Silverstone
210	Circuit de Spa-Francorchamps
220	Suzuka International Race Course
226	Watkins Glen International
232	Circuit Zandvoort
238	Index
240	Picture Credits

Page 2 Mike Hawthorn on the grid for the 1957 French GP at Rouen.
Left Tony Brooks in a Ferrari D246 takes Massenet at Monaco in 1959.

Introduction

T he first Formula 1 World Championship began in 1950 at the former bomber training base RAF Silverstone. It was an airfield circuit still owned by the Ministry of Defence and even though petrol was rationed, there were enough spectators keen to spend their coupons to get to Northamptonshire to make the event a success.

Grand Prix racing with motor cars was a lot older. From the moment the Benz Patent-Motorwagen hit the streets in 1885 there had been a myriad of different competitions, most notably the Gordon Bennett Cup (1900 to 1905) and in south-western France the first motor race to claim the title 'Grand Prix'. The Grand Prix de Pau of 1901 was run on a single lap over 300 kilometres using roads in the foothills of the Pyrenées. It was won by Franco-British aviator, Maurice Farman, who would go on to build the Goliath, long-distance passenger plane.

France was an early adopter and innovator in motor manufacturing at the turn of the twentieth century, so it was no surprise that it was a French car that won the first national race, the French Grand Prix of 1906. The Automobile Club de France closed public roads outside the city of Le Mans for a 103-kilometre circuit, raced over six laps on Saturday and six on the Sunday. Ferenc Szisz and his riding mechanic came home first in a Renault and boosted national sales of the marque.

Full-throttle international racing began in Europe after World War I with the establishment of Monza in 1922, Spa-Francorchamps in 1925, the Nürburgring in 1926, Monaco in 1929

and Reims in 1932. All five circuits would host races in the first two years of the nascent Formula 1, while both Monza and the Nürburgring were intended as test facilities to help their national motor industries.

It is only Reims-Gueux that no longer hosts motorsport in any form, but the pit garages, grandstands and race control buildings have been preserved in close to their original form, a remarkable preservation act by les Amis du Circuit de Gueux. The doyen of British motorsport writers, Nigel Roebuck, has lamented that no other sport treats its heritage with such disregard but the buildings at Reims are a striking example of what can be done. The reverse is true of a French circuit 250 kilometres to the west.

The final grand prix run at Rouen-les-Essarts took place in 1968, a first victory for 22-year-old Ferrari driver Jacky Ickx, although the race was most remembered for a shocking accident that claimed the life of French driver Jo Schlesser. Racing continued in the junior formulae until the early 1990s at Rouen until its final closure in 1994. Then, in 1999, disregarding the example of the Reims enthusiasts, the local authorities demolished every race building.

However, those armed with vintage photos of the grands prix can still find the odd small feature that has survived from the races of the 1950s. While the banked terraces on the hillside above the hairpin Virage du Nouveau Monde have become wooded, there is still a small set of concrete steps leading into them that can be matched with vintage motorsport shots of Piers Courage, Graham Hill and Dan Gurney.

The antithesis of this is Monaco. The track that spans the two communes of La Condamine and Monte Carlo has become a museum piece that F1 visits for what is effectively a time trial on the Saturday and a parade (with a certain amount of jeopardy) on the Sunday. This was ably demonstrated back in 2018 when Daniel Ricciardo's MGU-K failed on his Red Bull on Lap 28 and despite the considerable loss of power, and only six out of eight gears functioning, he managed to keep the lead for 50 laps to the chequered flag.

Monaco may be an anachronism, but it's also a fantastic example of how safety in F1 has evolved from its earliest days, when photographers loitered at the side of an open track. In the 1950s and early 1960s, the run from the chicane exit along the harbour front to Tabac had no barrier between the racing line and the water, only the occasional mooring bollard. Today there is Armco and catchfencing and cushioning Tecpro

Opposite **Juan Manuel Fangio takes a corner in his Ferrari-Lancia D50 on his way to victory at the non-championship Syracuse Grand Prix in 1956. The Syracuse event was a pre-season F1 race which was held 16 times between 1951 and 1967. Run partly on local roads in Sicily, very little of the circuit is left today.**

Above **The magnificent pre-war pit and race control buildings at Reims-Gueux that were saved by the local commune and a determined band of enthusiasts. The original pit garages on the right stretched much further down the road, and were demolished before the preservationists were able to step in.**

Below Clay Regazzoni (11) leads Ferrari team-mate Niki Lauda into Mirabeau corner at the start of the 1974 Monaco Grand Prix. Ronnie Peterson (1) in the Lotus-Ford has dived down the inside making the most of the limited opportunities to overtake on the streets of the principality.

Opposite top right Piers Courage, driving a BRM, accelerates out of the Nouveau Monde hairpin during the 1968 French Grand Prix at Rouen-les-Essarts on his way to sixth place. Beyond the car, a set of concrete steps leads to a hillside packed full of spectators (see also page 199).

Opposite top left Although the local authorities have done their best to erase any trace of the old circuit at Rouen, the concrete steps leading into a forest remain as a small vestige of the fearsome track.

Opposite bottom Max Verstappen leads Fernando Alonso's Aston Martin into Mirabeau during the 2023 Monaco Grand Prix. It is rare to see an overtaking move into Mirabeau in a modern grand prix. No longer do fans line the railings on the approach to the corner.

barriers on the outside of Tabac. Stranded cars are immediately hoisted from the circuit under a Virtual Safety Car, and if a vehicle should catch fire – as occurred to poor Lorenzo Bandini at the Monaco Grand Prix of 1967 – the race is swiftly stopped.

Safety is the reason that many circuits have been changed over the years. The old Österreichring was a great example of a flat chat blast around some perilous corners set in the beautiful Styrian hills. The often-maligned Hermann Tilke managed to preserve some of those essential elements when he redrafted it as the A1-Ring, but the fearsome 180mph Bosch Kurve could not be preserved, while complaints from neighbouring properties meant that the new circuit was drawn well within the boundaries of the old.

Drivers' favourite Spa-Francorchamps was rescued in 1983 by John Hugenholtz who cut out the lethal Burnenville corner and the Masta kink to create a circuit less than half the size of its predecessor, but with just as many challenges. The hairpin at La Source is no different in radius from when Ascari, Moss and Fangio rounded it – only now the road signs to Malmedy and Stavelot are gone and the memorial to the Great War, which lay beyond, has been replaced by the pit lane.

Hugenholtz also had a hand in designing the original Zandvoort circuit which made a recent comeback to the F1 calendar. This time it was Tilke Engineering which adapted the post-war track. With limited space to create the run-off needed for an FIA Grade 1 circuit, corners were banked and in

the process gave drivers two racing lines to follow, something ruthlessly exploited by Fernando Alonso in the 2023 Dutch Grand Prix. Dig a little deeper into the history of Zandvoort and it turns out the main straight was intended as a German *paradestrasse*, built when victory in Europe seemed a possibility. Even more bizarre is the sight of the monumental stone grandstand at the Norisring. The circuit at which Mexican star Pedro Rodríguez lost his life, and at which Max Verstappen's comprehensive outdriving of Esteban Ocon in European F3 caused Helmut Marko to race for his signature, sits on the old Nazi parade ground at Nuremberg.

Continuing the theme, the Goodwood and Silverstone circuits are both former RAF airfields, but whereas Goodwood refused to add the chicanes needed to slow cars down and faded from the events calendar, Silverstone has become the focus of Britain's booming motorsport industry. While Goodwood has been re-opened as a historic gem, perfect for vintage racing, Silverstone boasts the impressive Wing building, a luxury hotel opposite and the new Aston Martin complex next door. In 1950 Silverstone and Reims were part of the inaugural World Championship. Silverstone demonstrates what can be done while both Goodwood and Reims gives a true glimpse of what racing was like in the past, and indeed, how far it has come.

Frank Hopkinson
July 2024

LIVERPOOL, ENGLAND

Aintree

THE FAMOUS RACECOURSE WAS A READY-MADE VENUE FOR MOTOR-RACING – UNTIL BRANDS HATCH CAME UP ON THE RAILS…

The Topham family had run the famous racecourse at Aintree since the 1840s, and after reviving the Grand National in 1946, following its World War II hiatus, Mirabel Topham looked at ways of making the most of its underused facilities. Although the Grand National was the highlight of the National Hunt season, the racecourse hosted few events the rest of the year. A visit to the Earl of March's Goodwood circuit, gave her the idea that motor racing could be a useful supplement to the race meetings.

Aintree was closer to the spectating public than bucolic Silverstone stuck out in the wilds of Northamptonshire. It also had large, permanent grandstands, and bricks-and-mortar spectator facilities and was well-versed in accommodating crowds of 100,000. The precisely measured 3-mile circuit was built in three months at a cost of £100,000 and opened in May 1954. Topham's great coup had been to persuade the organizers of the British Grand Prix to alternate the race between Aintree and Silverstone, with the Liverpool circuit taking the odd years and the British Racing Drivers' Club-owned Silverstone the even.

The initial race in 1955 was a home triumph for Stirling Moss who became the first British driver to win his home grand prix, leading home Mercedes' team-mate Juan Manuel Fangio by 0.2 seconds. Moss, forever deferential to his two-times World Champion team leader, was never sure if he had won the race on merit, or if the gentlemanly Fangio (well on the way to

Opposite The front row for Aintree's 1955 debut F1 race. Jean Behra (2) in a Maserati at left with Juan Manuel Fangio centre and Stirling Moss right, both in Mercedes W196 cars.

Above Aintree's Grand National course runs anti-clockwise, while the motor-racing circuit switched to running clockwise for its first F1 race. The grandstands of 1950s vintage have been updated and supplemented over the years and were actually closer to the motor racing action than the horse racing.

Left Mercedes drivers (left to right) Karl Kling, Juan Manuel Fangio and Stirling Moss pose with team boss Alfred Neubauer at the 1955 British Grand Prix.

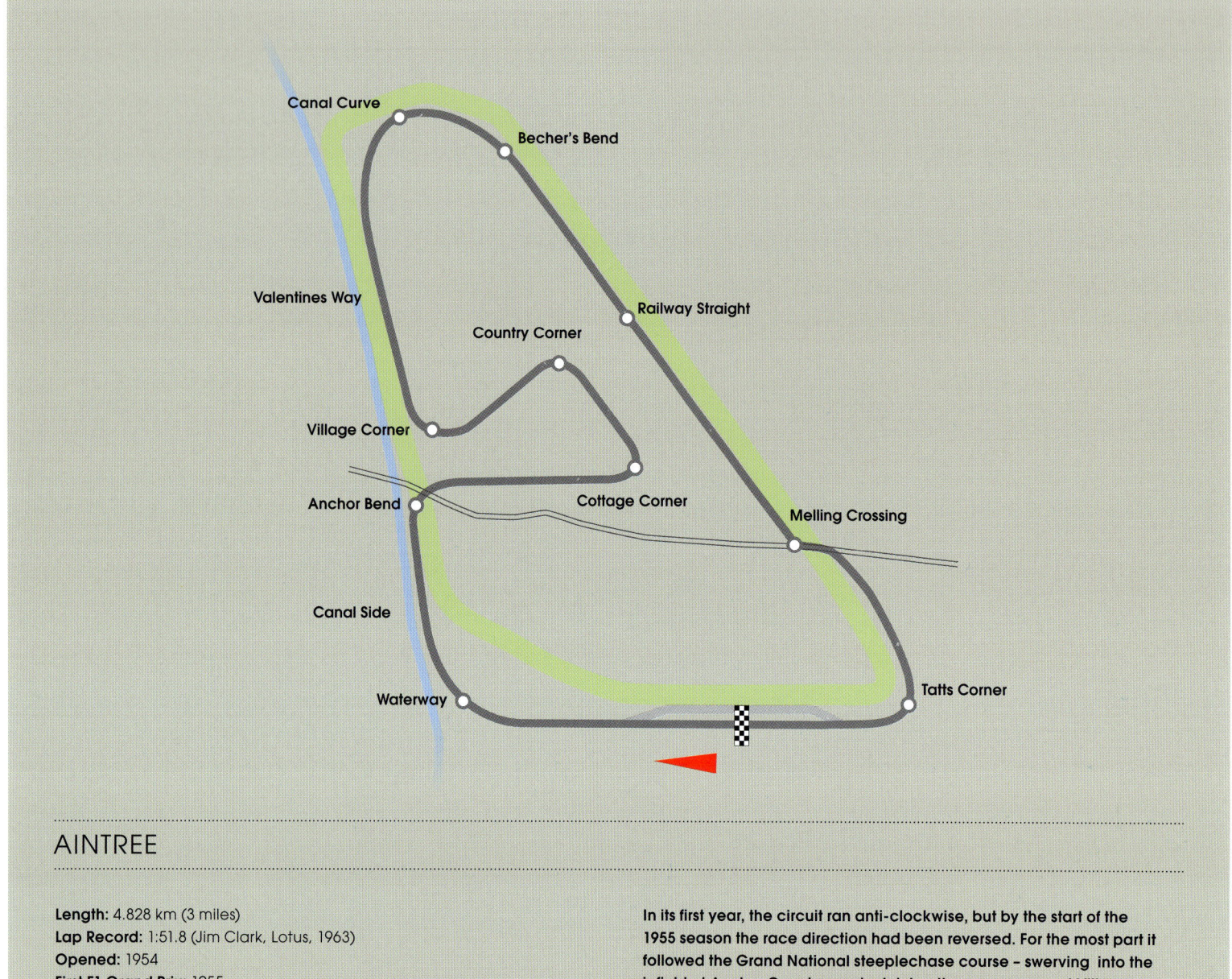

AINTREE

Length: 4.828 km (3 miles)
Lap Record: 1:51.8 (Jim Clark, Lotus, 1963)
Opened: 1954
First F1 Grand Prix: 1955
Last F1 Grand Prix: 1962
Number of F1 Grands Prix hosted: 5
Number of laps: 90
Race winning fact: The first race in 1955 provided Mercedes with a 1-2-3-4, with Stirling Moss leading home Juan Manuel Fangio, Karl Kling and Piero Taruffi

In its first year, the circuit ran anti-clockwise, but by the start of the 1955 season the race direction had been reversed. For the most part it followed the Grand National steeplechase course – swerving into the infield at Anchor Crossing and rejoining the race course at Village Corner, a detour which added four corners to the total.

his third title) had gifted him the victory. It is certain that throughout the 1955 season, the all-conquering Mercedes W196 was the class of the field and in grands prix Moss and Fangio formed what was known as 'the train' with Moss able to follow just a few feet behind his team leader. Mercedes team boss Alfred Neubauer was never too happy watching his drivers race so closely, fearful that one mistake could take out both cars, but Moss reassured him that 'Juan Manuel simply did not make mistakes'.

When Formula 1 returned in 1957, Mercedes had exited the sport and Moss achieved another landmark win. Driving for Vanwall, Stirling put his car on pole and led the race before a misfire forced him to retire. With driver swaps still eligible, the team brought in fellow Vanwall driver Tony Brooks, still suffering the effects of an accident at Le Mans, and Moss took the car. He rejoined in ninth place and took the lead with 20 laps still to run. Thus Moss and Brooks shared the honour of being the first British drivers to win a Formula 1 grand prix in a British car.

In 1959 it was the rear-engined Cooper of Jack Brabham that showed the direction of travel of F1 car design, beating Moss in a front-engined BRM; while in 1961 Ferrari demonstrated that they had overtaken the upstart English 'garagistas' with Wolfgang von Trips leading home Phil Hill and Richie Ginther, all driving the Ferrari 'shark nose' 156.

Jim Clark, in the Climax-engined Lotus 25 took victory in what proved to be the final F1 grand prix just a year later, 1962.

Left A programme for the 1959 British Grand Prix featuring the all-conquering Vanwall. In 1958 it had won the very first International Cup for Formula One Manufacturers today known as the Constructors' Trophy. However with team founder Tony Vandervell's failing health and the upsurge in competitiveness of the rear-engined Coopers, Vanwall entered only a single race in 1959, the British Grand Prix, from which Tony Brooks retired.

Above Cars head down the Sefton Straight (Aintree's land owner was Lord Sefton) heading towards the Melling Crossing kink in the International Daily Mirror Cup race of 1963.

Top Looking out across a flat expanse of racecourse, spectators not only got a purpose-built grandstand, they could see the whole course from where they sat. Here, the rain descends at the start of the 1961 grand prix with the 'shark nose' Ferraris on the right of the front row.

Above To limit damage to the course, temporary crossings were set up for race cars. Spanish nobleman and playboy Alfonso de Portago is the only driver to compete on both grass and tarmac, riding the Grand National as a gentleman jockey, before driving a sports car on the grand prix course. He was scheduled to drive for Ferrari in the 1957 British Grand Prix, but was killed competing in the Mille Miglia.

Above Race winner Wolfgang von Trips and second place Phil Hill with the indomitable Laura Ferrari at Aintree in 1961. In Michael Mann's recent film of the 1957 Mille Miglia, Ferrari, the central character of Laura Ferrari was played by Penelope Cruz.

Above Phil Hill in the Ferrari 'shark nose' 156 approaches Cottage corner in the 1961 race. The car was a convincing winner of both Formula 1 titles in 1961. It was updated for the 1963 and 1964 seasons and the shark nose dropped in favour of a conventional aero intake, before being superseded by the Ferrari 158.

Despite the far superior facilities, Aintree's lack of run-off areas in fast corners combined with concrete pillars close to the track – especially at the fast Melling Road kink – proved to be too great a hurdle. The Brands Hatch circuit in Kent would take over from 1964.

Aintree was still able to host sports car racing and the Aintree Circuit Club hosted races and sprints on the shorter club circuit until 1999. After a period of insolvency the club was able to celebrate the 50th anniversary of the grand prix track by helping to organize the 2004 Aintree Festival of Motorsport. More than 250 historically significant racing cars turned up on a bright November weekend with Sir Stirling Moss, Tony Brooks and Roy Salvadori all in attendance.

ANDERSTORP, SWEDEN

Anderstorp Raceway

WHEN THREE SWEDISH CLUB RACERS DECIDED TO BUILD A CIRCUIT OF THEIR OWN, THEY NEVER IMAGINED IT WOULD BECOME PART OF FORMULA 1 FOLKLORE

S ven 'Smokey' Asberg, a cigar permanently clamped between his teeth, was the driving force behind the Anderstorp race circuit. Sven led a group of three local racers intent on making a marshland site near their home town into a race track. His plan was to get investors to finance the scheme by combining the circuit with an airfield – the main straight would be the runway, and a daily service to Stockholm would surely be attractive to local business leaders...

Following World War II there had been many airfields that were turned into circuits, such as Silverstone, Goodwood, Snetterton and Thruxton. Anderstorp would effectively be a circuit turned into an airfield.

By 1966 Asberg had the finance he needed to begin construction. Leading Swedish F1 racer Jo Bonnier helped design the track, which made its debut under the banner of the Scandinavian Raceway in 1968, and for good measure won the opening sports car race. Apart from incorporating a runway as part of the main straight it was unusual in that the pits were half a lap away from the start/finish line. The short straight on which they were located was deemed too short a run to the first corner and so they were placed earlier in the lap.

However Asberg was not done with the project yet. Having achieved the dream of an Anderstorp race track, he wanted to go one better and bring

Opposite Vittorio Brambilla (9) in the March-Ford leads Patrick Depailler (4) in the Tyrrell-Ford at the start of the 1975 Swedish Grand Prix. They are followed by Jean-Pierre Jarier in the UOP-sponsored Shadow and the Martini Brabhams of Carlos Reutemann and Carlos Pace. Niki Lauda (12) is slow away in the Ferrari from fifth on the grid.

Below Today, the Anderstorp Raceway caters for domestic series, with the start/finish line now moved opposite the pits.

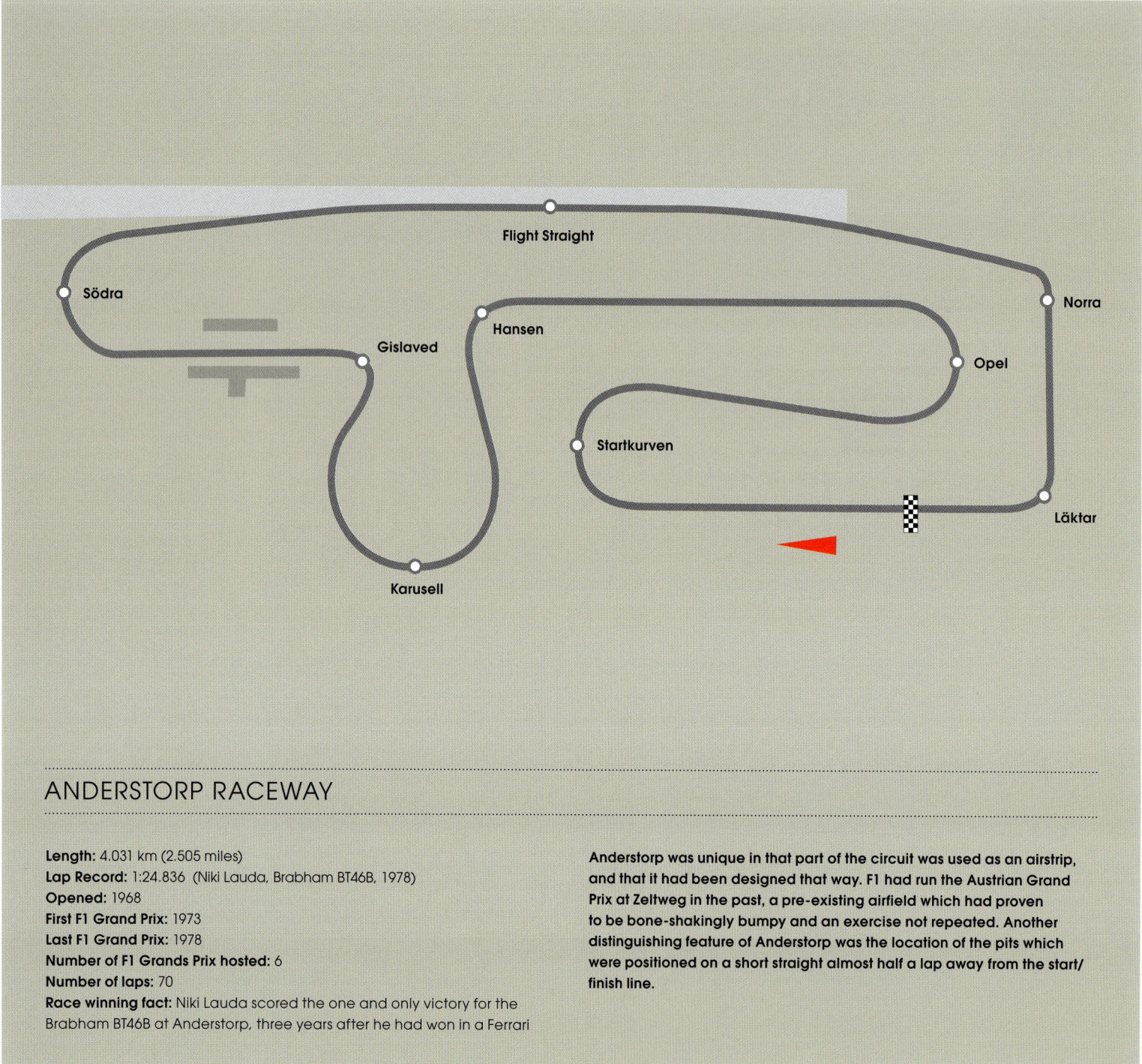

ANDERSTORP RACEWAY

Length: 4.031 km (2.505 miles)
Lap Record: 1:24.836 (Niki Lauda, Brabham BT46B, 1978)
Opened: 1968
First F1 Grand Prix: 1973
Last F1 Grand Prix: 1978
Number of F1 Grands Prix hosted: 6
Number of laps: 70
Race winning fact: Niki Lauda scored the one and only victory for the Brabham BT46B at Anderstorp, three years after he had won in a Ferrari

Anderstorp was unique in that part of the circuit was used as an airstrip, and that it had been designed that way. F1 had run the Austrian Grand Prix at Zeltweg in the past, a pre-existing airfield which had proven to be bone-shakingly bumpy and an exercise not repeated. Another distinguishing feature of Anderstorp was the location of the pits which were positioned on a short straight almost half a lap away from the start/finish line.

an F1 grand prix to Sweden. Bonnier, a constant presence on the grid through the 1960s and one of the key advisors to John Frankenheimer's *Grand Prix* film had put the country on the F1 map. As his career was coming to a close in 1971, fellow Swede Ronnie Peterson was on his way to second place for March in only his second World Championship, the timing was perfect.

Asberg duly got his debut grand prix in 1973, by which time Ronnie Peterson had switched to Lotus. The home crowd almost got the perfect result, Peterson put his car on pole and was leading the race until the closing stages when a deflating rear tyre allowed the McLaren of Denny Hulme past and he had to settle for second.

Anderstorp got the reputation for producing quirky results – in 1976 it was the venue for a Tyrrell-Ford 1-2 from Jody Scheckter and Patrick Depailler in the revolutionary (and legal) six-wheel Tyrrell P34. Two years after that, Brabham turned up with their Brabham BT46B 'fan car', the product of wily design engineer Gordon Murray. The fan was supposedly for cooling purposes, but in the era of ground effect cars it assisted downforce and helped suck the car to the track. Niki Lauda won the race at a canter while there was furore in the paddock about the legitimacy of the device.

Brabham proved to the stewards that it did indeed cool the car, but it came at a time when owner Bernie Ecclestone was courting the other privately owned teams in FOCA, the Formula One Constructors Association and preparing himself to tackle the behemoth that governed the sport. To appease his fellow team owners he withdrew the car for the next race, but the result stood.

Ronnie Peterson had scored a podium place in 1978 for what would prove to be his and the country's final grand prix. Three months later he died after medical complications from an accident at the Italian Grand Prix at Monza (an accident for which his good friend James Hunt blamed Riccardo Patrese). With fellow Swedish F1 star Gunnar Nilsson dying from cancer soon after, the 1979 Swedish Grand Prix was abruptly cancelled.

Today, what was the Scandinavian Raceway has been renamed the Anderstorp Raceway and hosts national events. There is a statue to Sven Smokey Asberg who died in 1992 – complete with cigar.

Top **Danish driver Jac Nelleman failing to qualify for the 1976 Swedish Grand Prix in a privately entered Brabham-Ford BT42. The airport was at its busiest during a grand prix weekend.**

Above left **The notorious Brabham BT46B 'fan car' which blitzed the opposition at Anderstorp in 1978 and was subsequently withdrawn by Bernie Ecclestone to placate his fellow team owners.**

Above **Home favourite Ronnie Peterson waits to go out in the Lotus 79 in what would prove to be the final Swedish Grand Prix in 1978.**

AUSTIN, TEXAS, USA

Circuit of the Americas

COTA IS ONE OF HERMANN TILKE'S BEST TRACKS, ENCOMPASSING SOME OF THE MOST THRILLING ASPECTS OF OTHER ESTABLISHED CIRCUITS

Following the unsuccessful, short-lived foray to Indianapolis, Formula 1 was keen to re-establish a grand prix in the United States. Teams and their multinational sponsors bemoaned the fact that the lucrative US market was untapped, and a lack of American Formula 1 drivers had failed to engage the large stateside motorsport audience.

So when race promoter Tavo Hellmund, aided by former World Motorcycle Champion Kevin Schwantz, conceived a purpose-built race circuit in Travis County near Austin, Texas, there was the chance to see a world-class facility emerge. Austin had already established its credentials as a party town hosting the ever-enlarging South by Southwest (SXSW) music and media festival since 1987. The city's motto is 'Keep Austin Weird'. Hellmund believed F1 could pick up on the Montréal vibe, where the city embraces the arrival of the Canadian Grand Prix each year, just across the river at Île Notre Dame.

The biggest investor in the project would be Texan billionaire Red McCombs who initially wanted to name the 900-acre site 'Speed City'. He had to make do with Circuit of the Americas, which he reasoned, '…reflects Austin's ideal location at the crossroads of North America from north to south, east to west. Also, it speaks to our state as a center of commerce and cultural exchange in this hemisphere.'

Construction work on the Hermann Tilke-designed circuit began in 2010 with a first grand prix pencilled in for 2012. Never ones to miss a promotional opportunity, Red Bull sent along

Opposite The race to finish the circuit in time for the inaugural grand prix in 2012 was almost as gripping as the race itself.

Left No-one better to drive the honorary first lap than a true American racing legend, Mario Andretti, at the wheel of his championship-winning Lotus 79 from the 1978 season. Ironically he was due to drive the Lotus-Renault R30 as well, but it wouldn't fire up.

Above The field piles up 'Phil Hill' to the first turn known as 'Big Red' in the 2022 race. Ten years after its debut the race was firmly established on the motorsport calendar.

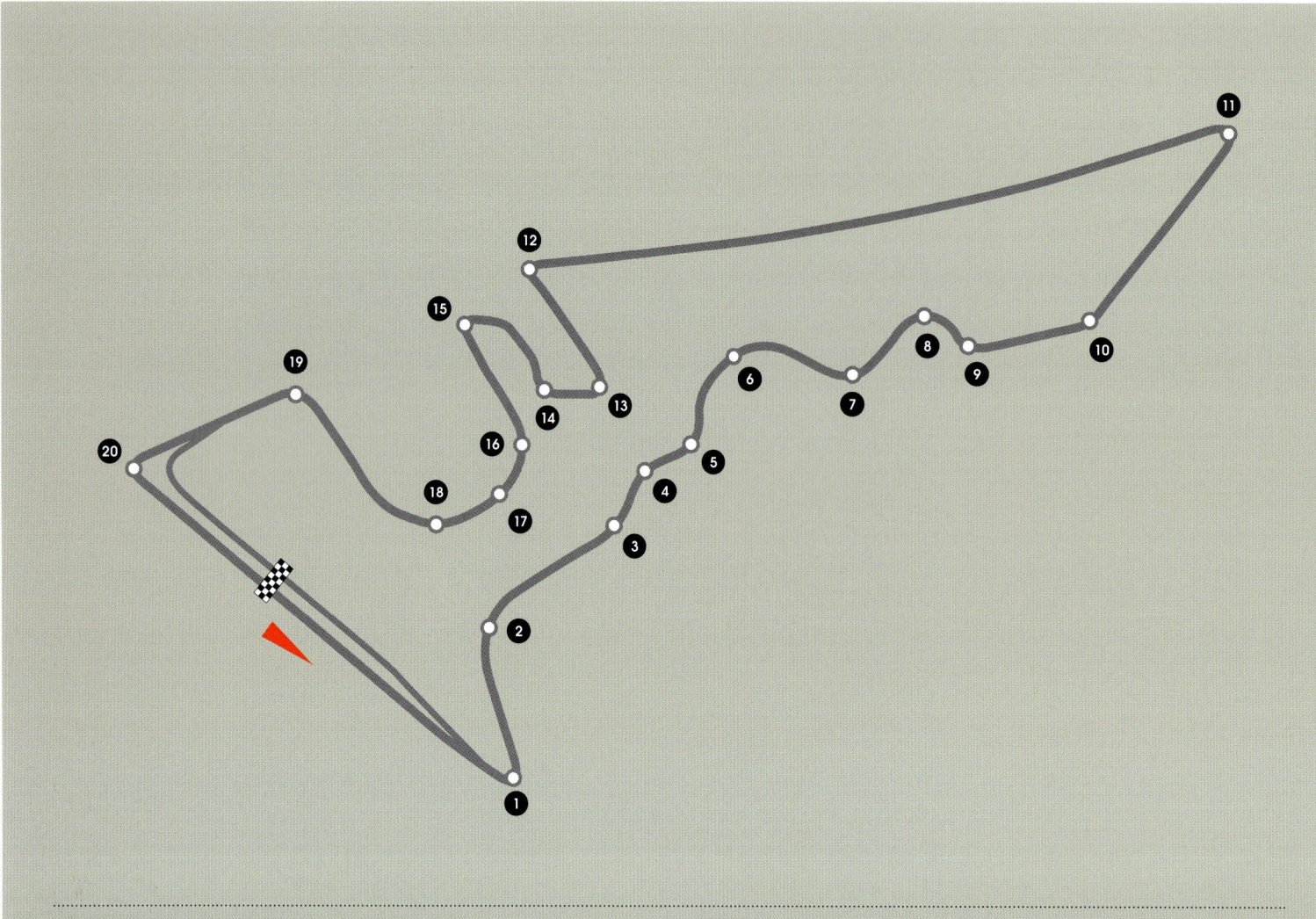

CIRCUIT OF THE AMERICAS

Length: 5.513 km (3.426 miles)
Lap Record: 1:36.169 (Charles Leclerc, Ferrari SF 90, 2019)
Opened: 2012
First F1 Grand Prix: 2012
Number of F1 Grands Prix hosted: 13
Number of laps: 56
Circuit Designers: Hermann Tilke, Tavo Hellmund and Kevin Schwantz
Race winning fact: Multiple USGP-winner Lewis Hamilton made it four wins in a row in 2017 on the way to his fourth World Championship

With 20 turns, the Circuit of the Americas was the first purpose-built track for Formula 1 in the United States. It is acknowledged as one of Hermann Tilke's best designs, aided by original promoter Tavo Hellmund and motorcycle champion Kevin Schwantz. Few changes have been needed since its 2012 debut, but in recent years there have been concerns over the bumpiness, exacerbated by F1's 2022 rule changes which introduced an element of ground effect, necessitating cars to be run lower to the ground.

David Coulthard in a heavily modified 'F1 car' – equipped with the kind of suspension Juan Manuel Fangio would have employed in his 6,000-kilometre panamericana road races – to reconnoitre the course and also throw in some donuts in downtown Austin.

Work was put on hold, though, when promoter and circuit owner fell out over supplementary funding from state and county. And Bernie Ecclestone's pursuit of a race on the New Jersey shoreline had an unsettling effect. In 2011, plans were revealed for the Grand Prix of America race entry in the 2013 F1 World Championship, run on a proposed 3.2-mile (5.2-km) Port Imperial Street Circuit through West New York and Weehawken. The race would have the Hudson River and Manhattan skyline as a spectacular backdrop. It was a serious proposal with Hermann Tilke completing a detailed circuit design. But could the US sustain two viable grands prix from a base of none?

In the end, McCombs and fellow investor Bobby Epstein bypassed Hellmund to get the 2012 grand prix done, when Ecclestone started threatening to strike it off the calendar. The race in New Jersey was dropped and F1 had its first ever purpose-built US Grand Prix track opened by the godfather of American motorsport Mario Andretti on 21 October 2012. Mario re-acquainted himself with the Lotus 79 in which he won the 1978 World Championship to complete the first official laps.

Formula 1 circuits work best with elevation changes and following a succession of what many critics considered as

Above The view from the COTA Observation Tower looking down on some of Tilke's 'borrowed' circuit elements. To the left is the stadium complex of corners inspired by Hockenheim and at top right is the high-speed Silverstone esses.

Left Four-time World Champion Sebastian Vettel executes some donuts as part of a demonstration run in downtown Austin ahead of the 2014 race. His 2011 championship-winning Red Bull RB7 points down Congress Avenue towards the Texas Capitol.

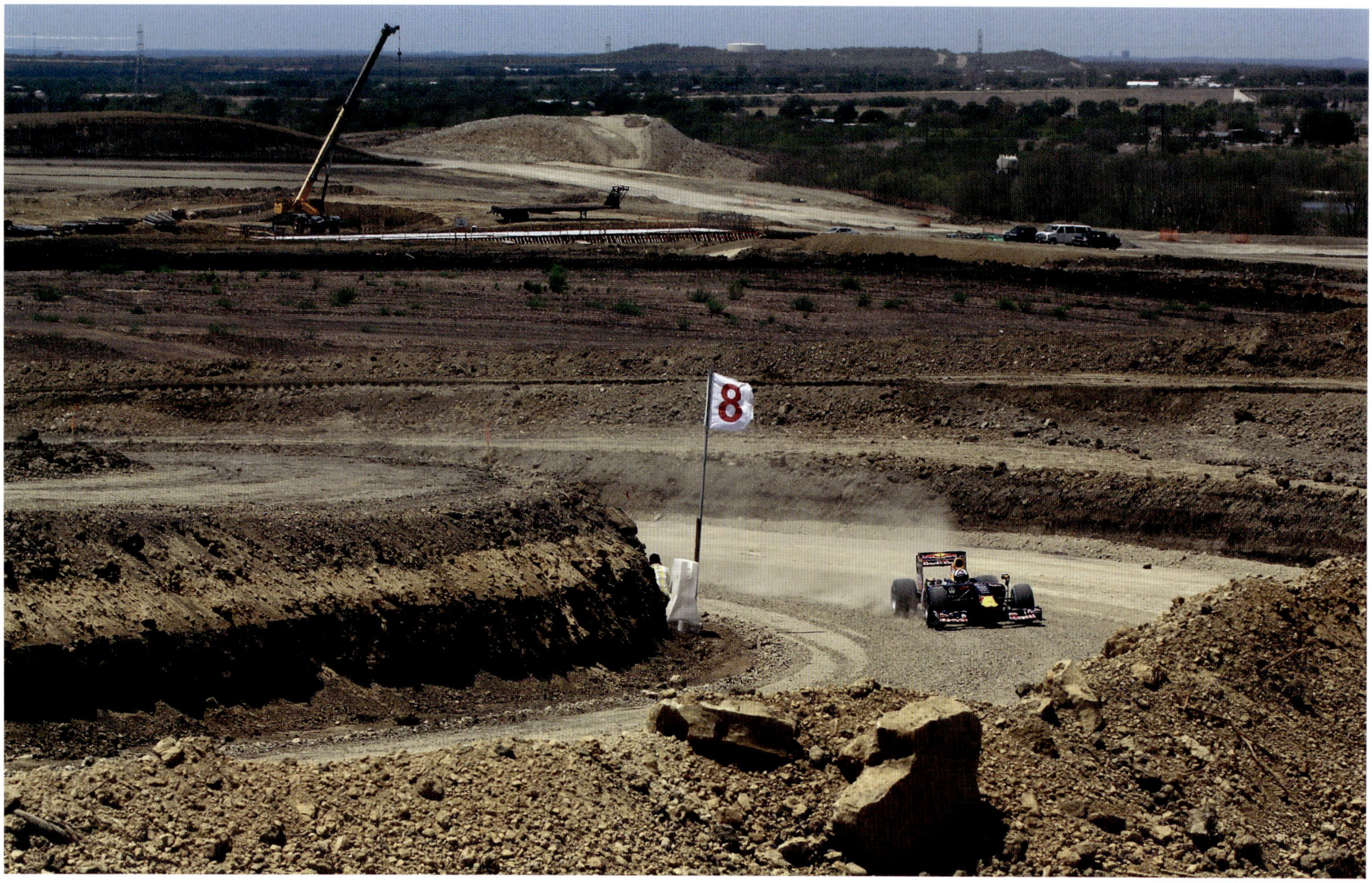
8

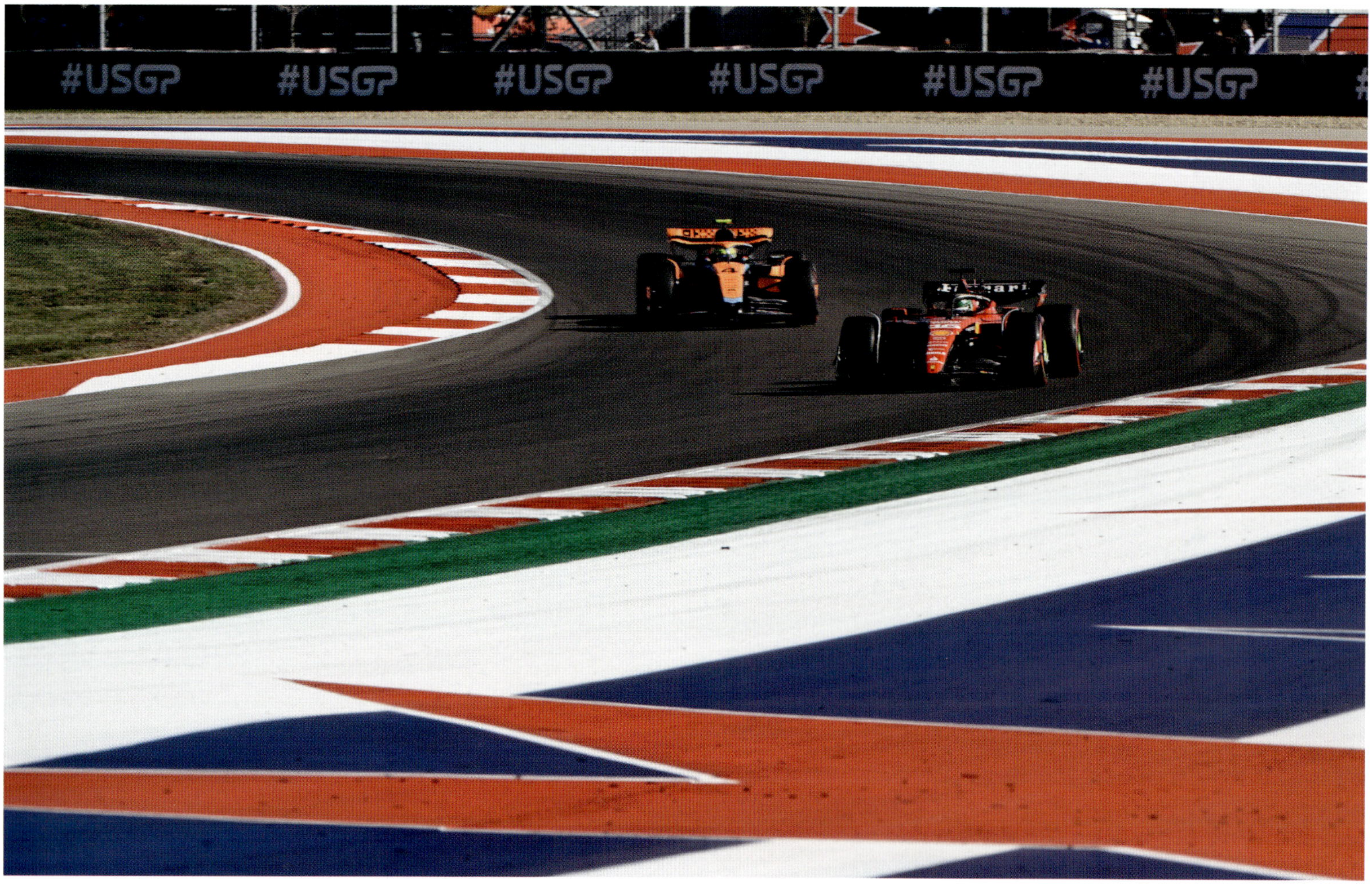
#USGP
#USGP
#USGP
#USGP
#USGP
#USGP

Opposite top David Coulthard rumbles his Red Bull demonstration car through Turn 8 of COTA during the early phase of circuit building in August 2011.

Opposite bottom Fast forward to 2023 and a great deal of earth moving later, McLaren's Lando Norris (4) pursues the Ferrari of Charles Leclerc (16).

Below Austin has been so long on the calendar that the great Michael Schumacher raced here. In 2012, his final season, racing for Mercedes, Michael steers into Turn 1. Disputing the asphalt is another former World Champion, Jenson Button, launching one up the inside in the McLaren-Mercedes on his way to fifth place.

'identikit' flat new tracks, such as Bahrain, Sepang, Shanghai and Abu Dhabi, the prospect of working with 141 feet of height change allowed COTA to establish a distinct identity. This was immediately apparent on the run to Turn 1 with cars taking on the 11% gradient of what is now nicknamed Phil Hill to the corner officially named Big Red, for the late McCombs.

Following the run uphill there was a succession of fast sweeps similar to the Maggots-Becketts sequence at Silverstone. Tilke adopted the process used in the 1991 re-design of Magny Cours which had imported corners from other established F1 circuits such as Estoril and Adelaide along with chicanes from the Nürburgring and Imola. In Austin the stadium section at Hockenheim was mimicked for the stands looking down on Turns 13, 14, 15 and 16 and Istanbul Park's challenging, multi-apex Turn 8 was replicated, though this time as a right-hander.

From an encouraging weekend attendance of 265,000 for the initial race of 2012, the numbers dipped. It was down to 224,000 three years later when Hurricane Patricia swept in with a deluge of rain, cancelling qualifying on the Saturday and forcing it into Sunday morning. Texas withdrew $5m of funding. However, a year later, bolstered by a fierce championship battle between team-mates Lewis Hamilton and Nico Rosberg, combined with good weather and the draw of a Saturday night concert from Taylor Swift, numbers recovered.

By 2021 there were 400,000 coming through the gates and with Liberty Media in charge of F1, Netflix's Drive to Survive

sustaining interest, the US demand was now robust enough to add a Miami Grand Prix with Las Vegas joining the party in 2023.

Drivers are enthusiastic about the blend of corners and overtaking opportunities presented by COTA, in addition to the larger-than-life Texan attitude to putting on a grand prix. However the 2022 technical regulations have brought problems. The reduction in ride height to create ground effect cars has emphasized how bumpy the asphalt has become.

'At the moment it feels like it's better suited to a rally car,' said race-winner Verstappen of the COTA surface. 'Like, I'm jumping and bouncing around. In an F1 car, you probably don't even see it as much because of course we are glued to the ground because of the downforce. I love this track, honestly, the layout is amazing, but we definitely need new tarmac.'

More scrutiny was placed on the track surface after Lewis Hamilton and Charles Leclerc were disqualified from the 2023 race. They had finished second and sixth respectively, but post-race checks discovered both cars had excessive wear to the rear skids which were outside F1 regulations, something that occurred after banging repeatedly against the track. That is not to take anything away from a circuit that feels to everyone like the first proper home of the USGP since Watkins Glen. And steered by the entrepreneurial instincts of promoter Bobby Epstein, the race is in good hands.

Opposite top **Looking down the hill to the start/finish straight, three months before the first scheduled race. Contractors worked around the clock to complete the Circuit of the Americas in time. The opening sprint uphill is unique in F1 as cars tackle a 113-foot (34.4 metre) rise.**

Opposite left **Lewis Hamilton celebrates winning the initial grand prix at Austin in 2012. He led home from Vettel, Alonso, Massa, Button and Räikkönen – five World Champions in the top six.**

Opposite right **Three iconic elements of a race in Austin – the Observation Tower, the state flag and multiple US Grand Prix winner Lewis Hamilton.**

Above **Only four years later and already COTA has proven to be a driver favourite. Cars line up before the parade lap in 2016 with the Mercedes of Hamilton and Rosberg on the front row ahead of the Red Bulls of Ricciardo and Verstappen.**

27

BERLIN, GERMANY

AVUS

TESTING GERMAN ENGINEERING TO THE LIMIT, AVUS POSED A TERRIFYING CHALLENGE WITH THE FEARSOME NORTH CURVE

AVUS stands for Automobil Verkehrs und ÜbungsStrasse, which translates to 'Automobile Traffic and Training Road'. Consisting of two parallel straights, each approximately 9.65 kilometres (6 miles) in length with two sweeping 180-degree curves at each end, AVUS was devised as a test track for the burgeoning German motor industry and opened in 1921.

The inaugural German Grand Prix was first held by the Automobilclub von Deutschland in July 1926 and the winner would prove to be one of the stand-out German motor-racing stars of the 1930s. The date of the GP coincided with a race in Spain, and the emergent Mercedes-Benz team, with one eye on export sales, chose to race their cars in San Sebastián not AVUS.

Rudolph Caracciola's parents had emigrated from Naples to Remagen near Bonn in the nineteenth century, and the young first-generation German was making a name for himself in sports car racing and hillclimbs. He was also working as a Daimler salesman in 1926 and managed to persuade the Mercedes office in Stuttgart to lend him a car for the AVUS race.

Opposite **The nearby Funkturm Radio Tower opened in 1926 and gave a panoramic view down onto the AVUS track and the flat, large-radius North Curve. By 1937 the circuit had been transformed, like much of Germany. Gone were the old entrance arches, a new art deco control tower building had been constructed next to the vertiginous 43-degree North Curve. The grandstand, or, AVUS Tribune, looks out over the start/finish line.**

Below **Today, the AVUS Tribune remains, sandwiched between carriageways; the North Curve banking has long been flattened (in 1967), the Control Tower is a hotel and the infield used as lorry parking.**

29

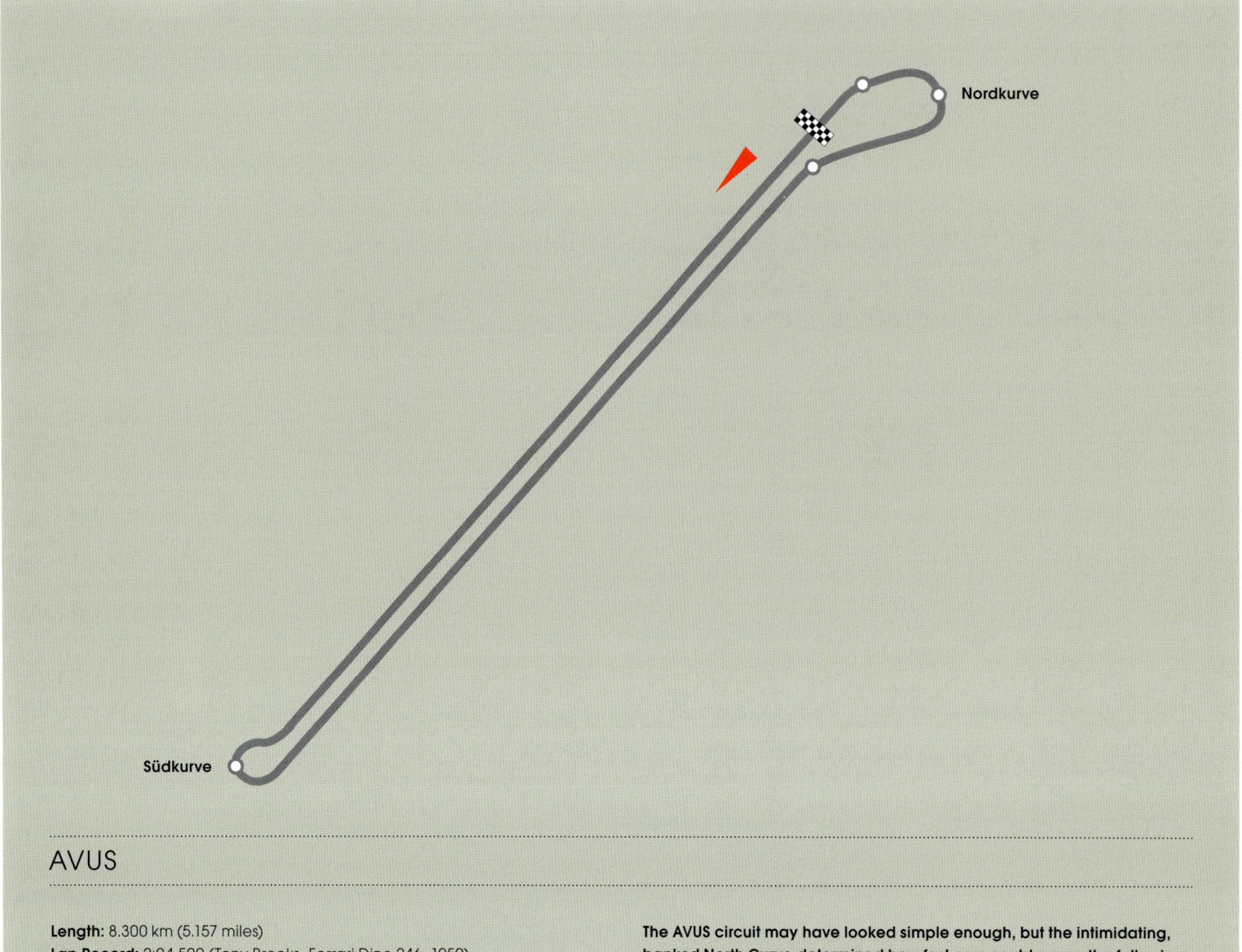

AVUS

Length: 8.300 km (5.157 miles)
Lap Record: 2:04.500 (Tony Brooks, Ferrari Dino 246, 1959)
Opened: 1921
Closed: 1998
First F1 Grand Prix: 1959
Number of F1 Grands Prix hosted: 1
Number of laps: 2 heats of 30 laps
Track Banking: 43°
Race winning fact: Tony Brooks' winning speed across the two heats was 143.3 miles per hour. A record at the time.

The AVUS circuit may have looked simple enough, but the intimidating, banked North Curve determined how fast cars could run on the following straight and the slippery brick surface needed maximum concentration. Despite the perils, in the 1959 race Masten Gregory driving for Cooper took the lead from Ferrari's Tony Brooks with an audacious pass on the banking. Jack Brabham called him 'the most fearless man I've ever known'.

On condition they entered the race as independents and not part of a works team, Mercedes agreed to lend Caracciola and Adolf Rosenberger two 1923, 2-litre 'Monza' cars. Given its proximity to Berlin, the race attracted a magnificent 230,000 spectators for a race which started disastrously for Caracciola. He stalled and his riding mechanic, Eugen Salzer, had to jump out and push-start the No.14 car. By the time they got underway they'd lost a minute to the leaders, including Rosenberger.

Conditions worsened. It started to rain. Caracciola started to pick off retiring cars and those slowing for the adverse weather. The North Curve was yet to receive its steep banking, but Rosenberger lost control there whilst overtaking a slower car, and crashed into the timekeepers' box, killing all three occupants.

Rosenberger survived the crash and would go on to co-found the Porsche company, providing the financial acumen for Ferdinand Porsche and Anton Piëch.

Caracciola was determined to finish the race despite the fog and rain, and in the absence of pitboards had no idea where he had finished when the chequered flag finally fell on lap 20. He had won. The German press were quick to baptize their new Regenmeister, or 'Rainmaster', for his skill in mastering the wet conditions, a title that Michael Schumacher would inherit in the 1990s.

A global economic depression and a world war separated the first and second grand prix run at AVUS. From 1927 the German Grand Prix was transferred to the 'safer' Nürburgring circuit in the

Left The 1937 event captured the public imagination and a staggering crowd of 380,000 cheered on the two German teams.

Below Rudolph Caracciola waits by his Mercedes-Benz 'Monza' to start the inaugural German Grand Prix in 1926. Beyond is the entrance to what was then described as the 'Automobil Strasse'.

Bottom Jo Bonnier (9) in a BRM and Tony Brooks (4) in a Ferrari lead the field at the South Curve after the start of the first heat of the 1959 German Grand Prix. Only nine cars would line up to take part in the second one-hour heat.

Right The old control tower, topped with a Nazi flag, stands at the exit of the steeply banked North Curve. This photo from 1937 shows an ERA driven by Charles Martin in the voiturette race for cars up to 1500cc

Below A view from the AVUS Tribune as a mixed field of voiturette cars – Maseratis, Talbots and ERAs – start the 1937 support race.

Above Previously used as a restaurant, office space and now a hotel, the control tower building has been preserved as a national monument.

Left Photographed in 2022, Iranian-born developer Hamid Djadda has brought the old grandstand back to life from a derelict, graffiti-covered shell. His plan is to make the reconfigured building (another listed monument) an event space.

Above Viewed from the corner of the Control Tower building, the North Curve was lined with potentially lethal flag poles should a car leave the circuit – the fate of French national hero Jean Behra.

Opposite left French driver Jean Behra (left) and the Porsche RSK, his final racing car. Driving on the brick-surfaced banking demanded the ultimate in concentration, with cars not settling down into a line and requiring constant steering input. In the wet it was doubly difficult.

Opposite right Ferrari proved to be the class of the field in the 1959 race filling the podium with (from left) Phil Hill, Dan Gurney and race winner Tony Brooks in the Dino D246. The AVUS tribune is beyond.

Eifel Mountains and AVUS hosted non-championship races.

With the rise of the Nazi party in the 1930s amid continuing success for French and Italian cars, there was political impetus to create dominant German race cars. Thus the Silver Arrows (Silberpfeile) of Mercedes-Benz and Auto-Union received major state sponsorship. For the 1936 summer Olympics, AVUS was used for the cycling road race, missing out the North Curve which was being transformed into 'the Wall of Death', a steeply banked 43° turn which would launch cars onto a scintillatingly fast following straight. Paved with brick, it was slippery when dry and even slippier when wet, with no retaining wall at the top to contain cars which veered towards the edge. For comparison, the Monza banking is 30°.

The Silver Arrows raced just once on the banked circuit, in 1937, in the 'Battle of the Streamliners' (Stromlinien). Having the status of a non-championship race, teams were allowed to run the kind of streamlined aerodynamic farings often seen in land speed attempts. Both companies practised extensively before the race, which revealed that top speeds on the main straight might reach 400km/h (248mph).

The race was divided into three seven-lap sprints with streamliners mixed in with conventional grand prix cars. In the second sprint Luigi Fagioli qualified his streamlined Auto Union Typ C with a time of 4 minutes and 8.2 seconds at an average speed of 284km/h (176mph) – just as the organizers had wished, the fastest motor racing lap in history and a mark not eclipsed till the late 1950s.

Fagioli's transmission then gave up and so only the Auto Union of Bernd Rosemeyer faced the three Mercedes drivers, Manfred von Brauchitsch, Hermann Lang and Rudi Caracciola in the final deciding sprint. Similar gearbox issues sidelined the favourite von Brauchitsch and Caracciola, so it was left to Hermann Lang to take victory for the Daimler-Benz team in his Mercedes W25 at an average speed over 258km/h (160mph).

After Auto Union star Rosemeyer was killed early in 1938 attempting a land-speed record on an autobahn, it was decided to suspend GP car racing at AVUS. A planned banked South Curve, for which a part of the Grunewald forest had been cleared, was put on hold.

In the post-war period, AVUS was halved in length, although not as many believe because the South Curve now lay in the Russian Sector of a divided Berlin, it was three kilometres inside. A non-championship Berlin Grand Prix of 1954 was dominated by Mercedes W196 drivers Karl Kling and Juan Manuel Fangio.

Finally AVUS got to host its one and only Formula 1 race with the 1959 German Grand Prix. Unusually the race was split into two parts with the winning time an aggregate of the two one-hour races. In an echo of the problems F1 would face when it raced at Indianapolis in 2003, it had been decided that tyre integrity could not be guaranteed for speeds of 242km/h (150mph) over a two-hour period, especially when combined with the hammering tyres took on the brick-lined North Curve.

Tony Brooks won both heats in a Ferrari D246 but the grand prix was overshadowed by the death of French ace Jean Behra in a support race the day before. Recently dismissed from Ferrari, Behra was competing in a Porsche RSK sports car. On the treacherously wet north turn Behra lost control, his car plunging over the top of the banking. Other drivers, such as Rosenberg in the 1920s and more recently journalist Richard von Frankenberg, had walked away from similar accidents, but Behra struck one of the flagpoles that lined the track as he was flung from his car.

By this time, the AVUS asphalt was also being used as an autobahn and in 1967 the north banking was dismantled to enlarge a junction near the Funkturm Radio Tower. Racing continued with a flat north curve allowing DTM races, until all racing ceased in 1999.

WEST KINGSDOWN, KENT, ENGLAND 🇬🇧

Brands Hatch

ONLY A SHORT DISTANCE FROM LONDON, BRANDS HATCH HAD THE POTENTIAL TO BECOME THE UK'S PREMIER TRACK, IF ONLY IT HAD MORE SPACE...

Brands Hatch started off life as a country cyclists' track. Situated close to the A20 London-Dover road and only 20 miles from central London, cyclists and subsequently motor-cyclists made use of the natural bowl-shaped topography for racing on a simple kidney-shaped circuit (clearly visible in the aerial photo opposite).

After the site was used to store military vehicles in World War II, it attracted interest from 500cc racers who raised £17,000 and converted the cinder track to tarmac. They competed using the only readily available racing machinery in Britain's austere post-war years – rear-engined machines powered by motorcycle engines, of which Cooper Cars were a major manufacturer (Stirling Moss was given one at 18).

From 1950 the first races at Brands Hatch were run anti-clockwise, with Paddock Hill Bend an uphill climb. Four years later, the quarter-of-a-mile loop up Pilgrim's Rise to Druid's Hill Bend was added and the circuit switched direction, thus making Paddock Hill Bend the tricky downhill challenge it remains to this day.

In 1960 further land was developed, taking the track out into the country at what used to be known as South Bank bend but was renamed Surtees in the 1970s. The circuit turned left and headed out through Pilgrim's Drop to Hawthorn Bend, turned 90 degrees right to Westfield, turned another 90 right towards Dingle Dell corner (now renamed Sheene's) turned 90 left at Stirlings, then through to Clearways where it rejoined the old

Opposite A multiple accident at the start of the 1976 British Grand Prix culminated in the exclusion of James Hunt's McLaren for the restart. But after fierce crowd protests the title contender was allowed to start a race which he went on to win. His infringement was taking a short-cut back to the pits, and he was subsequently disqualified.

Above Nigel Mansell glances in his mirrors as he leads Williams-Honda team-mate Nelson Piquet through Paddock Hill Bend during the 1986 British Grand Prix.

Left An aerial view of Brands Hatch from 1955 showing the Druids Hill extension (left) to the original kidney-shaped circuit. The grandstand on the main straight has just been built and the much longer grand prix extension will follow in 1960.

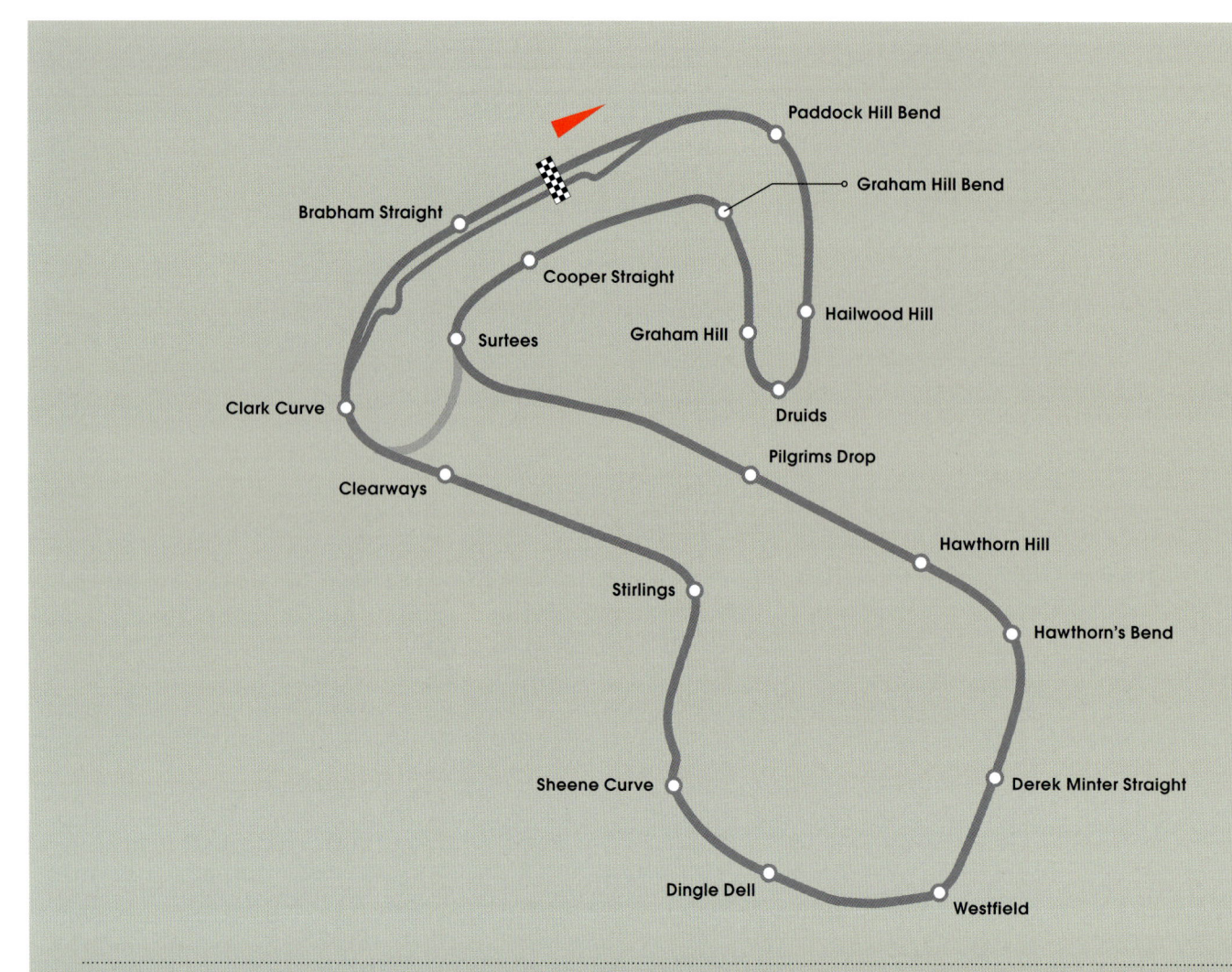

BRANDS HATCH

Length: 4.207 km (2.614 miles)
Lap Record: 1:09.593 (Nigel Mansell, Williams FW11, 1986)
Opened: 1950
First F1 Grand Prix: 1964
Last F1 Grand Prix: 1986
Number of F1 Grands Prix hosted: 14
Number of laps: 75
Race winning fact: Nigel Mansell showed his potential, winning ahead of two World Champion team-mates (Rosberg and Piquet) at Brands in the circuit's final two F1 races

Brands Hatch circuit owners made the right call when they changed the direction of running from anti-clockwise to clockwise. It introduced one of motorsport's most challenging corners, the downhill Paddock Hill Bend, scene of many racing incidents in every formula. Bernie Ecclestone bought the track with the view of re-installing the British Grand Prix in Kent, but ancient woodland and local housing put paid to any expansion plans and he reverted to putting pressure on Silverstone to improve.

---

club circuit. At 2.4 miles in length it was now long enough and testing enough to host grands prix.

The circuit's entrepreneurial Press Officer, John Webb, was made Circuit Director and aided by finance from the new circuit owners he was able to invest in the kind of facilities that made it worthy of hosting the 1964 British Grand Prix. Right on London's doorstep it took just seven weeks for all 12,400 grandstand seats to be sold out.

It was hardly surprising, given that the drivers' title that year was a fight between Brits; reigning World Champion Jim Clark for Lotus, John Surtees in a Ferrari and Graham Hill in a BRM. Clark practised in the Lotus 33 but raced and won with the Lotus 25, Hill was second and Surtees completed the podium in third place and would go on to win the 1964 championship. Today, all three have corners at Brands which bear their name.

From 1964, Brands Hatch alternated with Silverstone in hosting the British Grand Prix, holding 14 GPs in all (12 British and two European) before Silverstone won an exclusive contract to stage the race from 1987.

The circuit has provided both drama and tragedy, claiming the lives of Joe Siffert (1971) and Henry Surtees (2009), son of John Surtees, who was hit by an errant wheel in a Formula 2 race and whose needless death hastened the introduction of the Halo device in F1.

Jacques Laffite, racing for Ligier in his thirteenth season, had just equalled Graham Hill's record of 176 grand prix starts

Above Jack Brabham (5) in his Brabham BT19 lines up on pole alongside team-mate Denny Hulme (6) and Dan Gurney (16) driving an Eagle, before the start of the 1966 British Grand Prix.

Right Phil Hill exits Druids Hill bend in his Ferrari Dino 246 during the 1960 Race of Champions – a non-Championship F1 race.

at the 1986 British Grand Prix, but was involved in a multiple car accident before he even got to Paddock Hill Bend. The irrepressible Frenchman broke both legs and his pelvis in what would prove to be his final F1 race.

It also provided two successive edge-of-the-seat victories and the emergence of Nigel Mansell as a serious championship contender when he won the European Grand Prix of 1985, beating former World Champion Keke Rosberg in the same machinery, and the British Grand Prix of 1986, beating former World Champion Nelson Piquet, who was now a team-mate.

But perhaps Brands' greatest contribution to Formula 1 has been the number of future grand prix stars who have won the annual end-of-season Formula Ford Festival. The competition for entry-level single-seaters has provided the career impetus for a host of F1 drivers in the past including Derek Daly, Roberto Moreno, Jenson Button, Julian Bailey, Johnny Herbert, Eddie Irvine, Roland Ratzenberger, Jan Magnussen, Mark Webber and Anthony Davidson.

Today Brands Hatch is managed by Jonathan Palmer's Motorsport Vision company and continues to host national series, and like Dijon-Prenois, the only F1 machinery on display is likely to be historic racers.

Opposite top **Piers Courage, heir to the Courage brewing dynasty, practises in a Lotus for the 1967 Race of Champions, held in early March.**

Opposite bottom **A poster for the 1968 British Grand Prix, a race that would be won by Jo Siffert in a Lotus-Ford. Three years later the circuit would claim his life.**

Top **Romain Grosjean turns into Druids Hill bend in the Lotus E23 Hybrid during a filming day in 2015. The PDVSA sponsored team included Pastor Maldonado and reserve driver Jolyon Palmer.**

Above left **Didier Pironi in the Ferrari leads Derek Warwick in the Toleman-Hart as they head towards Surtees corner during the 1982 British Grand Prix.**

Above right **Brands Hatch still hosts historic F1 machinery, this race from the 2023 Masters Racing Legends series with cars from 1966 to 1985 in their original racing livery. Steve Hartley bunches up the pack through Clearways in his McLaren MP4/1.**

CLERMONT-FERRAND, FRANCE

Circuit de Charade

IT WAS BILLED AS FRANCE'S ANSWER TO THE NÜRBURGRING, BUT UNLIKE THE GERMAN CIRCUIT, IT RELIED HEAVILY ON LOCAL ROADS AND WAS TOO CLOSE TO ROCK WALLS

It all started with Gordon Bennett. In 1899, the owner of the *New York Herald* newspaper, James Gordon Bennett Junior offered the Automobile Club de France a trophy to be raced for annually by the automobile clubs of the USA and continental Europe.

Teams would race in national colours and late-to-the-party-Britain had to choose a different colour from its traditional colours of red, white or blue, as these had already been taken by the USA, Germany, and France respectively. British Racing Green was adopted. The winning country got to host the following year's race and so, after Léon Théry triumphed for France in 1904, a course was selected which would take in the home of Michelin tyres, Clermont-Ferrand.

The road course for the 1905 Gordon Bennett Cup stretched over a circuit of 137km mostly mountainous roads in the Auvergne. After four circuits of the course, a total of 548km, Frenchman Léon Théry was again victorious in his chain-driven 96hp Richard-Brasier (built in Ivry-sur-Seine by Henri Brasier and Georges Richard). It was the final year of the cup.

Fast forward to the early 1950s and successful French Formula 1 driver Louis Rosier wanted to celebrate the 50th anniversary of Théry's historic victory with a road race on the outskirts of Clermont-Ferrand. Backed by the Automobile Club of Auvergne and its president Jean Auchatraire the race was scheduled for 1955... until events at Le Mans cast doubt on all aspects of motor racing. On Saturday evening Henri Levegh's Mercedes was

Left French motorsport hero Louis Rosier (right) and co-driver Juan Manuel Fangio pose near their Talbot Lago car before the 1951 Le Mans race.

Below The Fédération Française du Sport Automobile (FFSA) help organize many racing series in France, including meetings at Charade. Some of this field of historic Formula Ford cars date back to a time when Circuit Louis Rosier hosted F1.

Opposite Denny Hulme in the Yardley McLaren leads Jackie Stewart's Tyrrell, but poleseitter Chris Amon, in a Matra, is long gone. The 1972 French Grand Prix was a race of attrition with ten cars sustaining punctures and a career-ending injury to Austrian racer Helmut Marko.

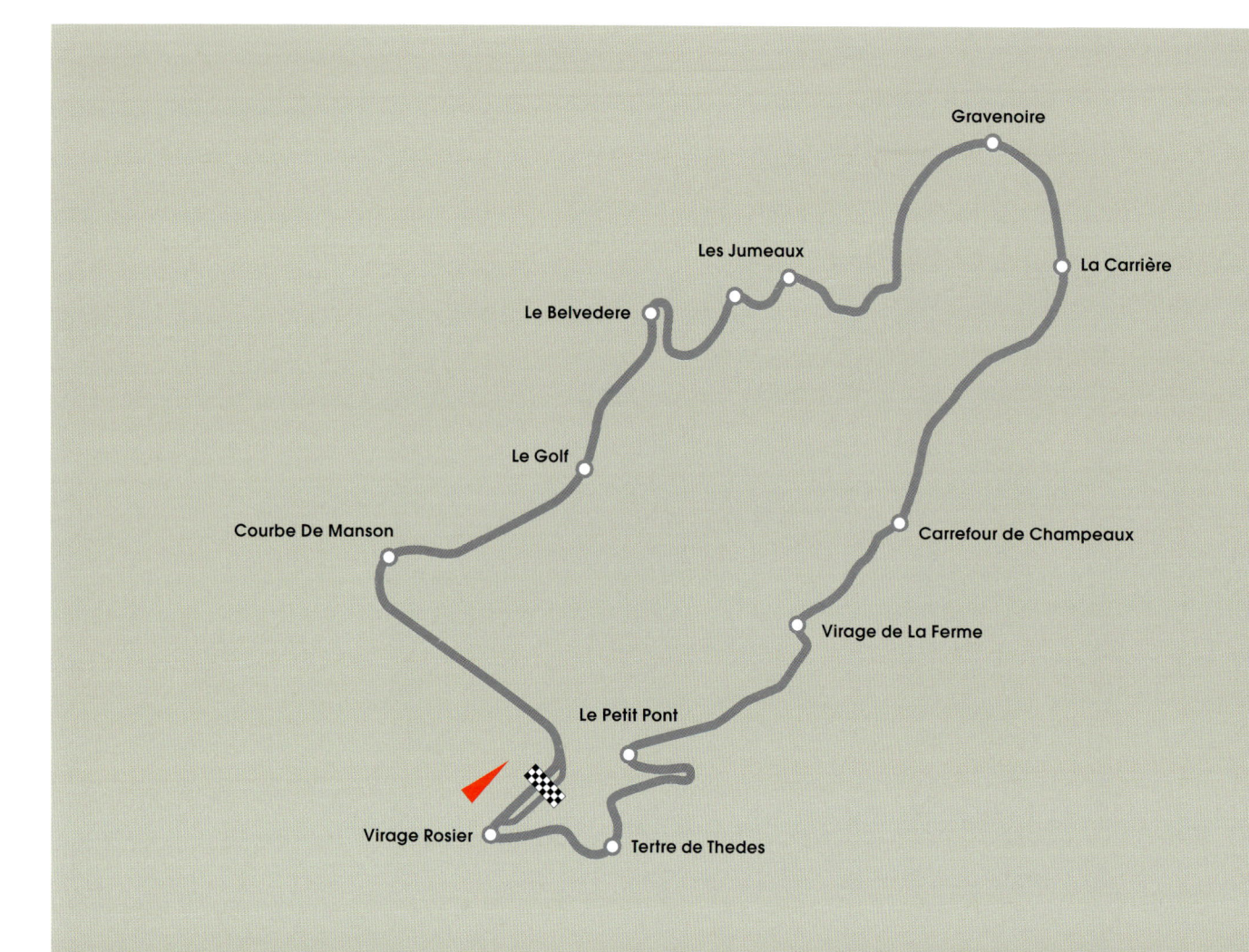

CIRCUIT DE CHARADE

Length: 8.055 km (5.005 miles)
Lap Record: 2:53.900 (Chris Amon, Matra MS120, 1972)
Opened: 1958
First F1 Grand Prix: 1965
Last F1 Grand Prix: 1972
Number of F1 Grands Prix hosted: 4
Number of laps: 38
Circuit Designers: Jean Auchatraire, Louis Rosier
Race winning fact: Jackie Stewart won in 1969 and 1972, proving himself to be the master of long circuits – he also won at Spa-Francorchamps and Nürburgring Nordschleife

The Circuit de Charade, or, as it was also known, Circuit Louis Rosier, made use of the public roads around the Puy de Dôme (a notable mountain climb on the Tour de France) which ran uncomfortably close to rockfaces and the detritus thrown off them soon made its way onto the racing line during grands prix. When F1 decamped to the more self-contained Dijon and Paul Ricard circuits, racing continued, until the public roads were abandoned in favour of a shortened track. Today's circuit still employs many of the bends originally raced by the fearless 'pilotes' of the 1960s.

launched into the crowd killing the driver and 83 spectators and injuring 120 more. Switzerland banned all motor racing, Mercedes withdrew from Formula 1 at the end of the season and the race in Clermont-Ferrand was cancelled.

Rosier himself was killed driving a Ferrari in a saloon car race at the Montlhéry circuit in 1956 and so it was left to Auchatraire to pursue Rosier's plan for the first mountain race track in France, sited at a safe distance out of town. Construction work started in May 1957 with pit garages, a control tower, a narrow pit straight and grandstand, with a new track linking six kilometres of sinuous public roads around the Puy de Gravenoire and Puy de Charade.

Opened in July 1958 at an event that packed in 60,000 spectators, the Formula 2 race was won by old stager Maurice 'Le Petoulet' Trintignant in a Cooper, but it was international motorcycle racing that really embraced the Circuit Louis Rosier. Starting in 1959, the French Motorcycle Grand Prix was won by John Surtees riding the 500cc MV Augusta. It hosted the race nine times until 1974 with wins for Phil Read, Giacomo Agostini and another rider, like Surtees, who would switch to four wheels, Mike Hailwood.

The mountainous terrain had many likening it to a French Nürburgring Nordschleife, but unlike its German counterpart there were no significant straights to alleviate the constant turning and rise and fall through more than fifty corners. In July 1959 Stirling Moss competed in a Formula 2 race at Clermont in a Cooper-Borgward and declared: 'I don't know a more wonderful

Above Chris Amon in the Matra MS120D recovers to third place after a costly puncture lost him the lead during the 1972 French Grand Prix. The racing line is just inches away from the rock face.

Left Lorenzo Bandini in the Ferrari 1512 during the 1965 French Grand Prix. For this debut race, the pole lap was set at 3:18.3 by Jim Clark. At the final race seven years later Chris Amon had got it down to 2:53.4.

Above **Two images from the movie shoot, including the Ford GT40 camera car driven by former World Champion Phil Hill. Director John Frankenheimer (in the raincoat) walks between cars on the front row. In the second photo Dan Gurney gives some last minute advice to actor Yves Montand who plays Ferrari driver Jean-Pierre Sarti.**

track than Charade.' He had won his 152nd race there with a fastest lap of 78mph, but F1 machinery would lap a lot quicker through the 1960s and early 1970s creating a feeling of nausea among some drivers.

Denny Hulme, like Moss, enjoyed the switchbacks: 'I loved that place, and it was always very kind to me,' he recalled. 'A lot of people used to wear open-faced helmets there so they could throw up as they went down the hills, left-right-left-right. I found that the best way was to hold your breath!'

The organizers managed to snag the French Grand Prix of 1965 (the 60th anniversary of the Gordon Bennett victory) but ironically no French driver took part. Jim Clark took victory in a Lotus 25, having won at Spa in the round before, and at Indianapolis in the race before that.

John Frankenheimer's cameras were present to film scenes of the 1965 race which resulted in an all-British podium of Clark, Graham Hill and Jackie Stewart. The movie *Grand Prix* would intercut footage from races at Charade over the 1965 and 1966 seasons and occasionally adapt the script to incorporate incidents in the races. On the Monday following the 1966 race 3,000 locals turned up as extras for scenes with Yves Montand, James Garner and French chanteuse Françoise Hardy.

Circuit de Charade would host four French GPs, returning in 1969, 1970 and 1972. The final race, in which Chris Amon set a new lap record of 104mph, brought into sharp focus the problems which would preclude any further F1 involvement. It was in the same race that a stone on the racing line was fired backwards

Left Henri Pescarolo in a Matra MS120 on his way to fifth place in the 1970 French Grand Prix. Closing in behind is the green and gold car of Jack Brabham on his way to third place.

Below Chris Amon in his Ferrari 312/69 during the 1969 grand prix. Amon would retire with engine issues from a race won by Jackie Stewart's Matra.

and penetrated the visor of Helmut Marko's helmet on Lap 8. Despite the excruciating pain and the sudden blinding in one eye the Austrian was mindful that he had 20 cars behind him and a collision within the tight track could have had fatal consequences: 'I only wanted to get out because the car was still almost full of 250 litres of fuel.' The future Red Bull advisor briefly lost consciousness and came to while being extracted from the car. Unable to find an eye surgeon to repair his damaged eye quickly, he lost the sight in that eye, his driving career over.

The Charade circuit could not compete with the newly built Paul Ricard track (1971) or Dijon (1974), and fell off the grand prix calendar. With no easy solutions to the safety issues from run-off areas, the classic road course was used less and less and finally closed in 1988. Happily the Council of Puy de Dôme stepped in and financed the building of the shortened course using the sections of track that had been built to link the two public roads. It was opened with a grand ceremony in June 1989, attended by racing luminaries such as Fangio, Moss and Jack Brabham. In his autobiography Brabham had described the organizers of the 1965 race as 'penny-pinching' because they hadn't allowed three entries 'only two, they said'. In those days drivers got start money.

Charade is now home to the Classic Racing School, runs track days and classic events, and is shaping up to become a centre for zero emission race cars, with a nearby 12-hectare solar park fulfilling a sustainable racing brief for the future.

PRENOIS, BURGUNDY, FRANCE

Dijon-Prenois

THE CIRCUIT DREAMED UP BY FRANÇOIS CHAMBELLAND WAS A REAL DRIVERS' CHALLENGE, BUT ALWAYS PROVED TO BE TOO SHORT TO MAINTAIN ITS PLACE ON THE CALENDAR

Given France's role in the rich pageant of motorsport history, it's surprising that the nation hasn't ended up with a grand prix circuit befitting its status and home to the Fédération Internationale de l'Automobile (FIA). Dijon-Prenois is perhaps the closest to an original racing circuit that the country has (i.e. developed *by* racers *for* racers), but it is a venue with a fatal flaw.

Reims, Rouen and Charade were all long race tracks that employed sections of local roads, but the facility built outside the village of Prenois near Dijon – the brainchild of former rugby-player François Chambelland among others – was a circuit that could be used year-round without the need to stop the traffic. But it was short. Despite his bold ambition to create an automotive centre in Dijon, the local city council didn't back Chambelland's vision, which slowed the development of plans originally drawn up in 1967 and commenced in 1969.

In laying out the circuit on undulating terrain, he was aided by French racing drivers François Cevert and Jean-Pierre Beltoise (Cevert's brother-in-law), but with limited finance he was restricted to building a shorter circuit than the 5km grand prix track he had envisioned. Even so, he was able to open the more compact version of his roller-coaster blast through the Burgundy countryside in 1972. Former rugby player, and Cooper and Brabham F1 driver, Guy Ligier drove the official opening lap.

It proved to be ironic that Ligier was given the honour of driving the opening laps at Dijon, as he was a close friend of

Opposite Niki Lauda (11) in the Ferrari 312T2 leads a pack of cars around Dijon's 'S' des Sablières in the 1977 French Grand Prix.

Above The track is still an important venue for French national series, in this instance the 2023 GT4 championship.

Left The Matchbox-sponsored Surtees of Jochen Mass catches fire in the pit lane during practice for the French Grand Prix in 1974. John Surtees supervises.

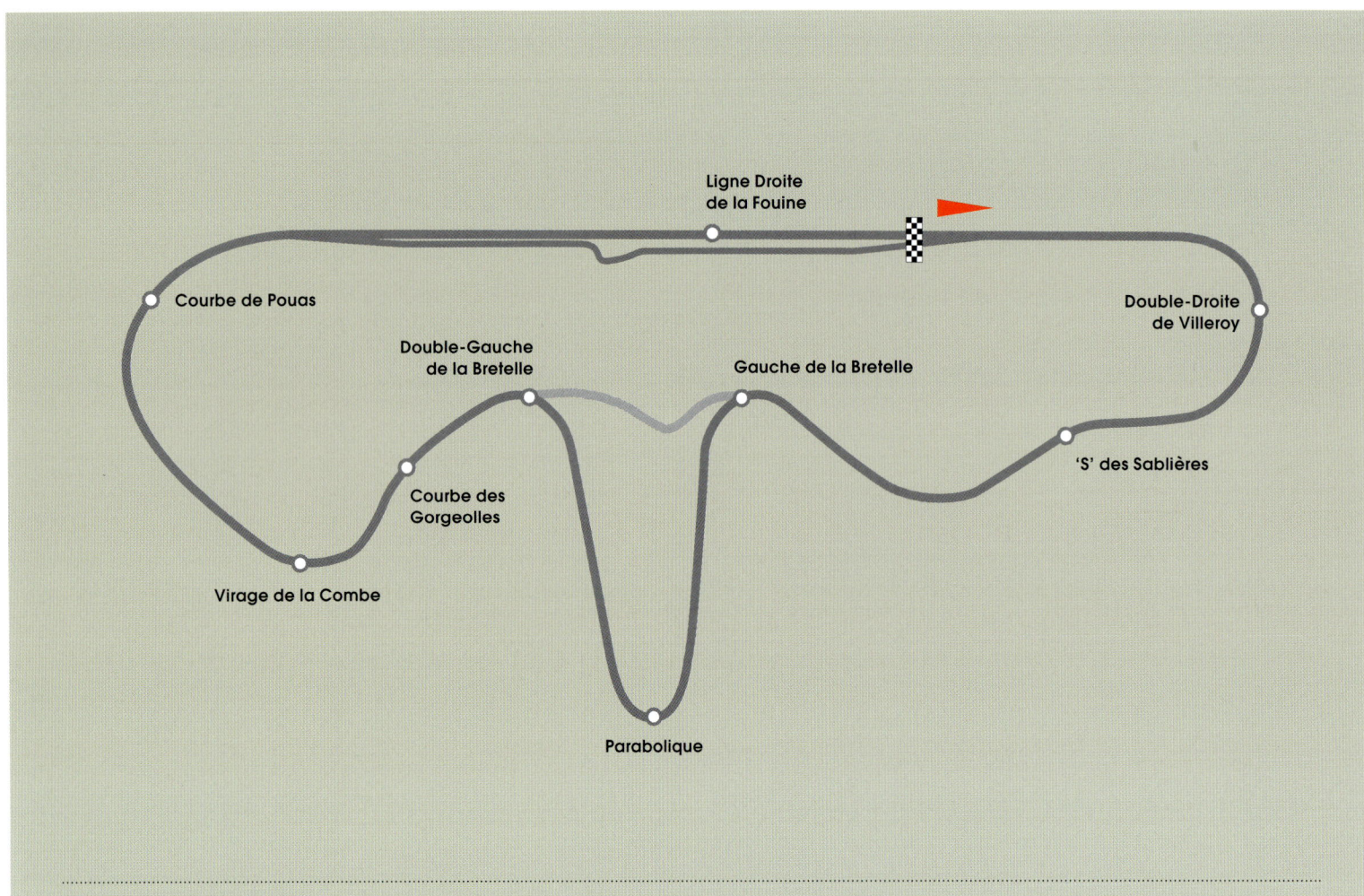

DIJON-PRENOIS

Length: 3.801 km (2.362 miles)
Lap Record: 1:05.357 (Alain Prost, McLaren MP4/2, 1984)
Opened: 1972
First F1 Grand Prix: 1974
Last F1 Grand Prix: 1984
Number of F1 Grands Prix hosted: 6 (5 French, 1 Swiss)
Number of laps: 79
Circuit Designers: François Chambelland, Jean-Pierre Beltoise, François Cevert and José Rosinsk
Race winning fact: No driver recorded a repeat win at Dijon. Ronnie Peterson (1974), Mario Andretti (1977), Jean-Pierre Jabouille (1979), Alain Prost (1981), Keke Rosberg (1982), Niki Lauda (1984)

Given more resources, the Dijon-Prenois circuit could have been the pre-eminent French F1 venue, given its proximity to a major French city and the rise and fall of its natural topography. French politics got in the way. However it remains seared into the memory of those who watched the closing stages of the 1979 race as it provided Renault with the first victory of the turbo era and the world TV audience with some epic closing laps, as Gilles Villeneuve wrestled second place back from the seemingly faster René Arnoux.

François Mitterand. The French president subsequently gave Ligier enormous state finance to resurrect the old Magny-Cours circuit near his home in Nevers in the 1980s and the investment in Magny-Cours effectively closed the door on any future expansion of Dijon.

With Charade hosting its final French Grand Prix in 1972 – the puncture-strewn race that exposed its limitations – and Paul Ricard taking over for 1973, the Dijon circuit got to host its first French GP in 1974. But the initial race immediately exposed Dijon-Prenois's limitation with the short lap of 2.04 miles/3.28kms taking just under a minute and the grid restricted to 22 of the 30 cars attempting to qualify. During the race, won by Ronnie Peterson's Lotus, back-markers were a constant problem and the nature of the fast, sweeping curves made it difficult for the leaders to make an easy pass.

Formula 1 departed to the Paul Ricard circuit for the 1975 GP, although the circuit was able to host the non-championship Swiss Grand Prix that year (Switzerland having banned motor-racing after the 1955 Le Mans tragedy). However if the French Grand Prix were ever to return, the lap length would need to be increased.

Chambelland persisted and although he could not finance the full 5km circuit, in 1976 he managed to include a new section which dived left downhill after 'S des Sablières' at a corner named 'Gauche de Bretelle' down a short straight to the 'Parabolique' hairpin then uphill to the twin-apex 'Double-

Left Tyrrell driver François Cevert along with his brother-in-law Jean-Pierre Beltoise helped lay out the initial circuit.

Below left Gilles Villeneuve's Ferrari crosses the line in front of Arnoux's Renault in what are widely regarded as the most rumbustious final laps of a grand prix.

Below right After the initial race in 1974, the French GP moved to Paul Ricard the following year and so the circuit organized a non-championship F1 race, the Swiss Grand Prix, for 1975.

51

Gauche de la Bretelle'. It was only an extra half a kilometre but it made all the difference.

The combination of extra track, the addition of slower corners, the original sweeping bends with elevation changes and some strange cambers made the new Dijon-Prenois a proper grand prix challenge and in 1977 the French GP returned, starting a biennial rotation with Paul Ricard, just as Brands Hatch had alternated with Silverstone.

Mario Andretti won the 1977 race for Lotus followed home by James Hunt and Gunnar Nilsson, but it was two years later that it earned its place in French motorsport history. The 1970s was a fine time to be a French motorsport fan with the greatest generation of F1 stars the nation had yet seen: François Cevert, Henri Pescarolo, Jacques Laffite, Patrick Depailler, Jean-Pierre Jarier, Jean-Pierre Beltoise, Jean-Pierre Jabouille, Didier Pironi, René Arnoux and Patrick Tambay all graced the grid in the decade, followed in 1980 by Alain Prost. *Paris-Match* celebrated the home-grown talent in 1977 with a photo opportunity of Jarier, Laffite, Depailler and Jabouille walking through a local cornfield with the village of Prenois beyond.

Renault had introduced their turbo engine in 1977 but it had been plagued with reliability issues. In 1979, the technology was coming good and Renault locked out the front row in Dijon qualifying with Jean-Pierre Jabouille on pole and René Arnoux in P2. In the race, Jabouille was leading with Gilles Villeneuve's Ferrari in second place being rapidly hauled in by third-placed René Arnoux as the final laps ticked down. Jabouille won the race, but all eyes were fixed on the titanic battle behind between Arnoux and Villeneuve. Having passed the French-Canadian on the 78th lap of 80, Arnoux began to pull away, but then the Ferrari closed rapidly on the start/finish straight and re-took second place in a haze of tyre smoke at the first corner starting Lap 79. Arnoux tried to repeat his pass at the beginning of Lap 80, but the two cars ran side by side through the first turn, bumping wheels which saw Arnoux get ahead before Villeneuve made a definitive final pass into Parabolique.

Ahead of them Jean-Pierre Jabouille had scored the first victory of the turbo era, the first Frenchman to win his home F1 grand prix, driving a French car, with a French engine, on French tyres (Michelin), using French fuel (Elf), but all the talk was of the epic duel for a lower step on the podium.

Alain Prost repeated the victory in 1981 and Dijon got to host another Swiss Grand Prix in 1982, but the 1984 French GP would prove to be its F1 swansong. Ironically the race was won by Niki Lauda in a McLaren en route to his third World Championship, denying Prost the opportunity of becoming the first French World Champion by half a point.

Although the teams enjoyed their short stay amongst the vineyards of the Côte de Nuits and Côte de Beaune, and that nearby Dijon had all the big-city facilities a circuit like Magny-Cours lacked, there was only one access road in which caused frustration and delay. And with the increasing speeds of F1 cars, lap times were edging towards the sub-minute mark again – Patrick Tambay's 1984 pole time was a 1:02-second lap.

Opposite Vittorio Brambilla with a very worn set of front tyres on his Surtees-Ford stops in the pit lane during practice for the 1977 French GP. John Surtees steps into frame from the right.

Below Today the pit garages have been rebuilt to accommodate modern racing series and the far greater number of pit boxes needed for large fields.

Bottom The 1982 Swiss Grand Prix was part of the official World Championship. Gordon Murray (white shirt) and the Brabham-BMW mechanics await the arrival of Nelson Piquet for the first mid-race fuel stop of the modern era.

Dijon-Prenois has continued to host national events, while rivals Paul Ricard and Magny-Cours have also fallen off the grand prix calendar. Despite Formula 1's owner Liberty Media professing a wish to keep historic races on the calendar, it seems grands prix in countries with no history of motorsport, such as Qatar and Azerbaijan with large piles of cash will always trump traditional races.

CASTLE DONINGTON, LEICESTERSHIRE, ENGLAND 🇬🇧

Donington Park

HOST TO THE MIGHTY SILVER ARROWS OF THE 1930S, DONINGTON'S PASSIONATE OWNER TOM WHEATCROFT SET ABOUT MAKING HIS CIRCUIT A MODERN GRAND PRIX VENUE

Donington Park is the only active British survivor of the pre-war racing scene. It took the laurels from the supercilious Brooklands brigade – 'the right crowd and no crowding' – when the crumbling concrete track began to get hazardous.

The estate land at Donington Hall had been used as a prisoner-of-war-camp in World War I, and when owner John Gillies Shields was approached by former TT motorcycle racer Fred Craner, with a view to putting on races for the Derby and District Motor Club, a deal for a trial race was struck.

In a matter of weeks a cinder track was marked out using mostly pre-existing estate roads and a crowd estimated at 20,000 turned up for the first race meeting on 25 May 1931. The venture would continue. In 1932 an expensive asphalt surface was added to attract four-wheel competition and at this stage the circuit still passed through the arches of Starkey's Bridge, swept through Coppice corner, which was still a coppice, and through the working farmyard beyond.

Formula 1's first World Champion, the uncompromising Giuseppe Farina, was among entrants at the first Donington Grand Prix of 1935 and the race distance of the parkland circuit increased with the addition of the Melbourne Hill loop. It was the grands prix of 1937 and 1938 that cemented Donington's place in motorsport history with the participation of the pride of Germany, the Silver Arrows cars. Four Mercedes-Benz W125s took on three Auto Union Typ Cs at the front of the race. Manfred von

Brauchitsch had claimed pole for Mercedes posting a lap time of 2:10, with Bernd Rosemeyer's Auto Union in P2. Predictably, German cars filled the first seven places; Prince Bira's Maserati was a distant 15 seconds in arrears in P8. Rosemeyer won the race from von Brauchitsch.

The following year's grand prix promised a re-match, that is until Hitler's continued occupation of the Sudetenland prompted an international crisis and the German teams made a hasty withdrawal of their machinery. Neville Chamberlain's dash to Munich may not have saved the countries from war, but it resurrected the grand prix which was another Silver Arrows whitewash, this time with Tazio Nuvolari's Auto Union coming home ahead of the Mercedes of Hermann Lang and British ace Richard Seaman.

One of the keen spectators at the 1937 race had been 15-year-old Tom Wheatcroft, born nearby in Castle Donington. After amassing a fortune in the building trade in the 1960s he put his money to good use by investing in a large collection of vintage motor racing cars as well as sponsoring drivers such as Derek Bell and Roger Williamson. Keen to restore his home circuit to its former glory he bought the 300-acre Donington estate in 1971 and set about the return of motor racing.

Donington had been used as a military vehicle depot in the war, but racing had not recommenced after hostilities ceased. The long process of rehabilitation was begun by Wheatcroft, permissions for a race track were obtained, and by 1977 the pre-war circuit for the most part, with a new start and finish straight

Opposite The start of the 1937 Donington Grand Prix. On the far right is Manfred von Brauchitsch's Mercedes W125 (3). Next to him is Bernd Rosemeyer's Auto-Union (5), then the Mercedes of Hermann Lang (2) and Richard Seaman (4).

Top The start of the 1983 European Grand Prix with the two Williams-Renaults of Alain Prost and Damon Hill locking out the front row.

Above Bernd Rosemeyer's Auto Union Typ C races to victory in the 1937 Donington Grand Prix.

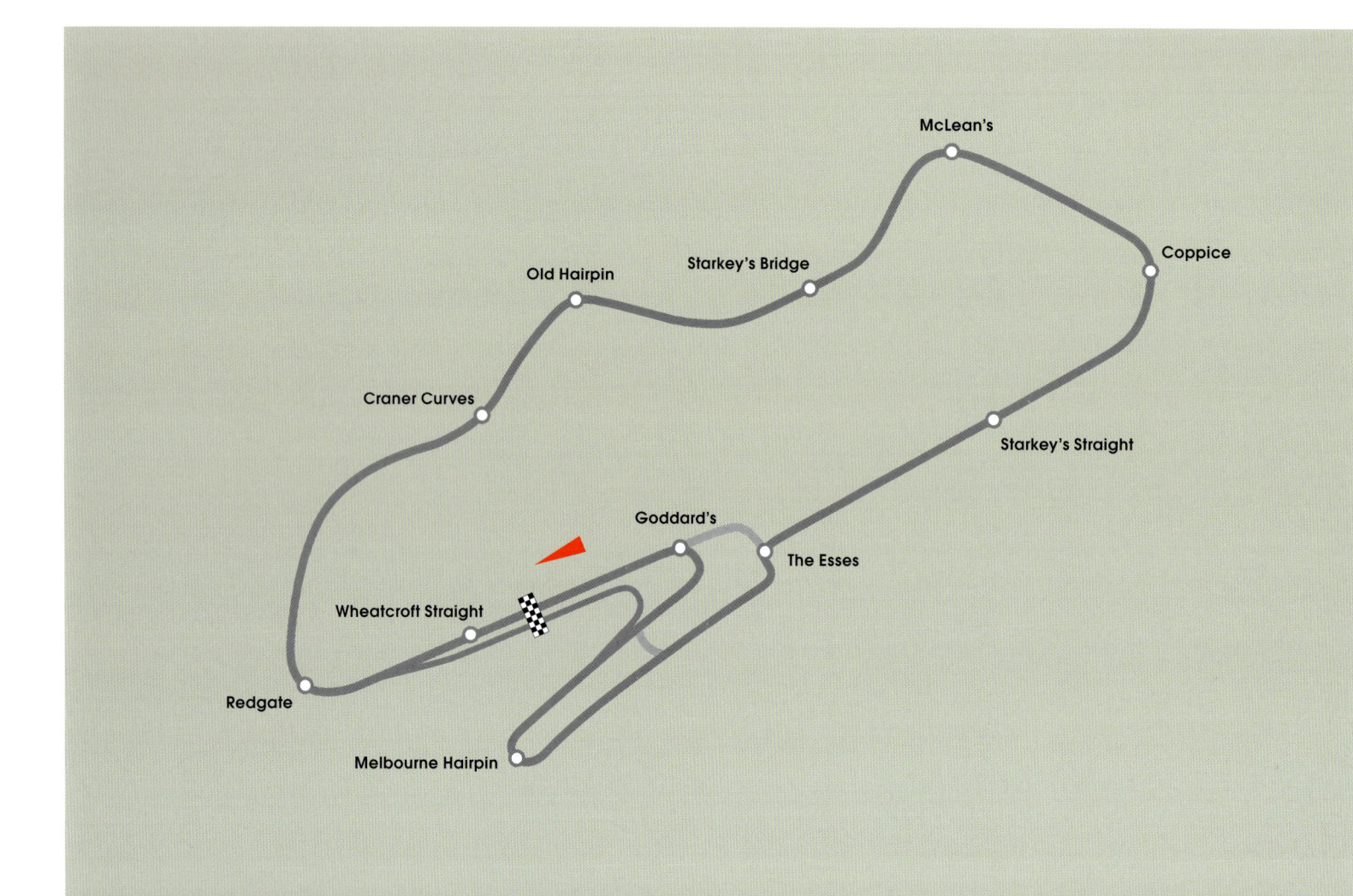

DONINGTON PARK

Length: 4.020 km (2.498 miles)
Lap Record: 1:18.029 (Ayrton Senna, McLaren MP4/8, 1993)
Opened: 1931
First F1 Grand Prix: 1993
Number of F1 Grands Prix hosted: 1
Number of laps: 76
Designer: Donington Estate, Fred Craner
Race winning fact: Ayrton Senna won from Damon Hill and Alain Prost in 1993, having made four pit stops compared to Prost's seven. He lapped the entire field bar Hill and won by a minute.

Britain's first full-length motorsport circuit attracted top European drivers in the 1930s. Local lad Tom Wheatcroft was there to watch the likes of Tazio Nuvolari and Bernd Rosemeyer thrill the crowd and would eventually buy the circuit at which he was a regular spectator. His ambition for it to become an F1 venue was finally realized in 1993, 20 years after he had suffered the heartache of watching his long-sponsored driver, Roger Williamson, perish in the 1973 Dutch Grand Prix.

---

leading to a new Redgate Corner, was ready for track action.

With its proximity to the M1 motorway it soon became a popular addition for national racing series, hosting cars up to F2/F3000 level. But Wheatcroft was hankering after a Formula 1 grand prix and ensured the track was brought up to the latest FIA spec, pushing back barriers, increasing gravel traps, improving access. Silverstone may have had the long-term contract for the British Grand Prix, but Brands Hatch had snared a European Grand Prix in 1985 and standalone GPs were a way of making money for Formula 1 when there was excess demand – Japan doubled up with the Asian Grand Prix and in the Schumacher era, the Nürburgring could regularly afford to host the European Grand Prix.

In 1993, the Japanese developer of the Autopolis circuit went bust and a last-minute replacement for the Asian Grand Prix was required. Donington seized the opportunity. The Sega European Grand Prix was run on 11 April 1993 and in the damp conditions at the start of the race Ayrton Senna produced an astonishing opening lap. Starting from fourth on the grid, Ayrton dropped a place after Michael Schumacher blocked him, but recovered from fifth to lead the race by the Melbourne hairpin. It was a virtuoso performance, but the soggy surrounds and limited pit facilities gave the weekend the impression of a national race meeting, not the third round of a World Championship.

Bernie Ecclestone and Max Mosley were two of Silverstone's harshest critics, constantly pressuring circuit owners the British

Left The great Italian ace Tazio Nuvolari is hoisted shoulder high after winning the 1938 Donington Grand Prix in an Auto Union.

Bottom Cars head off on the parade lap of the 1993 European Grand Prix. Though Senna (8) started from P4 on the grid he slipped behind Karl Wendlinger at the start of the race.

Below Michael Schumacher is widely regarded as one of F1's 'regenmeisters', but conditions during the 1993 grand prix proved too much and he spun into the gravel and retirement on Lap 22.

Below Cars round the Melbourne Hairpin during the 1937 Donington Grand Prix. Raymond Mays and Earl Howe – both driving ERAs – sandwich the Auto Union of Rudolph Hasse. Hasse joined the National Socialist Motor Corps during World War II and died on the Russian front in 1942.

Bottom Ayrton Senna on his way to what many think is the greatest opening lap in F1, at Donington Park in 1993. Here he passes great rival Alain Prost to take the lead. Contrary to popular belief, despite his prowess in the wet, Ayrton didn't enjoy driving in rain, once telling Brazilian journalist Jayme Brito, "Do you think I enjoy only seeing 5cms in front of me!"

Racing Drivers' Club to invest in the track. Frustrated by the lack of progress, there was an opportunity for Donington to replace Silverstone, but it would require massive investment. The Wheatcroft family didn't have the finances, so they sold a 150-year lease on the circuit to Donington Ventures Limited, who also, it turned out, didn't have the finances.

Despite obtaining a multi-year deal to hold the British GP, a new circuit design by Hermann Tilke and initial earthworks, the project ground to a halt with the work unfinished. It was not until Jonathan Palmer's Motor Sport Vision company (who also operate Oulton Park and Brands Hatch) became involved in 2017 that a clear future for the circuit could be mapped out. The chance of a return for F1 is long gone.

Above When the circuit was originally laid out it passed through many features on the estate including a coppice, the farmyard and an arch of Starkey's Bridge.

Left Many of the trees on the estate have been felled and cleared over the years. After the track swoops down the Craner Curves and through the Old Hairpin it no longer passes under Starkey's Bridge – which is still available for photo opportunities.

CHICHESTER, WEST SUSSEX, ENGLAND

Goodwood Circuit

AN INTRINSIC PART OF FORMULA 1 HISTORY, TWO OF THE SPORT'S GREATEST NAMES BOWED OUT AT THIS FORMER BATTLE OF BRITAIN AIRFIELD

With a boom in post-war racing interest, many former RAF airfields in Britain were turned into motor-racing circuits. Thruxton, Snetterton and the bomber training airfield at Silverstone all started to host races. RAF Westhampnett at Goodwood had been a satellite station for nearby RAF Tangmere in Chichester and an important emergency landing field in the Battle of Britain. It was from this airfield that Douglas Bader made his final sortie in August 1941, baling out over German-occupied France.

In 1946, Squadron Leader Tony Gaze, who had flown Hawker Hurricanes from the airfield during the war, suggested to the landowner, motor-racing enthusiast, the 9th Duke of Richmond and Gordon, that the airfield's perimeter road would be ideal for a circuit. The Duke had competed at Brooklands in the 1930s and in 1936 had staged his own private hillclimb with fellow Lancia enthusiasts on the course by Goodwood House that is now used for demonstration runs during the Festival of Speed.

On 18 September 1948 the Goodwood Motor Circuit was officially opened by the Duke with a lap of the circuit in his rakish Bristol 400. The meeting had attracted 15,000 spectators and racing was established.

In 1951, Formula 1's original World Champion, Giuseppe Farina, won the Goodwood Trophy race in his Alfa Romeo 159 at a speed in excess of 95mph (153km/h), so in a bid to contain speeds from Woodcote through to the start/finish line, the chicane was introduced. At first made of straw bales and

Opposite **Happier times for Stirling Moss as he wins the 1956 Glover Trophy in a Maserati.**

Top **Cars line up for the start of the Glover Trophy for racing machinery from 1961-1965 at the Goodwood Revival Meeting.**

Above left **Goodwood is keen to celebrate its RAF history along with its motorsport heritage.**

Above right **Sir Jackie Stewart has been a regular participant at the Goodwood Revival meetings, seen here on the grid in 2019.**

boards, from 1953 it became a much sturdier obstacle, a brick wall. When the circuit was restored for the Goodwood Revival meeting from 1998, mindful that the racing machinery jousting into the chicane could be worth millions, it was remade using polystyrene blocks. But made to look like bricks.

The annual Easter Monday meeting became the highlight of Goodwood's year with the top race, the Glover Trophy, more often than not run with Formula 1 machinery. It was in this race in 1962 that Stirling Moss crashed out at St Mary's bend in an accident that left him in a coma for 38 days and effectively ended his racing career. He had qualified his Walker Lotus 18/21 on pole, but a gear selection problem had forced him back into the pits and he emerged two laps down on Graham Hill's

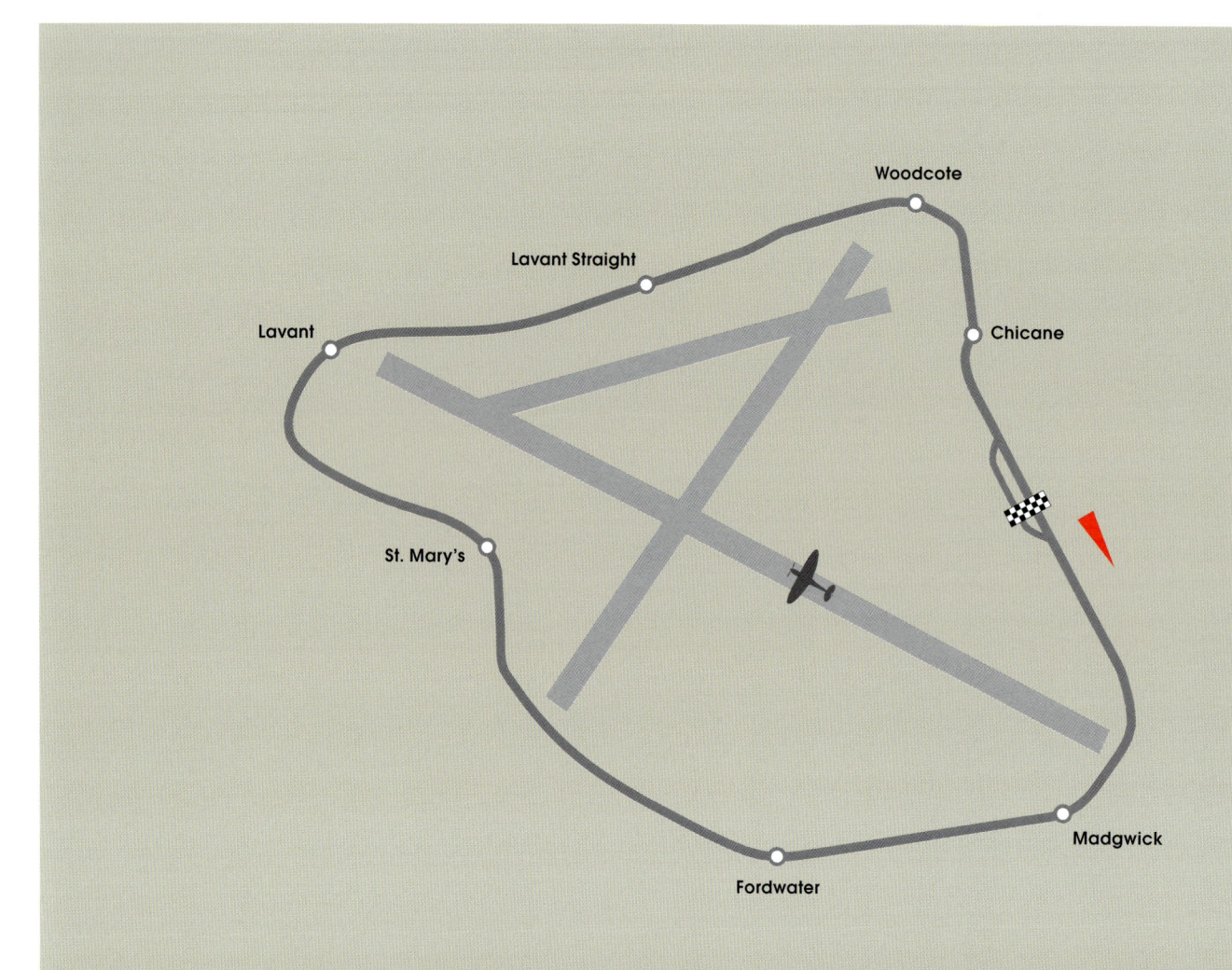

GOODWOOD CIRCUIT

Length: 3.862 km (2.400 miles)
Lap Record: 1:20.4, (Jim Clark/Jackie Stewart, Lotus/BRM 1965)
Opened: 1948
First Non-Championship F1 race: Richmond Trophy (1950)
Non-Championship F1 races: Richmond Trophy (1949–1954), Goodwood Trophy (1950–1955), Glover Trophy (1954–1965), Sussex Trophy (1955–1960)
Number of laps: 12
Race winning facts: Nino Farina won the 1951 Goodwood Trophy in an Alfa Romeo 159, while Prince Bira took the 1951 Richmond Trophy, and Froilán González won the 1952 race in a Ferrari 375.

A classic airfield perimeter circuit, Goodwood had aristocratic backing as it formed part of the estate of racing enthusiast the Duke of Richmond. Mothballed as a competition venue after 1966, it continued to be used for testing all kinds of racing machinery including the Can-Am sports cars in which McLaren drivers Denny Hulme and Bruce McLaren trounced the opposition in 1967, 1968 and 1969. The team would win again in 1970, but without their founder.

leading BRM and set off in a bid to get the fastest lap. Whilst trying to unlap himself from Hill his car left the road in a barely spectated part of the circuit and the unresolved mystery of how the infallible Moss had crashed began.

Speeds were ramping up. Goodwood's race-lap record of 1:20.4 was recorded jointly by Jim Clark and Jackie Stewart in 1965, a speed of 107mph. The Duke and members decided that for safety reasons racing would come to an end in 1966 – the addition of more chicanes was anathema to the spirit of Goodwood, even though they already had one in place.

The circuit was still available for testing and events through the 1970s, but there would be no wheel-to-wheel action. Even so, Bruce McLaren was killed in a testing accident at Goodwood. His McLaren Can-Am car crashed on the Lavant Straight when the rear bodywork came adrift at speed. The sudden loss of downforce unsettled the car, which spun, left the track, and hit a marshals' post.

However, that was not the end of the Goodwood story. In 1998, five years after launching the Festival of Speed in the grounds of nearby Goodwood House, and 50 years to the day after the Goodwood Motor Circuit was opened, the Earl of March (Freddie March's grandson) held the Revival Meeting for historic racers.

Period dress from the 1940s and 50s was a necessity and with the circuit buildings restored to their postwar splendour only the intrusion of modern safety devices spoiled the uncanny

Below Jim Clark, a regular competitor in sports car races, exits the chicane in his Aston Martin DB4GT Zagato during the Goodwood Tourist Trophy in 1961. One chicane was enough for the Duke of Richmond – after more were suggested to reduce speeds on the circuit the decision was taken to remove Goodwood from the motorsport calendar.

Bottom Very little has changed at the chicane in the intervening years, apart from the value of the cars taking part. This photo is from the 2022 Revival meeting showing a TVR Griffith in action.

illusion that Goodwood had entered a timewarp. The meeting has proved a roaring success, and along with the Festival of Speed in June it is the chance for old racers to catch up with each other and occasionally be reunited with their now-historic racing machinery.

HOCKENHEIM, GERMANY

Hockenheimring

IN THE PAST, MERCEDES' HOME CIRCUIT HAS ADAPTED WITH THE TIMES, BUT THE TIMES NOW CALL FOR MASSIVE RACE HOSTING FEES

The original Hockenheim was a triangular-shaped motorcycle circuit opened in 1932. The only feature recognizable to F1 fans was added in 1938 – the Ostkurve was a long, fast, sweeping curve that marked the far end of the circuit and returned cars in the direction of the pits. Though heavily modified over the years it would remain part of the challenge until 2001.

Following the upheavals of World War II and inevitable damage to the site, Hockenheim was then forced to redraw the circuit to the east of the new Mannheim-Walldorf autobahn. Using the substantial compensation offered for the land, the circuit owners were able to create a new start/finish straight and configure the final turns of the lap into a 'stadium section' or 'motodrome'. What would become a cauldron of noise in the Schumacher era was suggested by Ernst Christ in 1961 with the final configuration executed by John Hugenholtz, designer of Suzuka, Zolder and Jarama.

In the 1960s the German Grand Prix was still the property of the Nürburgring Nordschleife, but growing driver unrest at the length of the circuit (and thus the distance from any fire marshals), the lack of barriers and run-offs had been growing. In 1969 Jackie Stewart had campaigned for – and got – a driver boycott of Spa-Francorchamps because race organizers refused to make necessary safety changes. After the fatal crash of Piers Courage at Zandvoort in 1970, drivers demanded the same of the Nürburgring. Without the time to implement the

Opposite Alain Prost (15) leads from pole in his Renault RE30 at the 1981 German Grand Prix.

Above Lewis Hamilton (44) leads Mercedes team-mate Valtteri Bottas (77) at what would become an incident-packed German Grand Prix in 2019.

Left The sturdy figure of Alfred Neubauer supervises a Mercedes test at an undeveloped Hockenheim in 1954.

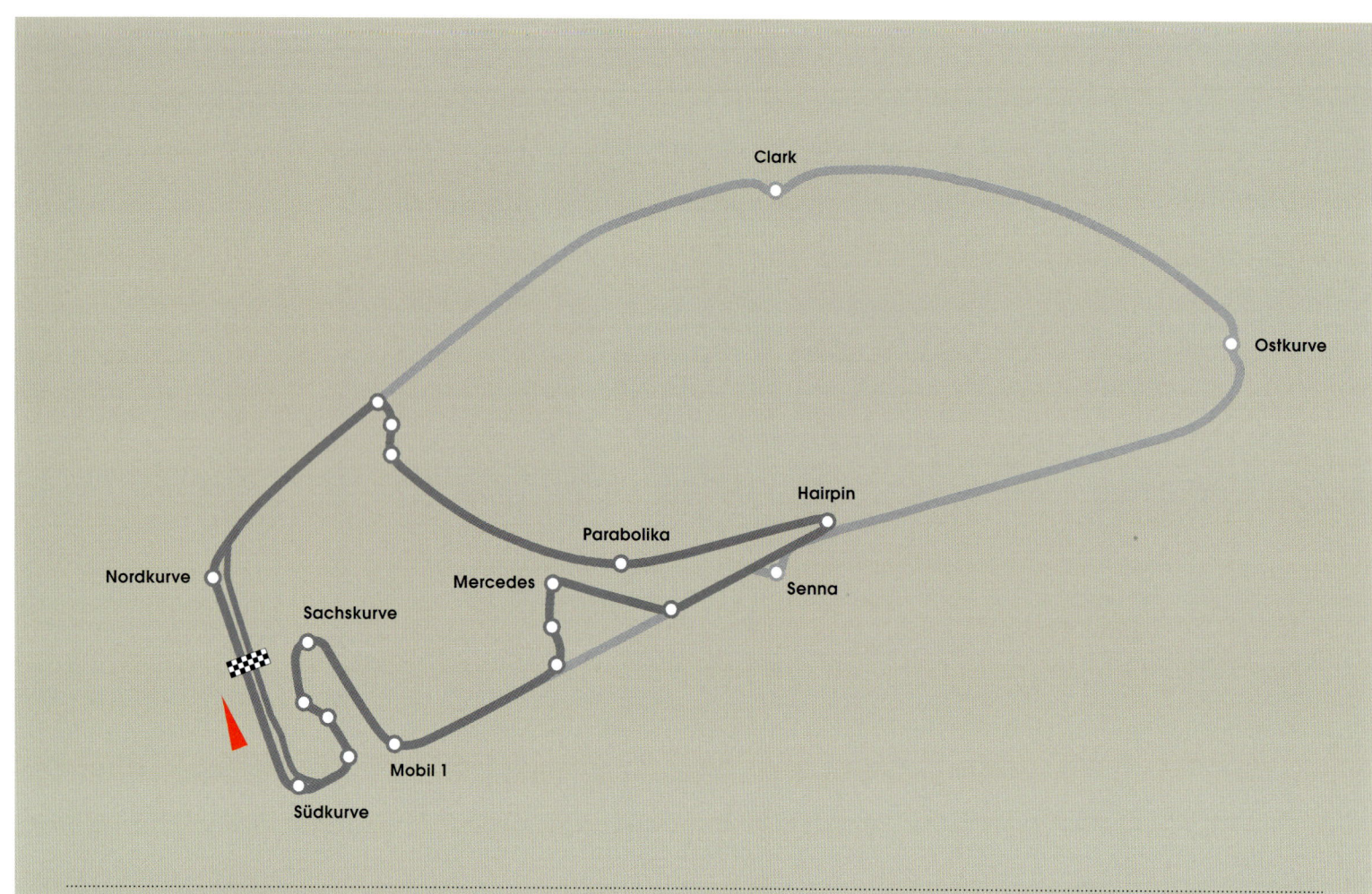

HOCKENHEIMRING

Length: 4.574 km (2.842 miles)
Lap Record: 1:13.780 (Kimi Räikkönen, McLaren MP4/19B, 2004)
Opened: 1932
First F1 Grand Prix: 1970
Last F1 Grand Prix: 2019
Number of F1 Grands Prix hosted: 37
Number of laps: 67
Redesigners: 1965 Stadium Section, Ernst Christ/John Hugenholtz – 2002 circuit reduction, Hermann Tilke
Race winning fact: Max Verstappen won the last race at Hockenheim in 2019 with wet conditions bringing out multiple Safety Cars. Daniil Kvyat scored Toro Rosso's first podium since 2008.

Hockenheim was seen as a much safer alternative to the Nürburgring and took over the German GP when drivers refused the trip to the Eifel Mountains. Over time, the long, spectatorless forest sections proved a burden, especially in 2000 when a disgruntled former Mercedes employee accessed the track, causing the dispatch of a Safety Car. Hermann Tilke created an overtaking-friendly shorter circuit and the new Hockenheim has provided many more thrills, even though it has failed to generate the crowds drawn by Michael Schumacher in his pomp.

work, the Hockenheimring stepped in to host the race.

Many thought it ironic that the circuit which had taken the life of Jim Clark, the greatest F1 driver since Fangio, in a minor F2 race in 1968 should be chosen on safety grounds. However Clark's accident had likely been caused by a tyre coming off the rim of his Lotus, sending the car spinning into the trees on one of the long, tree-lined straights.

A wary F1 returned to a modified Nürburgring in 1971 until Niki Lauda's fiery accident of 1976 resulted in the grand prix transferring permanently to Hockenheim. Following the Clark accident, two chicanes had been inserted on the main forest straights – Bremskurve 1 and Bremskurve 2 – and metal barriers had been erected around the circuit perimeter. It had slowed

Opposite top left **Jim Clark (left) photographed moments before going out in the F2 race that would claim his life.**

Opposite centre **Clark's Hockenheim memorial was originally the simple cross placed at the side of the tragic accident. But with the changes to the circuit it has been enlarged and moved closer to the stadium.**

Opposite top right **Having wrested the German GP from the Nürburgring, the organizers were keen to advertise their race and prove it could be a success.**

Opposite bottom **Jochen Rindt (2) in the Lotus 72C leads Clay Regazzoni (15) and Jacky Ickx (10) through the stadium section, much loved by Hermann Tilke, in the 1970 German Grand Prix.**

WORLD CHAMPION
1963 and 1965
INDIANAPOLIS 500
1965
JIM CLARK
7.4.1968
25 Grand Prix Wins
1962 to 1967
racing with
TEAM LOTUS

GROSSER PREIS VON
DEUTSCHLAND
VERANSTALTER: AUTOMOBILCLUB VON DEUTSCHLAND
Verkaufspreis
DM 2,–
AvD
Offizielles
Programm
2. August 1970
MOTODROM
HOCKENHEIM
Weltmeisterschaft · Formel.1

MOTOREN
SIE GEWINN

cars down, but Hockenheim was still considered a fast blast through the trees.

Patrick Depailler suffered a fatal accident near the Ostkurve in 1980 while testing for Alfa Romeo which precipitated the addition of a third chicane in 1982. It was at this hastily assembled chicane in the 1982 race that Nelson Piquet, enjoying a commanding lead in his Brabham-BMW and having just posted the *schnellste runde*, came up to lap Chilean driver Eliseo Salazar in an ATS. Salazar's front right tagged the rear left of the Brabham and both cars demolished the tyre walls of the chicanes, careering harmlessly to the side of the track. An enraged Piquet stormed out of his car waving, gesticulating, aiming punches and kicks at his fellow South-American in a classic piece of grand prix footage. It was only afterwards, when BMW chief mechanic Karl Heinz Öfner disassembled the engine, that he spotted a defective piston pin which would have grenaded the engine. Salazar had saved BMW from an embarrassing failure at their home race.

By 1992, the Ostkurve chicane had been reconfigured and in 1994 the remaining chicanes were tightened. By the late 1990s the fast blast through the trees, which many regarded as soulless and a poor test of F1 machinery – more like the circuits of the 1950s with their 'flying kilometres' than anything else – was slated for change. Germany's first World Champion Michael Schumacher was packing in the fans who only got to blow their airhorns for 45 laps. The radical 1999 plan eliminated the spectatorless section of track that ran through the trees.

Top **Alain Prost and René Arnoux lock out the front row for Renault in 1982, followed by Nelson Piquet's Brabham-BMW BT50 and Patrick Tambay in a Ferrari 126C2. As the turbo-engined cars outpaced the normally aspirated Ford runners, Hockenheim became a race which emphasised the disparity.**

Above **The race control buildings would struggle to meet the standard expected for a modern F1 venue, despite the addition of the Baden-Württemberg centre overlooking the stadium complex.**

Above **The first corner at Hockenheim has often proven to be a pinch point, causing accidents, but in 2001 Prost driver Luciano Burti managed to get airborne before he got there, causing more financial misery to his beleaguered team.**

Left **An aerial view of the shortened circuit from 2012 with the distinct outline of the old track stretching through the trees out to the Ostkurve (bottom right).**

Below Spectators viewing at the Ostkurve in 1989 with a chicane now in place to reduce speeds.

Bottom After the track was shortened for 2002, the long run through the trees was left to re-wild.

Right The approach to the Ostkurve and its spectator banking photographed in 1980. The flowers placed on the Armco are for Patrick Depailler who suffered a suspected suspension failure while testing mid-season for Alfa Romeo, his car impacting the barrier at massive speed.

Left Érik Comas watches as marshals douse his Ligier-Lamborghini after he tripped up going through the Ostkurve chicane during practice for the 1991 German Grand Prix. This is the chicane made famous by Nelson Piquet throwing punches at Eliseo Salazar after they collided during the 1982 race.

Below The two Haas cars of Romain Grosjean and Kevin Magnussen – in the short-lived Rich Energy livery – exit the hairpin in practice for the final Hockenheim GP in 2019.

The new Hermann Tilke-designed circuit retained the essential elements of the stadium section with the track extending no further east than the old Bremskurve 2, or Senna Kurve as it had been renamed.

From 2002, 67 laps would make up a grand prix distance and provide far more spectator engagement. Gone was the old forest section with its simple trackside memorial to Jim Clark now sitting beside a race track that had been turned into a forest track – and gone, too, was the old Ostkurve.

Despite the enhanced overtaking opportunities, the increased grandstand capacity and some dramatic grands prix starts as cars piled into the tightened first turn, the Nordkurve, the race struggled financially. Germany had a new, charismatic, multiple World Champion in Sebastian Vettel, followed by a dominant Mercedes team but still the crowds stayed away.

In a bid to stem the losses the circuit agreed to alternate hosting of the German Grand Prix with the New Nürburgring, which was enduring its own struggle to balance the books. With new race venues clamouring to thrust money into Bernie Ecclestone's and subsequently Liberty Media's pockets, the German Grand prix disappeared, like the Ostkurve, in 2020.

Above An emotional Patrick Tambay wins the 1983 San Marino Grand Prix for his friend Gilles Villeneuve.

Right Carlos Reutemann's Williams is jammed between the Renaults of Jean-Pierre Jabouille and René Arnoux at the start of the only Italian Grand Prix to be hosted by Imola, in 1980.

Opposite After the pit complex was rebuilt there were changes to the track. Although the building at left is new, the grandstand prominent in the 1983 image shows that the circuit ran closer to spectators before.

IMOLA, EMILIA ROMAGNA, ITALY

Circuit Enzo e Dino Ferrari

DESPITE THE BEAUTY OF ITS SETTING AND THE PASSION OF ITS FANS, THE CIRCUIT AT IMOLA WILL ALWAYS BE LINKED TO THE TRAGIC EVENTS OF 1994

Like so many of the circuits in this book, an *autodromo* at Imola was first promoted by motorcycle racers. Citing the need to boost local employment they successfully lobbied for a new road from close to where the double corner Rivazza lies today, all the way through to Tosa. This could then be linked up with another road from Tosa to Rivazza and *presto*, they had a circuit.

Located tight against the Santerno River on one side, the track, laid out in 1950, follows the bends of the river out to the Tosa hairpin, then winds up through rolling Emilia Romagna countryside to Variante Alta (now officially Curva Gresini) before swooping back down to the double left-hander of Rivazza and returning to the pits.

The essential shape of Imola hasn't changed in 70 years, but it has introduced a variety of speed-calming chicanes to keep cars within the bounds of safety. Located an hour's drive from Ferrari's base at Maranello, there has been a long association with the Scuderia, indeed, Enzo himself attended the ground-breaking ceremony in 1950. And when the circuit opened in October 1952 he sent along Alberto Ascari and 'Gigi' Villoresi to try out a Ferrari 340 Sport.

Following the death of Enzo's son, 'Alfredino' from muscular dystrophy in 1956, after which he buried himself in grief, the owners made the shrewd decision to rename the circuit Autodromo Dino Ferrari. It was therefore no surprise that with the passing of the 'old man' in 1988, that his name would be added to the title.

CIRCUIT ENZO E DINO FERRARI

Length: 4.909 km (3.05 miles)
Lap Record: 1:15.484 (Lewis Hamilton, Mercedes W11, 2020)
Opened: 1953
First F1 Grand Prix: 1980
Number of F1 Grands Prix hosted: 31 (1 Italian, 4 Emilia Romagna, 26 San Marino)
Number of laps: 63
Race winning fact: Michael Schumacher has the most wins at Imola with seven between 1994 and 2006 – six of them in a Ferrari.

The original circuit at Imola was fast-flowing, but like its fellow Grade 1-rated Italian circuit, Monza, has been neutralized over the years by chicanes and corner tightening to keep speeds in check. Having fallen off the F1 calendar in 2007, there seemed little prospect for a return, but the Covid emergency of 2020 provided the perfect opportunity for teams to rediscover what a pleasant experience it was racing in Emilia Romagna – and also pay tribute to the memory of Ayrton Senna, whose statue has become a point of pilgrimage.

Formula 1 machinery competed on the circuit for the first time in 1963 with the ubiquitous Jim Clark claiming victory. Sixteen years later it would be Niki Lauda in a Brabham-Alfa taking a non-championship win in the Dino Ferrari Grand Prix where F1 teams took note of how much less frenzied Imola was in comparison to Monza. The facilities had steadily been improved through the 1970s, so when a dispute erupted with the Italian Grand Prix organizers, the unthinkable happened. Monza would not host the race in 1980, it would be Imola.

The debut grand prix was notable for a massive accident involving tifosi favourite Gilles Villeneuve, whose Ferrari punctured on Lap 5, wrecking his Ferrari 312/T5 in the approach to the Tosa hairpin. The slight curve near the spot would bear his name from 1984 and a proper chicane was inserted there from 1995 in the wake of the 1994 fatalities.

Monza, having improved the circuit facilities, re-established its position as the natural home of the Italian Grand Prix in 1981. Attendance at the 1980 Imola race had been encouraging, but any talk of alternating with Monza on an annual basis was swept aside. Instead, Imola's owners managed to persuade the FIA that they would be the suitable venue for an extra San Marino Grand Prix, which they would run from 1981 through to 2006.

Increasing speed was checked with chicanes at Variante Bassa and Variante Alta. But the flat-out Tamburello corner, just after the start, had proven to be dangerous; there was little run-off to the concrete wall, beyond which lay the Santerno

Top Didier Pironi leads Gilles Villeneuve into the Tosa hairpin on the final lap of their intra-team duel in 1982.

Above Pironi crosses the line a few metres in front of Villeneuve. The repercussions of what the French-Canadian believed was a betrayal would have fatal consequences.

Left A subdued Villeneuve watches his team-mate spray the champagne on the podium. By season's end Gilles would lose his life in a qualifying accident and Pironi's championship hopes would end in a horrific career-ending accident at Hockenheim.

Below left Although some thought Senna reckless on track, serious accidents affected him deeply. Here he discusses the implications of Lotus driver Martin Donnely's horrific accident at the 1990 Portuguese GP with great friend Sid Watkins, the FIA Medical Delegate.

Below right With his trademark helmet design in the Brazil national colours Ayrton goes through last-minute preparations with Williams race engineer David Brown before the 1994 San Marino Grand Prix.

Bottom Senna leads into the Tosa hairpin in 1994 closely followed by Michael Schumacher's Benetton with team-mate Damon Hill back in fourth place.

Below A 2021 aerial view of the circuit at Imola looking down on the Tosa hairpin. The Santerno River to the left has limited changes to the track and so speeds have been reduced into the two corners of the 1994 tragedies using chicanes; Tamburello at top left and Villeneuve at centre bottom, reducing the speed into Tosa.

Right The drivers take a moment to remember Ayrton Senna on the anniversary of his death, before the 1995 San Marino GP. From left: Nigel Mansell, Jean Alesi, Heinz-Harald Frentzen, Michael Schumacher, Damon Hill and Aguri Suzuki.

river, so no room for extension, and the track there was bumpy. In 1987, Nelson Piquet was injured after crashing his Williams FW11B at Tamburello in practice – a tyre failure resulted in a violent collision with the wall and half the rear end of the car was torn off. In magnitude, it was a far greater impact than the one which killed Senna and after a trip to hospital, FIA Medical Delegate Sid Watkins would not sign Piquet off to race. In fact Piquet's injuries had been so serious, he felt the need to conceal their full extent from the team, in case they sidelined him in what was a World Championship contending year.

In 1989, a wing failure on Gerhard Berger's Ferrari sent him straight on into the wall at Tamburello and with the world's TV audience watching in horror, the car caught fire with the driver stuck inside. Mercifully, fire marshals were on the scene immediately, but the seconds had passed agonisingly slowly till they arrived. It was a relief to everyone when Berger emerged with burns to his fingers the only lasting physical injury.

Then came what looked like the least serious of the three Tamburello crashes, but on a weekend when F1 was already in mourning. After Rubens Barrichello's Jordan had catapulted off the track on Friday at the Variante Bassa chicane sending the Brazilian driver to hospital, Roland Ratzenberger's Simtek fractured its wing following a spin and an off-track excursion at the Acque Minerali chicane. Coming through the fast Villeneuve kink it failed, lodged under the front car which went on unabated into the banking at Tosa. He was killed by the 314km/h (195mph) impact.

Right The distinctive stone pines of the Variante Alta, now renamed Curve Gresini after motorcycle star Fausto Gresini. Though, like Parabolica at Monza which was officially named for Michael Alboreto, most refer to it by its former name.

Below Ferrari's Charles Leclerc took a podium in front of home fans in the 2024 race.

Above There was a pre-race commemoration for both Roland Ratzenberger and Ayrton Senna ahead of the 2024 race, with the flags of Austria and Brazil displayed along with the two drivers' respective helmets. Senna's statue near Tamburello is a place of regular pilgrimage.

Left Max Verstappen leads Oscar Piastri at the start of the 2024 race. With increasing pressure on the F1 schedule from new countries bidding for a grand prix it will be increasingly difficult to keep an Imola race on the calendar.

Senna's accident followed on the Sunday. The opening laps of the race had been run behind the Safety Car after a startline collision between Pedro Lamy and JJ Lehto's stalled Benetton. Back underway, Senna's leading Williams speared straight off into the wall at Tamburello. It looked serious, but eminently survivable. Except a suspension arm had bent backwards and penetrated the Brazilian's helmet.

Following F1's bleakest weekend since 1960, the sport moved quickly to improve track safety on all grand prix circuits. Imola responded to the tragedy by creating a chicane at Tamburello and another at Villeneuve to lessen speeds on the approach to Tosa. Racing continued through to 2006 when the inadequate pit facilities and the pressure from new countries wishing to host a race forced San Marino off the Formula 1 calendar.

Away from the spotlight, Imola rebuilt the pit complex, removed the Variante Bassa, extended the pit lane, and tightened the second Rivazza. But only a major shift in policy would bring a grand prix back – and in 2020 that arrived in the form of the Covid-restricted season.

Portimao made its debut, the much-missed Istanbul Park returned and F1 rediscovered how much it liked racing at Imola compared to some of the desert car parks it had been forced onto. The race was sponsored by the Emilia Romagna region and although the 2023 event had to be cancelled due to widespread flooding in the region, it returned in 2024.

INDIANAPOLIS, INDIANA, USA

Indianapolis Motor Speedway

FORMULA 1 AT THE HOME OF AMERICAN MOTORSPORT WASN'T THE EASIEST OF MARRIAGES AND NOBODY WAS SURPRISED WHEN THEY WENT THEIR SEPARATE WAYS

Like the ovals in Montlhéry in France and Brooklands in England, the speedway at Indianapolis was built to test both road-going machinery and race cars. Indiana-born entrepreneur Carl G. Fisher had racing experience gained in France and in 1905, mindful that the French led the world in producing automobiles, with famous names such as Renault, Peugeot, DeDion-Bouton, Delahaye and Panhard, he felt that a lack of a test track was holding American manufacturers back.

His home state was forging ahead with many small-scale businesses and a great way to advertise their product would be the biggest and best race track. Fisher lobbied that 'Indianapolis is going to be the world's greatest center of horseless carriage manufacturer, what could be more logical than building the world's greatest racetrack right here?'

He found the 328-acre Pressley Farm five miles outside of Indianapolis and, together with fellow investors, incorporated the Indianapolis Motor Speedway in 1909. Early races on the 'dirt' track proved dangerous and the owners moved rapidly to replace it with 3.2 million 10-pound bricks – thus 'the Brickyard' was born. There were originally three race meetings staged by the speedway on three major holiday weekends (Memorial Day, Fourth of July and Labor Day) but this was reduced to one epic race on Memorial Day – the Indianapolis 500.

Gradually the bricks were replaced with asphalt sections, until all that was left was a token yard of bricks at the start/finish.

When Formula 1 was conceived in 1950 the sport's organizers wanted to include the US and bizarrely the winner of the Indy 500 scored points towards the World Championship until 1960, even though the specialized machinery needed to go fast on the high-speed oval was quite different to the demands of almost all the F1 circuits. There would be the occasional F1 visitor in the 1960s with tyre failure damaging Jim Clark's Lotus suspension in 1964 before the Scot won the race a year later, and a then-colossal $166,621 prize, in the Lotus 38.

Under the guidance of Tony George, the number of race events began to expand in the 1990s. After Watkins Glen was deemed too dangerous, Formula 1 had cast around for a suitable venue for the US Grand Prix. The races at Las Vegas,

Opposite The 1955 Indianapolis 500 in progress at the Indianapolis Motor Speedway (IMS) when it really was a 'brickyard'.

Above Kimi Räikkönen heads off from P2 on the 2005 grid with no intention of returning to his grid slot after the parade lap. Unlike IndyCars, F1 tackled the IMS in a clockwise direction.

Right By the time of the British invasion in 1966, a win at Indy no longer counted towards the World Championship. Jim Clark (right) finished runner up to race winner Graham Hill (centre) while Jackie Stewart was Rookie of the Year. Clark had won the race for Lotus in 1965, the first win for a rear-engined car at the Indianapolis 500.

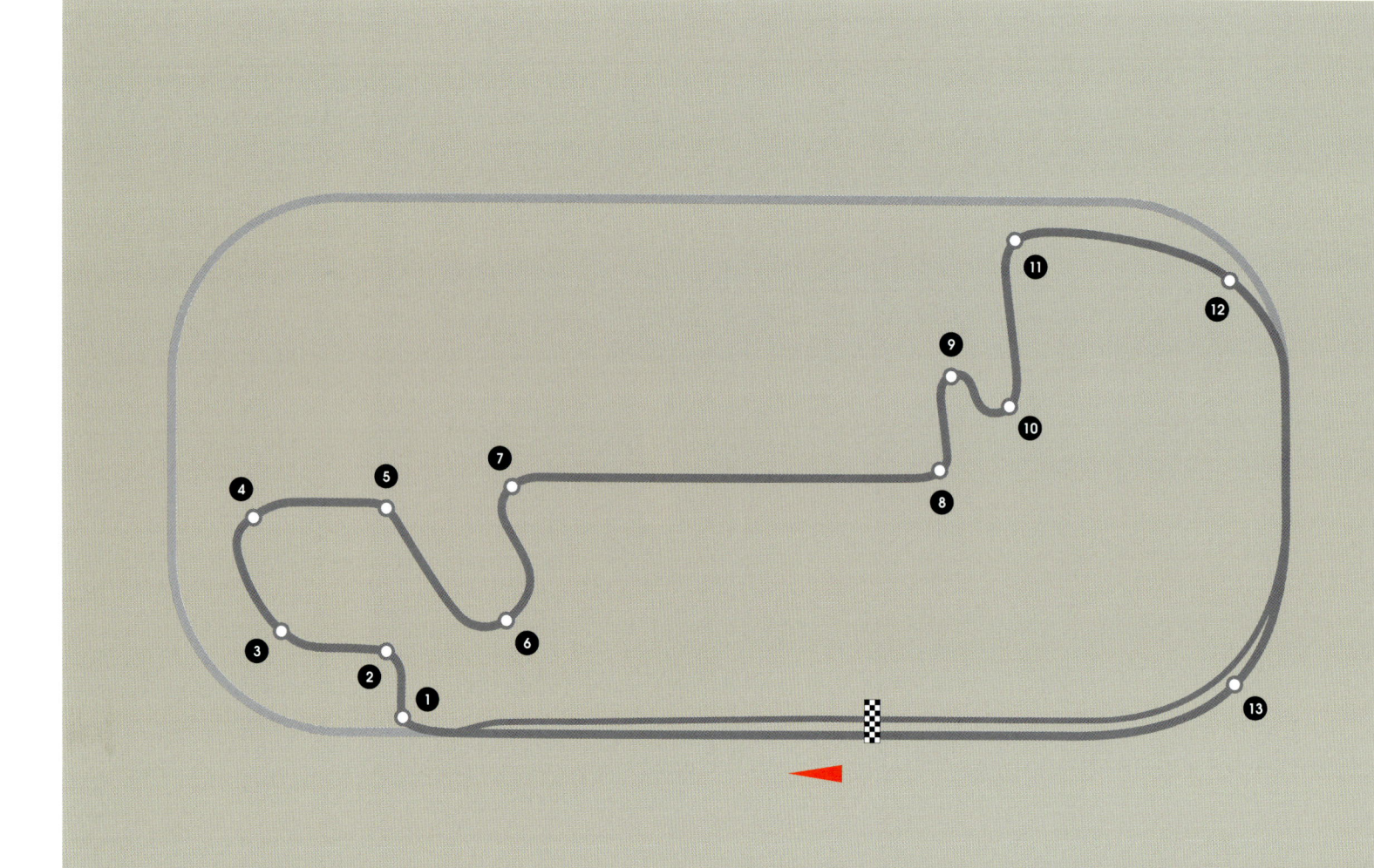

INDIANAPOLIS MOTOR SPEEDWAY

Length: 4.190 km (2.605 miles)
Lap Record: 1:10.399, (Rubens Barrichello, Ferrari F2004, 2004)
Opened: 1909
First F1 Grand Prix: 2000
Last F1 Grand Prix: 2007
Number of F1 Grands Prix hosted: 8
Number of laps: 73
Designers of F1 circuit: Kevin Forbes and Hermann Tilke
Race winning fact: Lewis Hamilton edged out Fernando Alonso in the final IMS F1 grand prix in 2007 in his challenge to become a rookie World Champion.

F1 racing at Indianapolis was always going to be a huge compromise, but Bernie Ecclestone had been under pressure from the teams to unlock the lucrative US market and a race at the home of American motorsport seemed hard to resist, even though set-up would be awkward. As one commentator put it: 'It's one frightening bend, one massive straight, an overtaking opportunity and the infield section is all the odd bits of track left in the Scalextric box.' The race's future in Indiana was hopelessly shackled by the 2005 Michelin tyre debacle. In Max Mosley's 2015 autobiography he reveals that Edouard Michelin opposed his election to an FIA post, and some believe that this was a long-harboured grudge.

Long Beach, Dallas and Detroit barely captured the public's imagination – unless they were a big fan of 90-degree turns – and after Phoenix in 1991, the US Grand Prix lapsed.

Then, in 2000, Bernie Ecclestone announced he had concluded a deal to run the USGP at the spiritual home of American motor-racing, Indianapolis. A 2.6-mile (4.2-km) circuit was built through the infield linking Turns 1 and the exit of Turn 2, limiting the amount of flat-out running. Even so, drivers were on full throttle right through the banked final corner (Turn 1 on the oval) and along the main straight for up to 25 seconds – the longest flat-out blast of any F1 circuit. Plus Indy fans had to adjust to the sight of cars travelling in a clockwise direction for once.

The first race was a record-breaker with an estimated 225,000 attending on the Sunday to see Michael Schumacher take the win in his third World Championship-winning year. Two years later he caused controversy by trying to engineer a dead heat with team-mate Rubens Barrichello. He was already World Champion that year, a season in which Ferrari had invoked team orders and forced Barrichello to hand the Austrian Grand Prix victory to Michael, even though he had no serious rival. It was a vain attempt at parity – given the sophistication of F1 timing – and Schumacher lost the race by 0.011 seconds.

Worse was to happen in 2005. Formula 1 was in the middle of tyre wars with three Bridgestone-running teams pitted against the majority of Michelin runners. In practice a series of tyre failures for the Michelin-shod cars pointed to the fact that they

Below The magnificent Indianapolis pagoda is an echo of the wooden original from 1913. With more than 250,000 permanent seats, it is the biggest sports venue in the world, let alone the biggest motorsport venue. However, for the F1 races, only a small proportion of the grandstands was used.

Right Ralf Schumacher was alarmed by the Michelin tyre failure that threw his Toyota into the wall during practice in 2005. It was then that the tyre company realized there was a major problem with integrity of the sidewalls. Bridgestone had data from their subsidiary Firestone which supplied the Indy Racing League.

could not withstand the loads of the Turn 1 cornering speeds. Bridgestone had tyre data from their American subsidiary, and understandably had not been keen to share it with their rival in advance. A solution was found to avoid the problem – a chicane at Turn 1 (not unlike one introduced at Montlhéry, and a device previous used in a Spanish GP). FIA boss Max Mosley in his remote Parisian office refused to accept the compromise. The circuit would not be changed on his autocratic watch.

Michelin could not guarantee the safety of their tyres and although all 20 cars formed up on the grid, after the parade lap, 14 returned to the pits leaving six cars to 'race' in front of a hostile crowd who resorted to throwing beer cans on the track. Michelin helped refund fans and the 2006 race was surprisingly well supported – even so, seven cars were eliminated in two accidents on the opening lap when Mark Webber collided with Christian Klien in Turn 1 and then, in Turn 2, McLaren's Juan Pablo Montoya made contact with teammate Kimi Räikkönen, before hitting Jenson Button, who in turn was hit by Nick Heidfeld, whose Sauber was launched into a triple barrel roll. In two corners there had been more action than in the previous year's 73 laps. That is, not counting the unabated arguments in the paddock.

The 2007 race proved to be the final F1 race at Indy after a Mexican stand-off between Tony George and Bernie Ecclestone over that perennial favourite for losing a grand prix – race hosting fees. It would not be until 2012 that Austin took its place on the F1 calendar and banished all thoughts of Indy for good.

INTERLAGOS, SÃO PAULO, BRAZIL

Autódromo José Carlos Pace

ONE OF FORMULA 1'S OLDEST STAGES, INTERLAGOS HAS MADE IT THROUGH TO THE MODERN ERA. BUT IT USED TO BE ALMOST DOUBLE THE LENGTH…

Interlagos has been a regular on the grand prix calendar, its long-time ramshackle character compensated by the passionate fans and the support of São Paulo drivers, Emerson Fittipaldi, Ayrton Senna, Rubens Barrichello and Felipe Massa. Barrichello grew up close to the circuit, but unlike the other three, never won his home race.

The circuit 'between the lakes' had been created in 1940 to run national events on an almost 8 kms track (5 miles) that stretched from a hillside start, down and around a lake and then curved back on itself many times before heading up the hill again from the final corner, Junção. Almost all the spectator viewing was from the hill looking down into this natural amphitheatre of switchbacks that included corners such as 'Beak of the Duck'/Bico de Pato and the horseshoe-shaped bend Ferradura.

When Formula 1 was established in the 1950s it had been the Argentinians Juan Manuel Fangio and 'Pampas Bull' Froilán González, who had a commanded a home race for a logistically challenging South American round in Buenos Aires. By the early 1970s it was a young Brazilian, Emerson Fittipaldi driving for Gold Leaf Team Lotus who was the exciting prospect, winning the USGP in his debut season.

In 1972 Fittipaldi became the youngest World Champion at 25 and so a home race in São Paulo was guaranteed to fill the stands. Come race day, it was team-mate Ronnie Peterson who put his Lotus on pole by 0.2 of a second, but a rear wheel

Opposite **In the days before they built grandstands opposite the pits Jean-Pierre Jarier qualified on pole in his Shadow-Ford for the fourth running of the Brazilian Grand Prix. With the extra-long circuit, his pole lap was a 2:29.**

Left **Cars set off for the parade lap before the sprint race in 2023. The size of the grandstand opposite the pits is limited by the road running behind it.**

Below **Colin Chapman and Barbro Peterson, wife of Lotus driver Ronnie, perch on the pitwall recording times during practice for the 1973 race.**

problem handed the race to Fittipaldi ahead of Jackie Stewart, who would be his main contender for the 1973 drivers' title. Emo won it again in 1974, but in 1975 he had to take a lower step on the podium when fellow São Paulista, Carlos Pace, won the race in a Brabham BT44B. It would be Pace's only grand prix victory, in 1977 he was killed in a light aircraft accident and in 1985 the circuit was renamed in his memory as the Autódromo José Carlos Pace.

As the decade wore on, so the circuit wore out. At the end of the 1970s there was strong criticism over the bumpy and uneven nature of the track, and Fittipaldi's F1 performances suffered from what biographer Steve Small described as 'a spectacularly ill-judged career move'. He had started up his own team, Copersuca/Fittipaldi and turned his 2nd place in the championship with McLaren in 1975 to 16th place with his own under-performing cars in 1976.

With the city unwilling to finance improvements, the race moved south to the new Jacarepaguá circuit built on a former swamp near Rio de Janeiro. Appropriately the new Brazilian star was Rio-born Nelson Piquet and for a decade he was the star of the show during the Brazilian Grand Prix weekend, winning twice in front of his home fans. As the 1990s approached, the FIA increased safety standards required by circuits and with Rio losing money, the Mayor of São Paulo, Luiza Erundina, saw an opportunity to snatch the grand prix back.

To make Interlagos more F1 relevant, the circuit was almost halved in length to 4.31 kms (2.67 miles) turning it from a

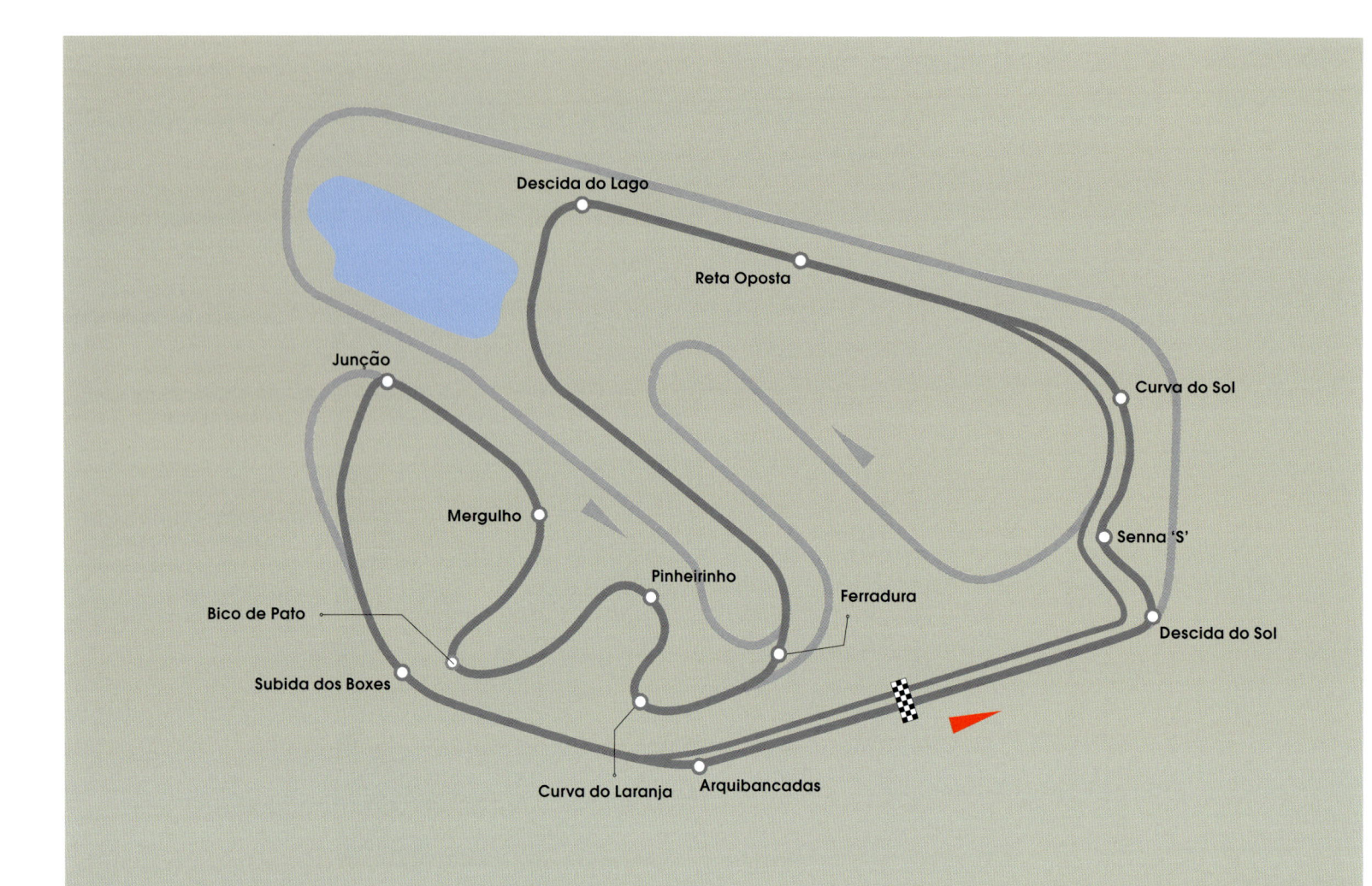

AUTÓDROMO JOSÉ CARLOS PACE

Length: 3.337 km (2.074 miles)
Lap Record: 1:10.540 (Valtteri Bottas, Mercedes W09, 2018)
Opened: 1940
First F1 Grand Prix: 1973
Number of F1 Grands Prix hosted: 40
Number of laps: 71
Major circuit change: 1990
Race winning fact: Ayrton Senna finally won his home race at the eighth attempt in 1991 – unlike local boy Rubens Barrichello who failed in 19 attempts (six of those with Ferrari).

When F1 first ventured to the city in the 1970s, the Interlagos circuit was a massive 7.960 km (4.946 miles) and the lap times were around 2:30. After the bumps proved too much in 1980, the Brazilian Grand Prix decamped to Rio de Janeiro. When F1 returned in 1990, with a packed circuit guaranteed by its World Championship-winning favourite son, Ayrton Senna on the grid, the shortened circuit proved to be a real success, frequently delivering dramatic races.

2:23 lap in 1979 to a 1:17 pole lap for Ayrton Senna in 1990. At the end of the start/finish straight, the track now cut left through the Esses, soon to become the Senna Esses, to join the inner loop of track and sprint downhill to Descida do Lago. Previously cars had come up the hill in the opposite direction.

Originally the track went around the outer curve and today, cars which miss their braking point for Turn 1, often end up going straight on into the run-off area that was the old track. Cars no longer looped down beyond the small lake but cut across the top of it before reaching the horseshoe-shaped Ferradura. And while the cars had previously swept around a gentle curve at Junção, this was now closer to 90-degrees, slowing the cars and putting an emphasis on engine power on the on the long drag uphill.

There have been minor corner reprofiles since, but the only real difference between the circuit of 1990 and today is the position of the pit lane, the entry to which is perilously close to the racing line. Hence the pit lane entry has gone backwards and forwards over the years, but mostly backwards towards Junção, to find the safest compromise. In 1999 the pit lane exit was also changed. Previously it had emerged onto the track at the bottom of the Senna 'S' and was a favourite place for marshals to collect carbon fibre, but from 1999 it joined on the downhill straight to Descida do Lago.

Interlagos has a reputation for sudden deluges. In 2003, running water across the track at Turn 3 created a car park of wrecked machinery behind the Armco, as six cars, one car

Below Jean-Pierre Jarier's Shadow-Ford out on track in 1975. One of the famous corners at the modern Interlagos is Descida do Lago (where Verstappen pushed Hamilton off during the 2021 race) or 'Lake Descent'. The old circuit went past the lake and then the circuit doubled back round and Jarier is about to make a 180-degree turn and go up Lake Descent.

Bottom The start of the chaotic 2008 race when Lewis Hamilton left it exceptionally late to win his first world title.

Right The grandstands were still undeveloped when Ayrton Senna put his McLaren-Honda MP4/6, on pole for the 1991 Brazilian Grand Prix.

after another, misjudged the grip and ran straight on into the barriers, including World Champion Michael Schumacher. The 2016 race was similarly chaotic. At the heart of it was Pirelli's poor-functioning full-wet tyre, which was hardly better than the intermediate, and drivers found themselves aquaplaning and spinning helplessly into the Armco at regular intervals. Romain Grosjean didn't even make it to the grid.

There were five safety cars and two red flags in all. One of them was brought out by Kimi Räikkönen's accident on the main straight. Another saw Felipe Massa slide his Williams into the barriers at what was supposed to be his final Brazilian Grand Prix, and with racing neutralized, mechanics came out of the garages all along the pit lane to applaud him as he walked

87

back to the Williams garage in tears.

In a roll of the dice, Verstappen was brought in from second place on Lap 43 for a set of inters to try and chase Lewis Hamilton down for the win. But then the rain started to get worse, and Max was called back for more wets, emerging in 14th place with 15 laps to go. He then embarked on a mesmerising charge through the field, (including 'Save of the Season' when he lost the rear on the main straight) charging past a succession of cars, all on the same tyres. He made it back to third place on a day when no-one was watching the winner. Toto Wolf described it as "really unbelievable driving. Physics are being redefined."

The Brazilian Grand prix was often the last race of the season and while the 2007 drivers' title went down to the final GP in São Paulo, the 2008 Interlagos showdown between Lewis Hamilton and Felipe Massa redefined the phrase 'taking it to the wire'.

In another chaotic wet race Felipe Massa took the victory while championship rival Lewis Hamilton was back in sixth place on the final lap when he needed to be fifth. Ahead of him Timo Glock had stayed out on slicks and was falling backwards when Hamilton passed him at Junção, effectively winning the drivers' title at the last corner, on the last lap, of the last race. Journalist Joe Saward noted that Massa 'took defeat with a grace and a style that one rarely sees in modern sport.'

Interlagos's place on the grand prix calendar has been likened to just-in-time production management. Every time F1 demands improvements to the circuit, the organizers respond just in time to renew the contract. After recent pit and paddock improvements, the circuit has never looked better. But with drivers preferring fewer races and teams ever mindful of the security problems getting personnel into the circuit safely, the clock may well be ticking.

Opposite top **Carlos Pace** driving a Brabham BT44B on his way to victory in 1975. It was the only win of his short career.

Above **The start of the grand prix in 2023 and already Alex Albon and Kevin Magnussen have tangled before the first turn.**

Opposite bottom **The chance of sudden heavy rain in Brazil is often a factor in races. In 2023 Lando Norris walks back to the pits after qualifying as the heavens open.**

Left **An aerial view of the Interlagos circuit from 2023 gives a good overview of the changes made to ensure Brazil's place on the F1 calendar.**

SAN SEBASTIÁN DE LOS REYES, MADRID, SPAIN

Circuito de Madrid Jarama

LIKE SO MANY EUROPEAN MOTOR-RACING CIRCUITS, THE LAYOUT OF JARAMA WAS LIMITED BY THE LAND AVAILABLE

It may have some of the most evocative corner names in Formula 1 – Farina, Fangio, Nuvolari, Ascari and Portago, but the Jarama circuit is more suited to two wheels than four. Given that it was designed by one of the architects of Suzuka, John Hugenholtz, that is surprising; but when the Dutchman was handed the brief in the mid-1960s by the Royal Automobile Club of Spain he had wanted more land.

The club had bought an area of scrubland at San Sebastián on the northern outskirts of Madrid (not to be confused with the northern coastal town of San Sebastián that hosted a grand prix between 1923 and 1930) and divided it between a golf club and a race circuit. The land allocated for motor-racing was smaller than Hugenholtz had envisaged which resulted in a compact circuit with tight switchbacks making maximum use of the land, though helped by elevation changes. In many ways it was a forerunner to the Circuit de Catalunya which would succeed it.

The track, pit buildings and brutalist concrete control tower were complete by February 1967, with an official opening in July. It was Jim Clark who won the first single-seater race for F2 machinery at Jarama later that month. Barcelona's street circuit, Pedralbes, had hosted the last Spanish Grand Prix in 1951 and 1954 and in a bid to re-instate the event the Royal Automobile Club hosted a non-championship F1 race at Jarama in 1967, which, inevitably, was won by Jim Clark.

This paved the way for Jarama's inclusion as part of the World Championship from the 1968 season, though the track was

Left Denny Hulme and Bruce McLaren sit on their respective McLarens as they wait for practice to begin at Jarama in 1968. The cars bear the original McLaren papaya paint scheme and treaded tyres. It will not be until 1970 that slicks become standard.

Opposite Jackie Stewart in the March 701 leads the McLaren of Denny Hulme and the Brabham of Jack Brabham as he jumps the pair of them at the start of the 1970 Spanish Grand Prix.

Below Today Jarama is home to the FIA Spanish Truck Grand Prix.

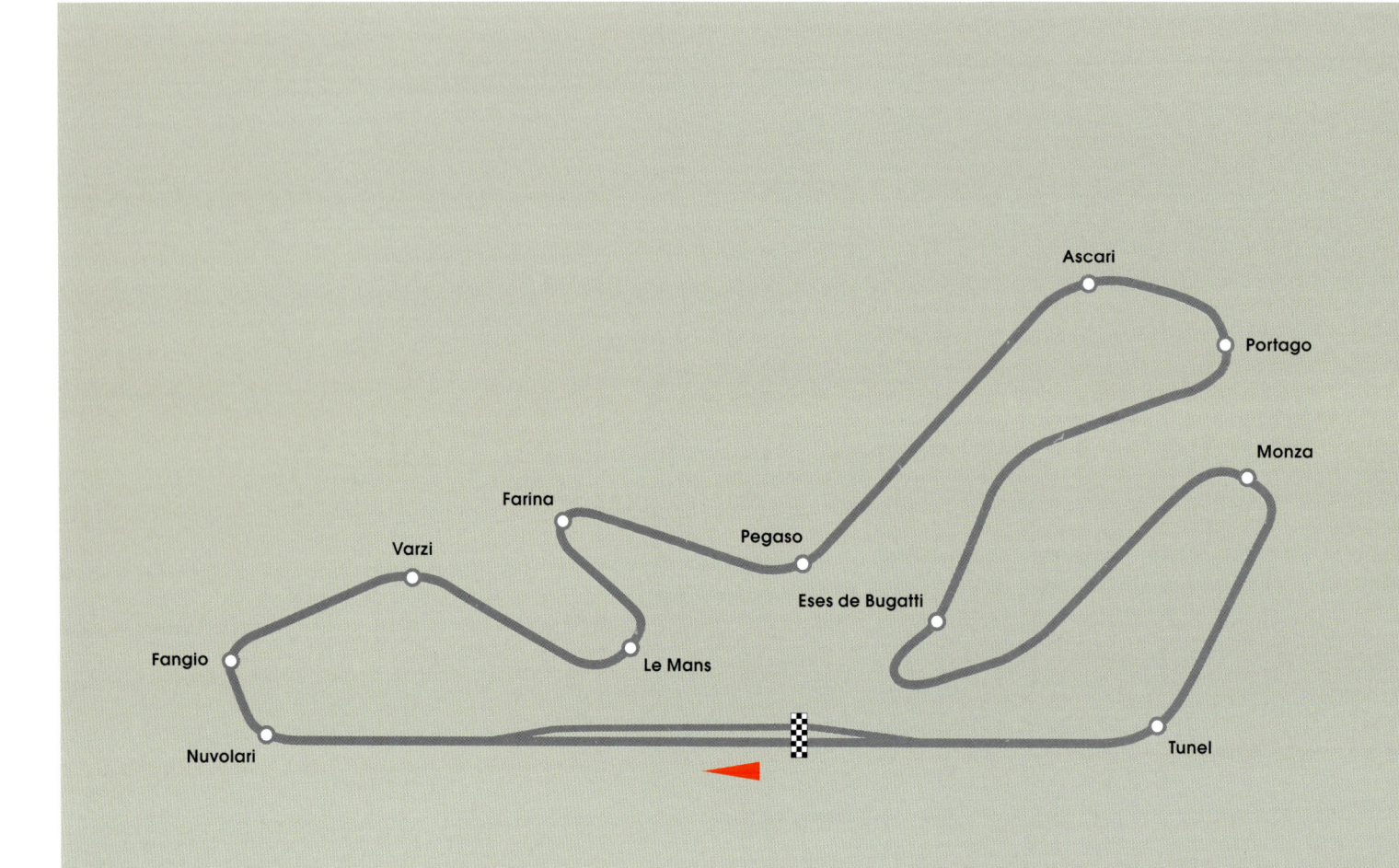

CIRCUITO DE MADRID JARAMA

Length: 3.404 km (2.115 miles)
Lap Record: 1:16.440 (Gilles Villeneuve, Ferrari 312T4, 1979)
Opened: 1967
First F1 Grand Prix: 1968
Last F1 Grand Prix: 1981
Number of F1 Grands Prix hosted: 9
Number of laps: 80
Designer: John Hugenholtz
Race winning fact: Gilles Villeneuve's 1981 grand prix victory was the final win of his short, 68-race career.

Although doubt has been cast on how much of both Suzuka and Zandvoort circuits John Hugenholtz designed, the narrow, twisty Jarama circuit is all the Dutchman's own. It hosted nine F1 races in its time, many run in chaotic fashion. Unwittingly it was also the circuit at the centre of a major row between the FOCA teams and the FIA in 1980, over finance and control of the sport. The race went ahead as a show of muscle from Bernie Ecclestone's FOCA, but the FIA refused to ratify the result, a win for Alan Jones in the Williams. That excision from the record books didn't stop Jones from becoming World Champion in 1980.

obliged to alternate with Barcelona's Montjuïc Park street course until 1975. In the wake of Jim Clark's death a month earlier, the mood at the initial grand prix was sombre. Drivers asked for more safety catch-fencing to be erected and when two inexperienced Spanish drivers were proposed to boost gate numbers there was talk of a driver boycott. In the race it was a case of last man standing as leader after leader retired with mechanical problems. The BRM team was not amused when Pedro Rodríguez crashed out on Lap 23 and spectators descended on his car 'like vultures' and removed many parts as souvenirs.

Two years later – the intervening Montjuïc race having endured its own safety problems in 1969 – Jarama was at the centre of another safety row and organizational chaos brought on by last-minute changes to the qualifying procedure. Only 16 of the 22 cars entered were allowed to start, which meant that drivers such as Rolf Stommelen in the Brabham-Ford, who had been 12th quickest in the first part of qualifying on Friday, was hauled off the grid.

Once the race got under way Jackie Oliver's BRM suffered a broken stub axle going into the Bugatti Esses and T-boned Jacky Ickx's Ferrari, puncturing the fuel tanks. Immediately 45 gallons of Avgas in the Ferrari went up in flames along with the BRM and it's similarly laden fuel load. Oliver was out of his car quickly, but Ickx was slower out, emerging with his overalls on fire, which were extinguished by a soldier at the side of the track. The fire marshals dispensed a lot of foam onto the track before they brought

Left The iconic brutalist control tower is central to many posters advertising races at Jarama.

Bottom After an early collision between Jacky Ickx in the Ferrari and Jackie Oliver in a BRM, the cars were left to burn throughout the 1970 race. Although both drivers escaped relatively unharmed, the teams paid a high price for the organizers' lack of proper safety equipment.

Below Jackie Stewart avoids the burning oil, water and extinguisher foam sprayed on the circuit in the 1970 grand prix. The idea of a race continuing with a burning car at the side of the track seems bizarre in the context of modern F1, but it was commonplace in the 1960s and 1970s.

Left Gilles Villeneuve in the Ferrari 126C angles his head to see how close Jacques Laffite is during the 1981 Spanish Grand Prix. Villeneuve finished 0.22 seconds in front of the Ligier-Matra and 0.58 seconds in front of John Watson's McLaren, seen here closing in. The five cars in shot finished within two seconds of each other.

Below Patrick Depailler in the Tyrrell-Ford about to be lapped by Niki Lauda's Ferrari in the 1974 Spanish Grand Prix.

Opposite top Fernando Alonso takes a run in the DTM-spec Aston Martin Vantage that he bought from engine builder HWA in 2023. The Jarama control tower behind has been updated in the intervening years.

Opposite bottom The Vantage DTM from 2019 was handed over to Alonso during a large fan event organized by his sponsor, Finetwork, in September 2023. Madrid now holds the contract for a street race between 2026 and 2035.

extinguishers to bear on the burning cars and the foam soon ran out. With the race lasting 90 laps, drivers had to negotiate through a foam ice rink – Jack Brabham spun his car twice – with the two flaming cars sat at the side of the track burning steadily throughout the rest of the race, while the water poured onto the wreckage created magnesium flare-ups. As an exercise in how not to run an F1 race, Jarama 1970 was a comprehensive success.

F1 speeds ramped up through the 1970s, exposing the limitations of the tight and narrow circuit. Things came to a head at the 1981 race when Gilles Villeneuve, driving the difficult-handling, new turbo-powered Ferrari 126C, was able to hold off far more agile cars. Gilles described it as 'like driving a big red Cadillac', but he managed to keep four cars behind him all the way to the flag. The top five were separated by an exciting 1.24 seconds, but it proved to be Jarama's final race. The circuit at Jerez would take over from 1986.

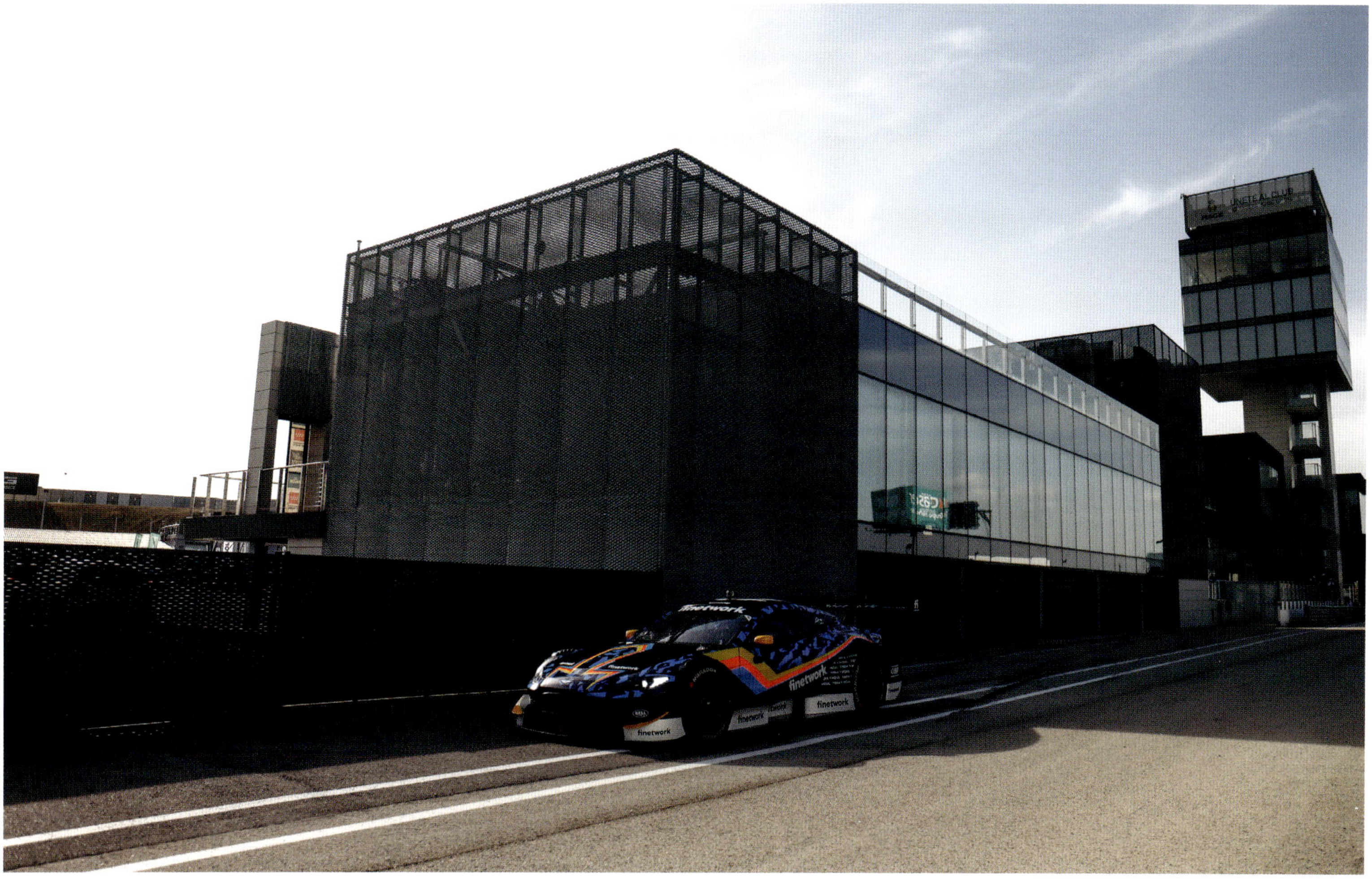
finetwork

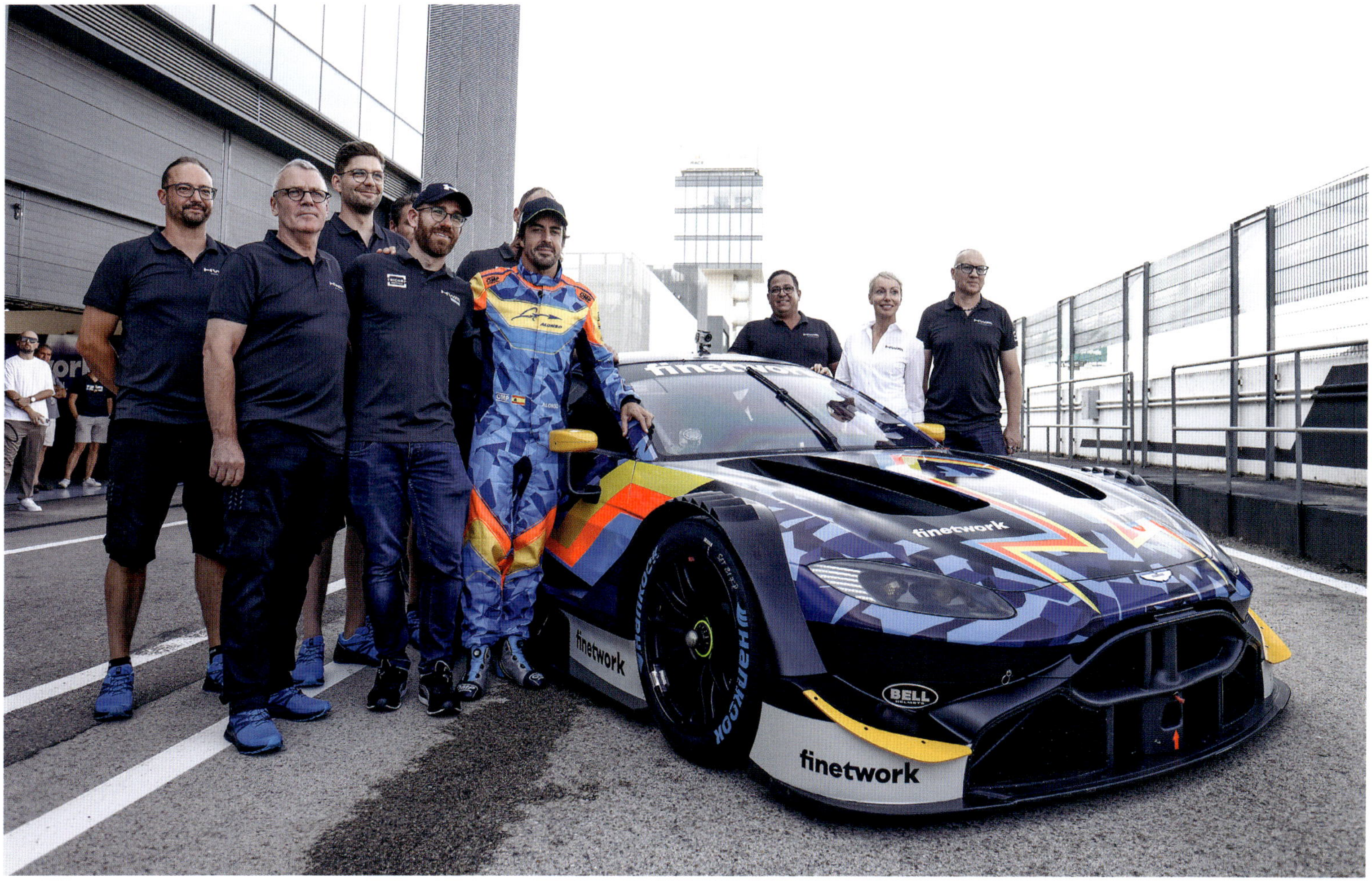
finetwork
finetwork
BELL
HANKOOK

Above Gilles Villeneuve (27) had very little luck in Vegas. After qualifying third he started from the wrong grid position and was disqualified.

Opposite After extended negotiations and considerable investment, Liberty Media pulled off the coup of a race down the Las Vegas Strip. Max Verstappen and Charles Leclerc go side by side into the first turn of what would be a memorable race.

LAS VEGAS, NEVADA, USA

Caesars Palace

IF FORMULA 1 COULD PULL OFF A GRAND PRIX IN DOWN-AT-HEEL LONG BEACH, SURELY A RACE IN LAS VEGAS HAD VERY GOOD ODDS

Race circuits once built can stand or fall on access roads and nearby accommodation. Aida in Japan and Yeongam in South Korea are two great circuits which failed when it came to providing nearby hotels. When Las Vegas casino-resort Caesars Palace put their money down on a grand prix for the 1981 season, that was not going to be a problem.

Always with an eye to expanding in America, Bernie Ecclestone had spent four years negotiating with the casino owners to host the event. Unlike the modern race, there had been no agreement with rival casinos or with Clark County and the race would take place on a Saturday afternoon. It was due to follow a week after the USGP (East) at Watkins Glen. But when the New York track failed to come up with payments to teams still owing from the 1980 race, the East Coast event was pulled, never to return.

The omens were still good for F1's Vegas debut: Chris Pook, the man who had successfully launched the Long Beach race was promoter. It was the season finale with the drivers' title on the line. There was local interest with two strong American drivers on the grid in former World Champion Mario Andretti and Eddie Cheever (who would score a podium the following year). And as team personnel were booked into Caesars Palace, there would be no queueing for two hours on the snarled up A43 to get into the circuit.

Creating a grand prix track of a sizeable length inside the casino's parking lot was the biggest challenge – that and drivers

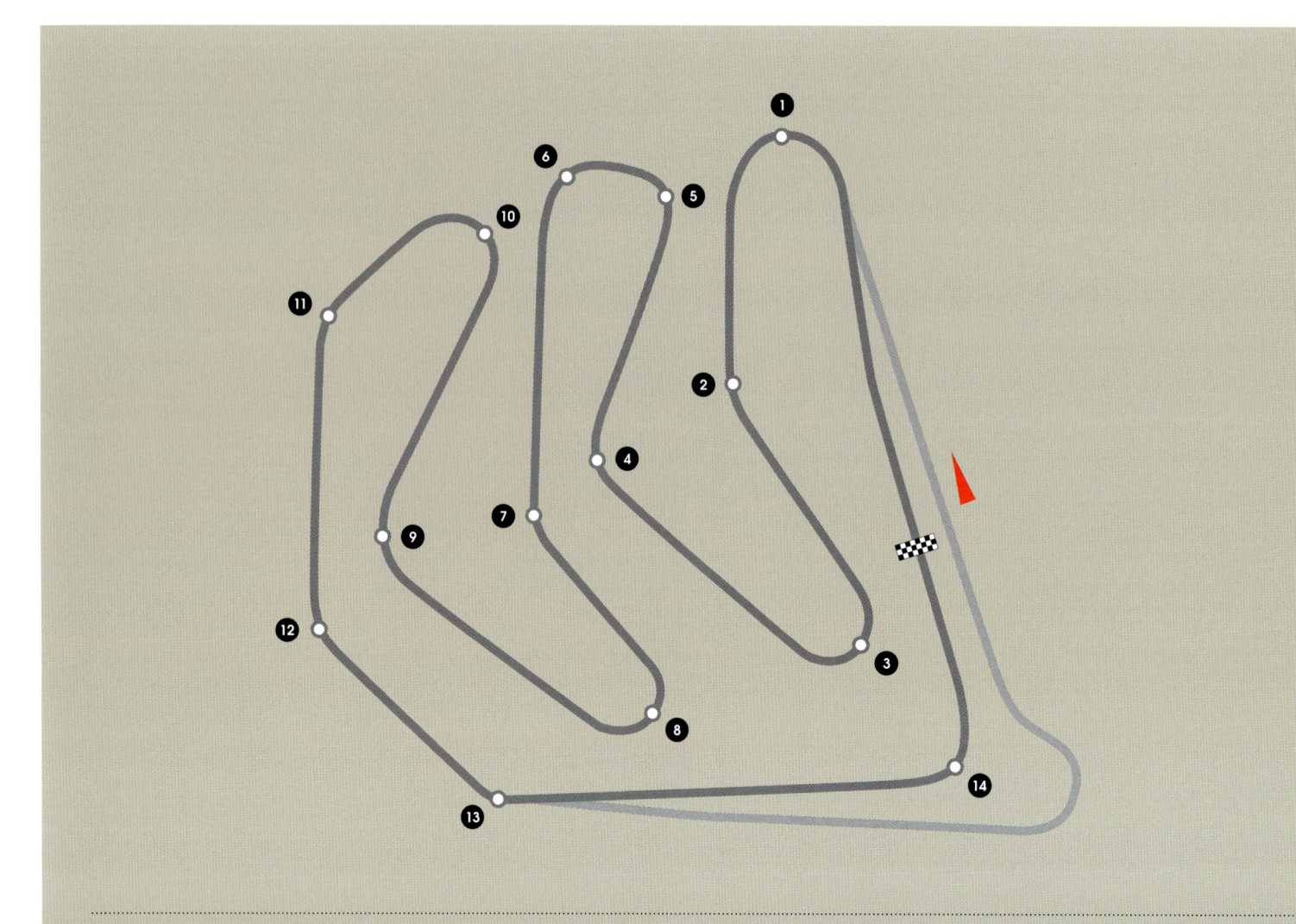

CAESARS PALACE

Length: 3.650 km (2.268 miles)
Lap Record: 1:19.369 (Michele Alboreto, Tyrrell 011, 1982)
Opened: 1981
First F1 Grand Prix: 1981
Last F1 Grand Prix: 1982
Number of F1 Grands Prix hosted: 2
Number of laps: 75
Race winning fact: Michele Alboreto won the 1982 race in a Tyrrell to become the 11th different winner in the season, a record number of winners.

The race at Caesars Palace was intended to draw in the high rollers for the weekend, just as the big boxing tournaments had at Caesars in the past. F1 didn't have the same drawing power as the preceding Sugar Ray Leonard vs Thomas Hearns fight. Nelson Piquet won the World Championship title for Brabham that weekend and team owner Bernie Ecclestone celebrated by taking to the gambling tables himself. Max Mosley revealed in his autobiography that Bernie then lost $100,000 playing with a group of elderly Chinese ladies.

coping with the heat, which could still be a factor in mid-October Nevada. The circuit had been designed to run anti-clockwise, unlike most race circuits on the calendar, putting a strain on under-used neck muscles. That, combined with a tight, bumpy and disorientating track, woven through a flat parking lot between metre-high concrete barriers, made the driving experience as testing as the accommodation was luxurious.

Spectators may have got a great view, encompassing the whole of the flat circuit, but none of the stands were covered. The photographers were aggrieved as they had no access to the infield to take photos on what was a critical race – the title-deciding grand prix. English photo-journalist Mike Doodson received last-minute permission from Chris Pook to access the infield, and then was arrested by Clark County police for entering a restricted area and marched into detention. He had to be freed by an incandescent FIA chief Jean-Marie Balestre.

The race proved to be a non-contest with Alan Jones in the Williams disappearing off into the distance from the front row, while Williams team-mate and polesitter Carlos Reutemann tried to keep ahead of championship rival Nelson Piquet. Reutemann slipped behind the Brabham driver with gearbox problems on Lap 17 and it was left to an exhausted Piquet to bring his car home in fifth place to take the drivers' title.

Although forthright Aussie Alan Jones described the circuit in 1981 as, "a goat track flattened out", time has mellowed him. When Las Vegas rebooted the grand prix in 2023 he thought it

Below left The course skirted the Sands Hotel and Casino (visible top right) made famous by Frank Sinatra and Sammy Davis Jr. Indeed, Sammy Davis dropped by to meet the drivers for the first running of the grand prix. Here, Didier Pironi gives team-mate Gilles Villeneuve a lift back to the pits during practice, after his car stopped on track.

Below right Michele Alboreto won the second grand prix at Caesars Palace in 1982, his first win, in the Tyrrell-Ford.

Bottom The cars pile into the first turn of what will be a disorientating succession of loops, in 1981.

Right **The much-vaunted Sphere employed in the 2023 race is not the first to appear in Las Vegas. Between 1980 and 1989 Caesars Palace had its own Omnimax Theatre dome.**

Opposite **As part of the F1 race preparations, organizers commandeered the Sphere as a changing backdrop to the race. Sergio Pérez in the No.11 Red Bull RB19 passes through during practice for the race.**

Below **Vainglorious President of the FIA, Jean-Marie Balestre – centre stage on the podium in suit – waits for his opportunity to grab the microphone in what was a typically disorganized podium ceremony. Drivers would regularly give him 'bunny ears' during his speech. The Caesars Palace podium, complete with laurel wreaths and attendant centurions was more elaborate than most, but low-key in comparison to today's podium ceremonies.**

Opposite bottom **Max Verstappen in an Elvis tribute racesuit takes the top step of Formula 1's grandest podium in 2023. These days the podium is carefully choreographed.**

was no worse than others on the grand prix calendar. "I have raced on circuits which are just as tight in Europe," he recalled. "It was quite technical to race." The problem was the anti-clockwise nature. "For the final six or seven laps, I would go through a left-hander and my head would fall over to the right and I would have to wait for the next right-hander for it to come back up again."

The inaugural race was not a financial success, failing to attract the high-rollers the casino was used to attracting for big boxing matches. A year later, and again the race would be the title decider, this time between Keke Rosberg for Williams and John Watson in a McLaren, who needed to win the race.

Intriguingly, for 1982 there had been a serious proposal to run the F1 race on the Saturday and a CART race around the perimeter oval on the Sunday. When Jean-Marie Balestre got wind of the plan he had moved the event forward and banned any future dual championship events alongside the North American single-seater series.

The 75-lap race was won by Michele Alboreto, driving a normally aspirated Tyrrell-Ford. In a season which saw the racing retirement, through injury, of Ferrari's Didier Pironi, there had been 11 different winning drivers and World Champion Rosberg achieved it with just a single race win.

Caesars Palace gamble on F1 had not come off financially, and the race was not continued in 1983, but lessons were learned for the future Las Vegas Grand Prix. For a start, Las Vegas looks best at night, when temperatures are more driver and spectator friendly. Also, it's best to get the entire city involved in the

project to promote the event. The new grand prix has been a tremendous success despite World Champion Max Verstappen's initial reluctance to embrace the showbiz aspects. And having a titanic, race-long battle for its debut grand prix was a suitable introduction to those who had come to Las Vegas out of curiosity.

100

WELCOME
VEGAS
salesforce

FERRARI
FIA Formula 1 World Championship
LAS VEGAS

LONG BEACH, CALIFORNIA, USA

Long Beach

LONG BEACH WAS AN INDUSTRIAL PORT CITY WITH A HISTORY OF MANUFACTURING, BUT THE GRAND PRIX HELPED TRANSFORM IT INTO AN UPSCALE RESORT

The Grand Prix of Long Beach was the vision of English ex-pat Chris Pook, who was working as a travel agent in the faded seaside resort south of Los Angeles. Long Beach's claim to fame in the mid-1970s was the presence of the RMS *Queen Mary*, the elegant transatlantic liner which had been turned into a hotel and casino. Pook had the idea to organize a motor race for F5000 cars around the city to draw tourists in. If Monte Carlo could do it…

At the time the city was a long way from the glittering Mediterranean venue for the Monaco Grand Prix, as former Brabham and McLaren driver John Watson told author Andrew Benson for his book, *Remarkable Motor Races:* 'It was the first street track in North America that F1 had raced on. It was very much a navy town. Not so much dodgy, but it didn't have the polish and glamour that Hollywood had. On the pit straight, there may have been a few little places, you might have called them dives. It had character, let's put it that way.'

It also had sun, sea and a huge spectator catchment area to draw from in Southern California and 46,000 turned up for the first race. With the infrastructure in place, Pook was able to engage the attention of Bernie Ecclestone and Long Beach stepped up to Formula 1 in March 1976 to host the USGP (West).

The circuit boasted some suitable West Coast names, with the two main straights of Ocean Boulevard and Shoreline Drive, and sandwiched between them the Long Beach Convention Center, where the paddock was located. In the races from 1975

Opposite The start of the race in 1980 with cars braking for the wide Queen's Hairpin at the end of East Shoreline Drive. Nelson Piquet in the Brabham BT49 leads from René Arnoux, Patrick Depailler, Jan Lammers, Alan Jones and Bruno Giacomelli. Further back, Mario Andretti in the Lotus 81 and Jean-Pierre Jarier in a Tyrrell make contact.

Right Drivers had to contend with steep city ramps. Here, Gunnar Nilsson in the JPS Lotus leads Hans Joachim Stuck in the yellow March followed by Jody Scheckter in a Tyrrell during the 1976 race.

Below A paddock like no other, Alan Jones levers himself out of the Saudia-sponsored Williams in 1980.

Bottom The start of the IndyCar race from 2023. Cars now turn left at the Toyota bend which has replaced the hairpin, before doubling back along West Shoreline Drive.

LONG BEACH

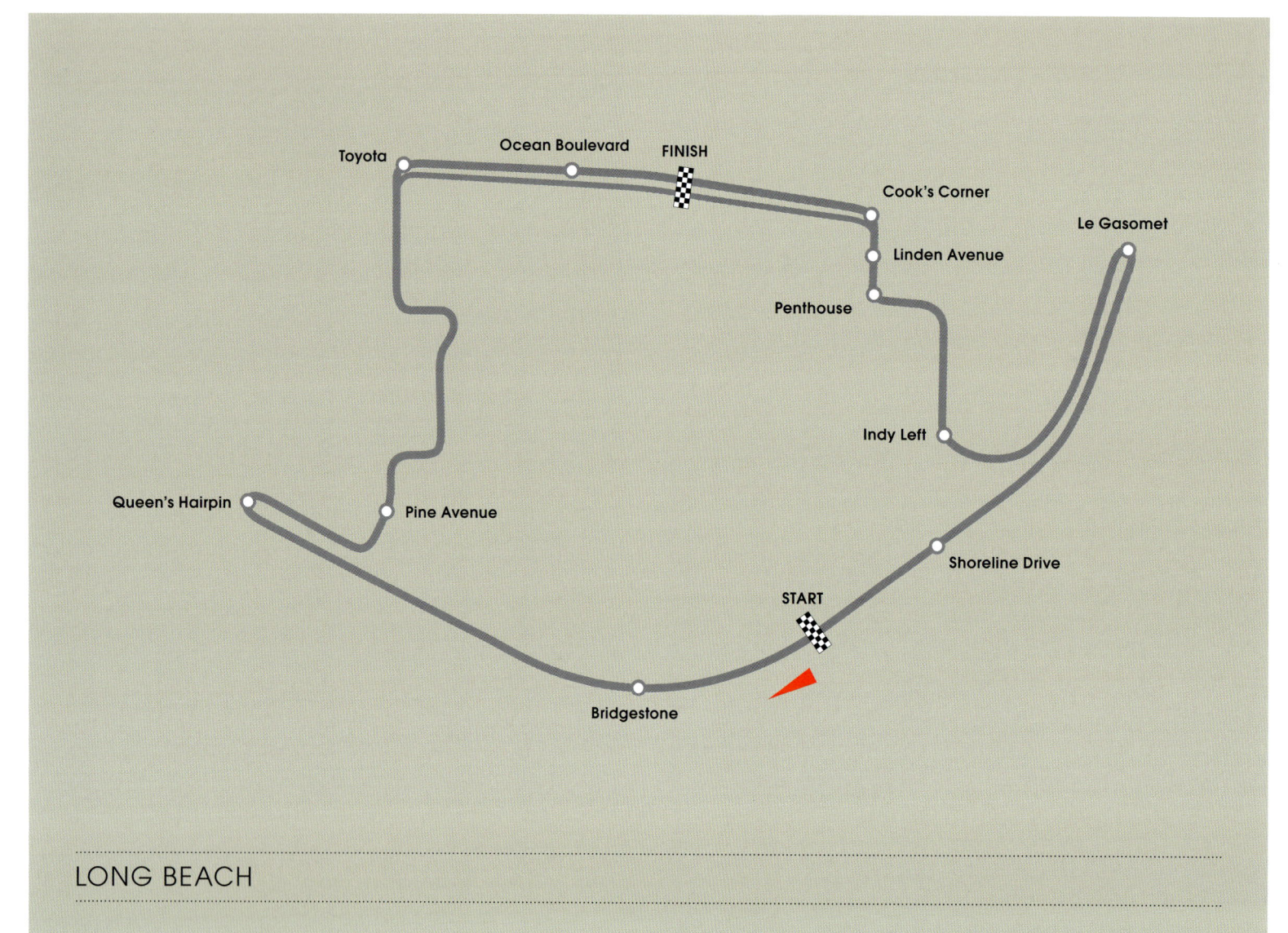

Length: 3.275 km (2.035 miles)
Lap Record: 1:28.33, (Niki Lauda, McLaren MP4/1C, 1983)
Opened: 1975
First F1 Grand Prix: 1976
Last F1 Grand Prix: 1983
Number of F1 Grands Prix hosted: 8
Number of laps: 75
Race winning fact: In 1983 McLaren duo John Watson and Niki Lauda not only started 22nd and 23rd, finished first and second, but they also lapped everyone except third place René Arnoux.

Long Beach started life with its pit complex on Ocean Boulevard in the Convention Center, with the start/finish line opposite. However early first corner pile-ups caused the organizers to move the start to Shoreline Drive to spread cars out, while the finish line remained on Ocean Boulevard. For what proved to be the final F1 race in 1983, the pit complex was moved to the position it occupies today along Shoreline Drive. The circuit plan above represents the race as it was in 1982 – when Nigel Mansell famously started the race with his Lotus in reverse, trying to get out of the way of team-mate Elio de Angelis, who had lined up incorrectly.

to 1977 there were multiple incidents in the first few tight, right-angle corners after the startline on Ocean Boulevard, similar to those seen at Baku in modern times. So, in 1978 the startline was moved to Shoreline Drive to space the field out, but the finish line remained on Ocean Boulevard. It was a logistical detail overlooked for the first race using that system and with no flag marshal on the new grid, cars overshot it.

Ferrari's Clay Regazzoni won the very first race, but interest in the event took off the following year when Mario Andretti, driving for Lotus, won a race-long battle with Jody Scheckter and Niki Lauda in front of 70,000 ecstatic spectators. He became the first American driver to win a US Grand Prix and described the experience as "even more satisfying than winning Indianapolis".

But the stand-out Long Beach memory comes from 1983 when John Watson set an F1 record that cannot be equalled whilst the grid has just 20 cars. Starting from 22nd on the grid (with McLaren team-mate Niki Lauda in P23) he won the race, the only driver to win an F1 grand prix from so far back. The two McLarens had qualified poorly because F1 was in the middle of one of its tyre wars – Goodyear vs Michelin. The Michelins were designed primarily for the heavier turbo cars of Renault and Brabham while the McLaren was a lightweight Cosworth-powered car, perfect for a street circuit, but unable to 'switch' the tyres on during low-fuel runs.

Once the car had a full load of fuel on board it carved through the field, Lauda leading the way and Watson following in close attendance before jumping his team-mate into the Shoreline Drive hairpin. It was the final dramatic race for F1 at the circuit – Ecclestone wanted to ramp up the hosting fee and Pook knew his financial limits. The Long Beach Grand Prix made the smooth and economically less stressful transition to IndyCar racing the following year. It has become a highlight of the North American open-wheel racing season, helped enormously by Toyota's sponsorship over three decades. With the steady gentrification of the city over 50 years, Long Beach really *has* become the Monaco Grand Prix of Southern California.

Above A very public driver briefing before the 1979 race at Long Beach with (from left), Riccardo Patrese, Clay Regazzoni, Patrick Depailler, Alan Jones, Hans Joachim Stuck, James Hunt, Niki Lauda and Emerson Fittipaldi.

Right John Watson on his way to a stunning win at the 1983 event from 22nd on the grid – a feat that is unlikely to be equalled any time soon with grids of 20 cars. The funnels of the liner *Queen Mary* are visible beyond.

Above Bruce McLaren raises his hand to indicate he is coming into the pits as he places his Cooper on the inside of the 180-degree Peraltada during practice for the non-championship 1962 Mexican Grand Prix.

Opposite The position of the pit lane hasn't changed, but the cornering speed of Peraltada has been reduced by cutting it in half, and cars now turn sharp right onto it after going through the stadium section.

Left Jim Clark leads teammate Graham Hill, both in Lotus 49s, during the 1967 Mexican Grand Prix.

MEXICO CITY

Autódromo Hermanos Rodríguez

THE IDEA TO SHOWCASE MEXICO'S DRIVING TALENT WITH AN INTERNATIONAL CIRCUIT HAD THE MOST TRAGIC OF BEGINNINGS

Mexico City's Autódromo Magdalena Mixiuhca was the idea of government advisor Pedro Natalio Rodríguez. He had two precocious sons who were racing cars from an early age – older brother Pedro raced a Jaguar XK120 from the age of 15, while younger brother Ricardo graduated from an Opel to a Porsche Spyder at the same tender age.

The brothers' daring exploits caught the attention of Luigi Chinetti, boss of NART (North American Racing Team), the organization responsible for selling Ferraris in the States, who promoted their business by going racing in the European sports car races. Chinetti was a regular at Le Mans. Racing for NART the brothers would go on to win the Nürburgring 1000km and Paris 1000km, at the ages of 19 and 21.

In 1958, Rodríguez Sr. had persuaded Mexican President Adolfo López Mateo that it would be good for Mexico to have its own dedicated race track to celebrate the achievements of Mexican drivers, not just his sons, and so an area was set aside in the Magdalena Mixiuhca Park to create a double race track. Like Monza, it would have a road course and an oval. For the oval there were two 180-degree banked turns, one of which, Peraltada, would be used on the grand prix circuit.

Fittingly, the first race, the Mexico City 500 Miles, held in December 1959, was won by Pedro Rodríguez with brother Ricardo in third. To prove to Formula 1's hierarchy that Mexico should be included on the F1 calendar, a non-championship race was organized for November 1962. By this time it was younger brother Ricardo who was the star. On his debut for Ferrari at the 1961 Italian Grand Prix he had put his car alongside World Championship leader Wolfgang von Trips and ahead of Phil Hill, who had been driving the Ferrari 156 all year.

The international field assembled for the race considered the circuit interesting, but there were concerns about bumps on the high-speed Peraltada, the lower portion of which was the pit lane entry. Those fears were tragically realized in practice. Ferrari had declined to send cars and so Ricardo Rodríguez was attempting to put his Rob Walker-entered Lotus-Climax on pole when he ran wide at Peraltada, hit the barrier and was thrown from the car. The 20-year-old died from his injuries. When the race was eventually run three days later, it was a chaotic affair, with drivers unsure of who exactly was starting the race.

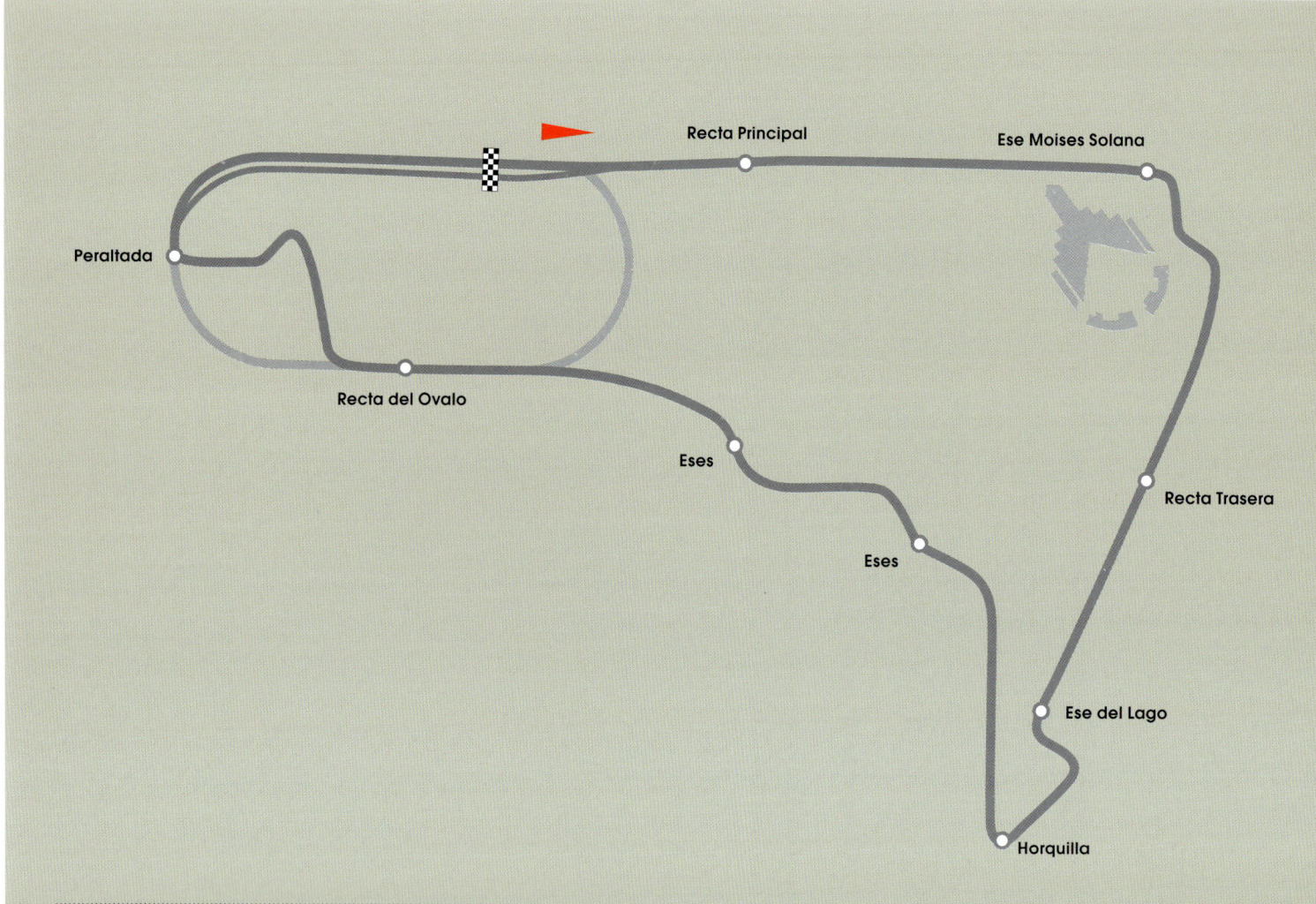

AUTÓDROMO HERMANOS RODRÍGUEZ

Length: 4.304 km (2.674 miles)
Lap Record: 1:17.774 (Valtteri Bottas, Mercedes W12, 2021)
Opened: 1961
First F1 Grand Prix: 1963
Number of F1 Grands Prix hosted: 23
Number of laps: 71
Circuit Designer: Oscar Fernández (1959), Hermann Tilke (2015)
Race winning fact: Max Verstappen is by far the most successful driver at the Mexican GP having won in 2017, 2018, 2021, 2022 and 2023.

The teams' regard set-up for grands prix at the Autódromo Ricardo Rodríguez as a considerable challenge. Formula 1 engines face a power loss in the mile-high atmosphere of Mexico City – 2,225 metres (7,300 feet) above sea level. The reduced oxygen density forces engines to work harder to generate the same power output as at lower altitudes. Turbochargers operate less effectively due to the lower air pressure. Brake settings need careful calibration to avoid overheating along with the downforce levels of the aero package.

Jim Clark won it after taking over Trevor Taylor's car but all the focus was on the loss of a national hero. The circuit would be renamed Autódromo Ricardo Rodríguez.

Races continued through the 1960s, buoyed by participation of Pedro Rodríguez from 1963 onwards, and sometimes run by NART in Ferrari F1 machinery. By 1970 he was driving a Yardley-BRM and his second place at the USGP at Watkins Glen, the previous round to the Mexican GP, had ramped up attendance considerably in the municipal park. Security had never been great in Mexico City with stray dogs wandering across the track and spectator fences breached. On race day 200,000 crammed into the circuit, lining the sides of the track, very much like a World Championship rally.

The common sense decision would have been to cancel the race – despite drivers such as Jackie Stewart and Rodríguez going out to talk to the crowd, they were not moving. Faced with a potential riot the teams agreed to go ahead in what was an uneasy grand prix, with no spectator fatalities, though Stewart did hit a dog which eliminated him from the running. There would be no return in 1971.

Pedro Rodríguez, who was fond of wearing a deerstalker hat round the F1 paddock, was having another strong season for Yardley-BRM in 1971 when he accepted a sports car drive at the Norisring which claimed his life (see page 156). The Mexican circuit would now be renamed the Autódromo Hermanos Rodríguez in 1972.

Left Ricardo Rodríguez (left) standing above his Lotus-Climax 24 on 11 April 1962, moments before going out and suffering a fatal crash at Peraltada.

Bottom The chaotic start to the 1962 grand prix. Jim Clark's car refused to start and he got a push-start from officials – and was then disqualified for having a push-start. He later took over Trevor Taylor's car and the duo shared the win.

Below Future team boss Roger Penske high on the Peraltada banking in a Climax-engined Lotus 24 ahead of the 1962 race.

Right A view looking down from above home plate at the Foro Sol baseball stadium in 2009.

Below There could have been tragic consequences at the 1970 race when the crowd encroached to the edge of the track and despite pleas from the drivers, refused to move back. Clay Regazzoni, Jackie Stewart, Jacky Ickx and Jean-Pierre Beltoise take it carefully.

Left Foro Sol is no longer a baseball stadium, the Red Devils having moved to a new stadium with more shade. It is now a cauldron of noise for Mexican motorsport stars in both F1 and IndyCar, the first series to make use of this clever reworking of an old track.

Below Home favourite Sergio Pérez tries an overambitious move at the start of the 2023 Mexican Grand Prix and his race is over at the first turn.

It looked like the Autódromo would fall back into national racing or developed for housing, but in 1986, after a group of local businessmen invested $10 million to restore the circuit, with high-security fences a priority, F1 returned. One of the highlights from Mexico's second stint was the 1990 race with Nigel Mansell in a Ferrari chasing Gerhard Berger's McLaren for second place and passing him on the outside of Peraltada, on the penultimate lap, on worn tyres. It remains one of the greatest F1 overtakes of all time. Mansell won the race in 1992 during his stroll to the World Championship in the Adrian Newey-designed FW14B, after which the race dropped off the schedule once more.

Fast forward to 2011 and a new Mexican F1 star joined the Sauber team. Sergio Pérez immediately impressed with his tyre-preserving skills and by the 2013 season was behind the wheel of a McLaren, while at the same time Esteban Gutiérrez slotted into his old seat at Sauber. Talks were started to resurrect the Mexican Grand Prix, which culminated in the race's return for 2015.

At 2,240 metres (7,350 ft) above sea level it has always represented an engineering challenge, but how could the old circuit be adapted for F1 cars, particularly Peraltada, which had no space for extra run-off? The solution had been found when ChampCar had visited in 2002. The circuit took a detour through the Foro Sol baseball stadium, home to Mexico City's Los Diablos Rojos, before exiting between grandstands and joining Peraltada at low-speed for the final quadrant before the start/finish straight.

New pits and paddock buildings were constructed and Hermann Tilke was brought in to reprofile many of the corners, especially Turns 1, 2 and 3, the favourite zone for wheel banging after the long run from the start line. He also put an extra corner into the Foro Sol section, slowing the cars in front of a planned podium building. Baseball has now left the stadium for good, moving further down the main straight to the remarkable, avant garde Estadio Alfredo Harp Helú stadium.

Foro Sol remains a cauldron of noise celebrating 'Checo' Pérez whenever the race comes to town. There is also a lot of pre-race sombrero wearing and face-painting to celebrate the annual *Dia De Los Muertos* (Day of the Dead), but how much longer Mexico might stay on the calendar should there be no Mexican driver on the grid, remains a moot point.

MONTE CARLO, MONACO

Circuit de Monaco

THE UNIQUE CHALLENGE OF MONACO ENSURES THAT SATURDAY IS FAR MORE IMPORTANT THAN THE RACE ON SUNDAY

Above Tony Brooks leads in the Ferrari going round the Gasworks Hairpin. Since 1959 substantial areas of the harbour have been filled in allowing the expansion of the pits.
Opposite The extent of the expansion can be gauged by the line of trees along Boulevard Albert, the one constant in both photographs.

It is the most famous grand prix in the world, but visitors to Monte Carlo unaware that a Formula 1 race was staged around its streets, would be staggered that it was possible. Yet when it was first proposed there were road races across Europe that passed through the centres of towns and villages, past front doors that locals nailed shut in case they should forget and step out in front of a roaring Bugatti during the event.

There were also other motor races with inviting Mediterranean backdrops – Pescara, Bari, San Remo and Naples all had their charms, but above anything else Monaco had money. It was and still is the home to many of the world's tax evaders, including a large proportion of the current grid.

It also had the veneer of royalty which helped attract the 'right crowd' for holidays in the sun. Glamorous Nice may have had La Croisette or the Promenade des Anglais, but Monte Carlo was not part of the *republique* – it had Prince Louis II and the famous casino.

So it was a blow to the esteem of the Automobile Club de Monaco when they were refused entry to the international governing body of motorsport clubs, the forerunner to the FIA. They were already established as a French national club, responsible for running the Monte Carlo Rally which had begun in 1911, and had assumed that joining would be a given. Except the majority of the Monte Carlo Rally takes place in Southern France. The grounds for refusal by the Association Internationale

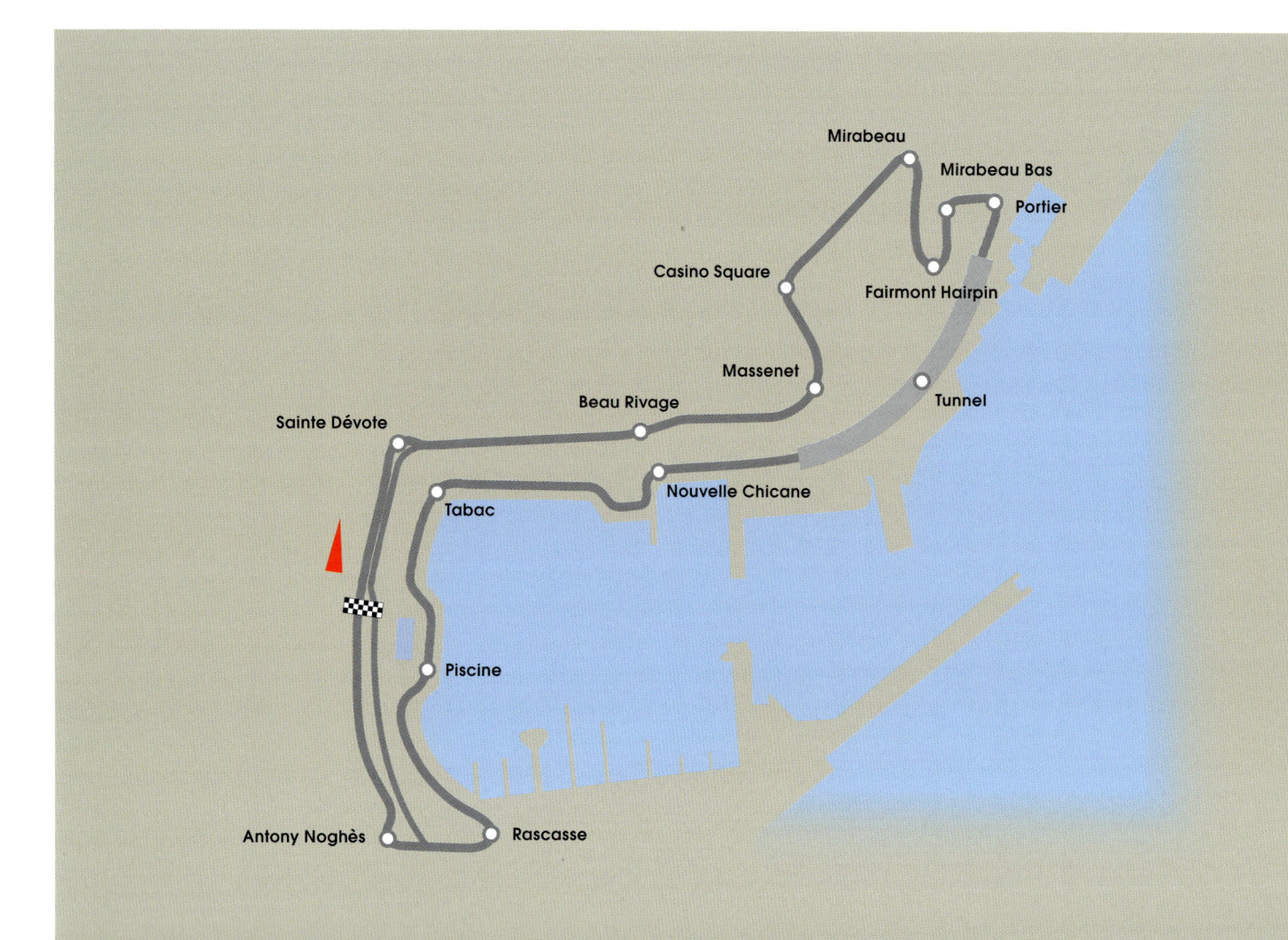

CIRCUIT DE MONACO

Length: 3.337 km (2.074 miles)
Lap Record: 1:12.909 (Lewis Hamilton, Mercedes W12, 2021)
Opened: 1929
First F1 Grand Prix: 1950
Number of F1 Grands Prix hosted: 69
Number of laps: 78
Circuit Designer: Anthony Noghès
Race winning fact: Graham Hill won at Monaco in 1963 and 1964 and in 1965 he had to take the escape road at the chicane on Lap 25. He got out, pushed his BRM back on the circuit and still won.

The Circuit de Monaco has many unique features. It was F1's first city grand prix track (followed by Pedralbes in Barcelona). It is the only circuit with a tunnel covering the race track. It has the slowest corner in F1, the 48km/h (30mph) Fairmont Hairpin and has the slowest pit lane speed limit. Constructing the circuit takes six weeks and the dismantling of it afterwards takes another three. To maximize use of the circuit, there is also a weekend of historic F1 racing with machinery from the years 1961-1965, 1966-1972 and 1973-1976.

Left William Grover-Williams in his race-winning Bugatti from 1929. Williams also won the Belgian Grand Prix at Spa-Francorchamps in 1931. Having grown up in France with a French mother he was bilingual and in World War II was recruited by SOE to help the French Resistance. He was captured by the Germans in 1943 and executed in March 1945.

Opposite top Cars lined up on Boulevard Albert for the start of the 1935 race. When the grand prix resumed after World War II the start line was moved to the harbourside, before the Gasworks Hairpin, but has since returned to its original position. In 1935 it was an all-Mercedes front row of Rudi Caracciola, Manfred von Brauchitsch and Luigi Fagioli.

Opposite bottom Grover-Williams with his Bugatti T51 before the 1933 race. He could only manage 7th in the 100-lap race won by Achille Varzi.

des Automobiles Clubs Reconnus were that the Monaco club did not run a motorsport event within its own boundaries. If they wanted admission to the top tier of motorsport clubs they would need to organize a race in Monte Carlo.

This was a challenge that wealthy cigarette manufacturer and Monaco resident Anthony Noghés, General Commissioner of the Automobile Club, was prepared to take on. He plotted out a course which went from the Boulevard Albert I (today's start/finish straight) up the hill to Casino Square, down to the Mirabeau Hotel where there was a sharp right, before dropping down to Monte Carlo Station. There, a tight left downhill hairpin led under the railway arches to Portier on the sea front (a sea front which has now been reclaimed for apartment blocks). Cars would drive a short stretch along the seafront before the tunnel, emerging on Quai des Etats-Unis with a small chicane slowing cars at the bottom of the hill – then known as Chicane du Port – before gaining speed on the short straight to Tabac, named after a harbourside tobacconist's. A left turn onto Quai Albert I, pointed cars towards the best overtaking spot on the circuit, the tight Gazometre hairpin, before returning cars to the start/finish line.

Although there have been a regular series of small adjustments to corners over the years, the basic Noghés track plan is still in place almost a century later.

The venture was approved by Prince Louis II who saw it as a way of extending the tourist season, the race taking place in the week of Ascension (40 days after Easter, and thus governed by when Easter fell each year). More importantly Noghés' circuit

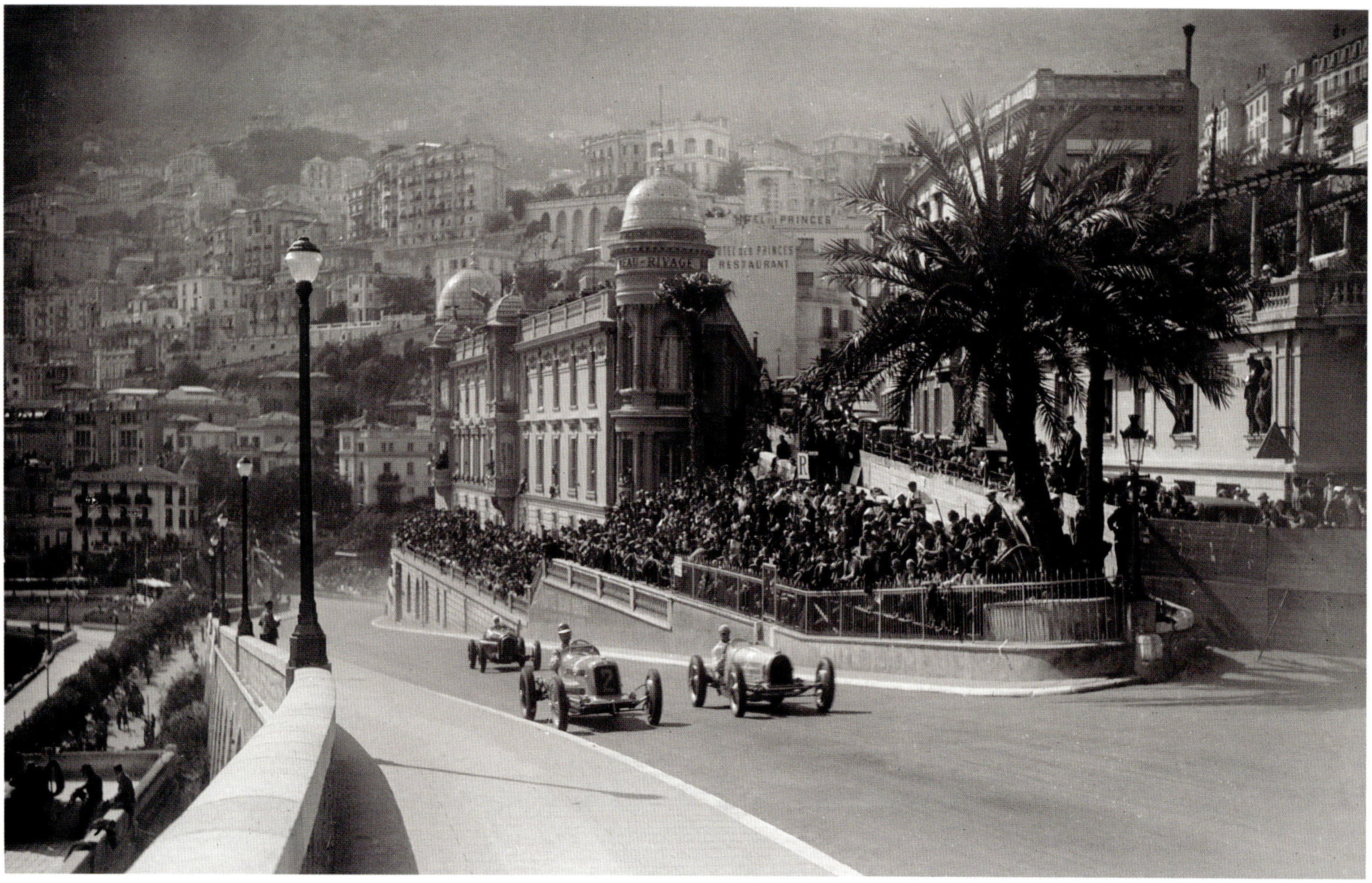
RESTAURANT

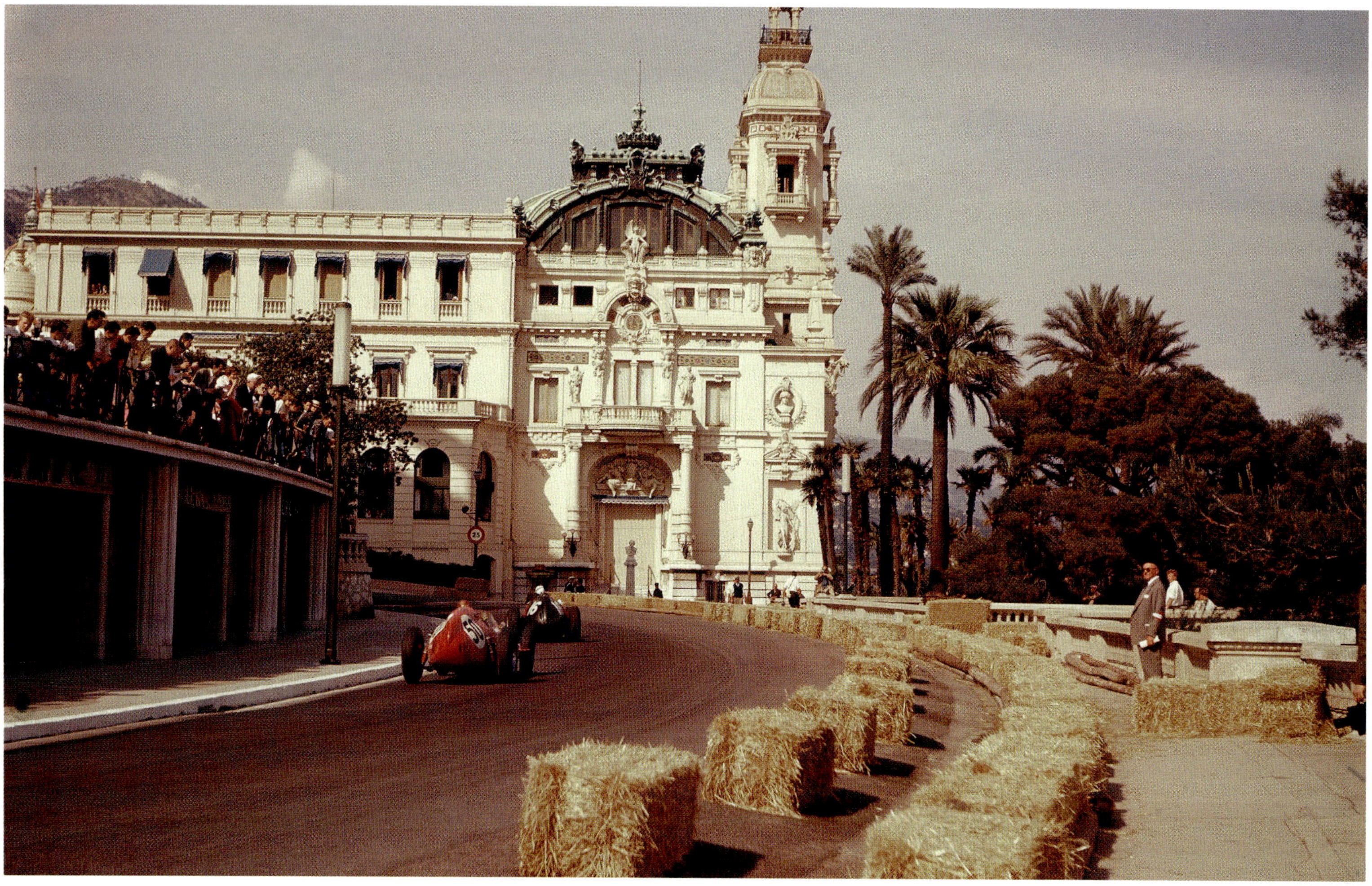

Opposite top **Cars stream up the hill, Beau Rivage, in the 1934 race. Narrower cars in the 1930s made it a potential overtaking spot.**

Above **Max Verstappen and Valtteri Bottas cover the same ground in 2021, though the opportunity to overtake today is rare and risky.**

Opposite bottom **Tony Brooks in the Ferrari D246 taking Massenet corner on his way to second place in 1959. The last victory for a rear-engined car at Monaco had come in 1957.**

Left **Lando Norris rounds Massenet in his McLaren with its special Ayrton Senna tribute livery. Senna was the master of Monaco, inexplicably hitting the wall at Portier in 1988 when leading the race by 50 seconds.**

Right Graham Hill rounds the Station Hairpin in 1964 driving a BRM. Unusually, that year Monaco was the first official F1 race of the season.

Below John Surtees takes the hairpin in his Ferrari 156 in the 1963 race, with the station buildings prominent to the left. The station was closed in 1965 as part of a plan by Prince Rainier III to free up more land for development.

Left Looking back towards the Mirabeau corner from the Fairmont Hairpin, the short sprint downhill represents an opening lap overtaking opportunity as cars back up to take the tightest corner in F1.

Below Charles Leclerc rounds what is now known as the Fairmont Hairpin. Since the station's demise it has been known as the Old Station Hairpin, Loews Hairpin (after the ugly hotel built there), the Grand Hotel Hairpin and now the Fairmont Hairpin.

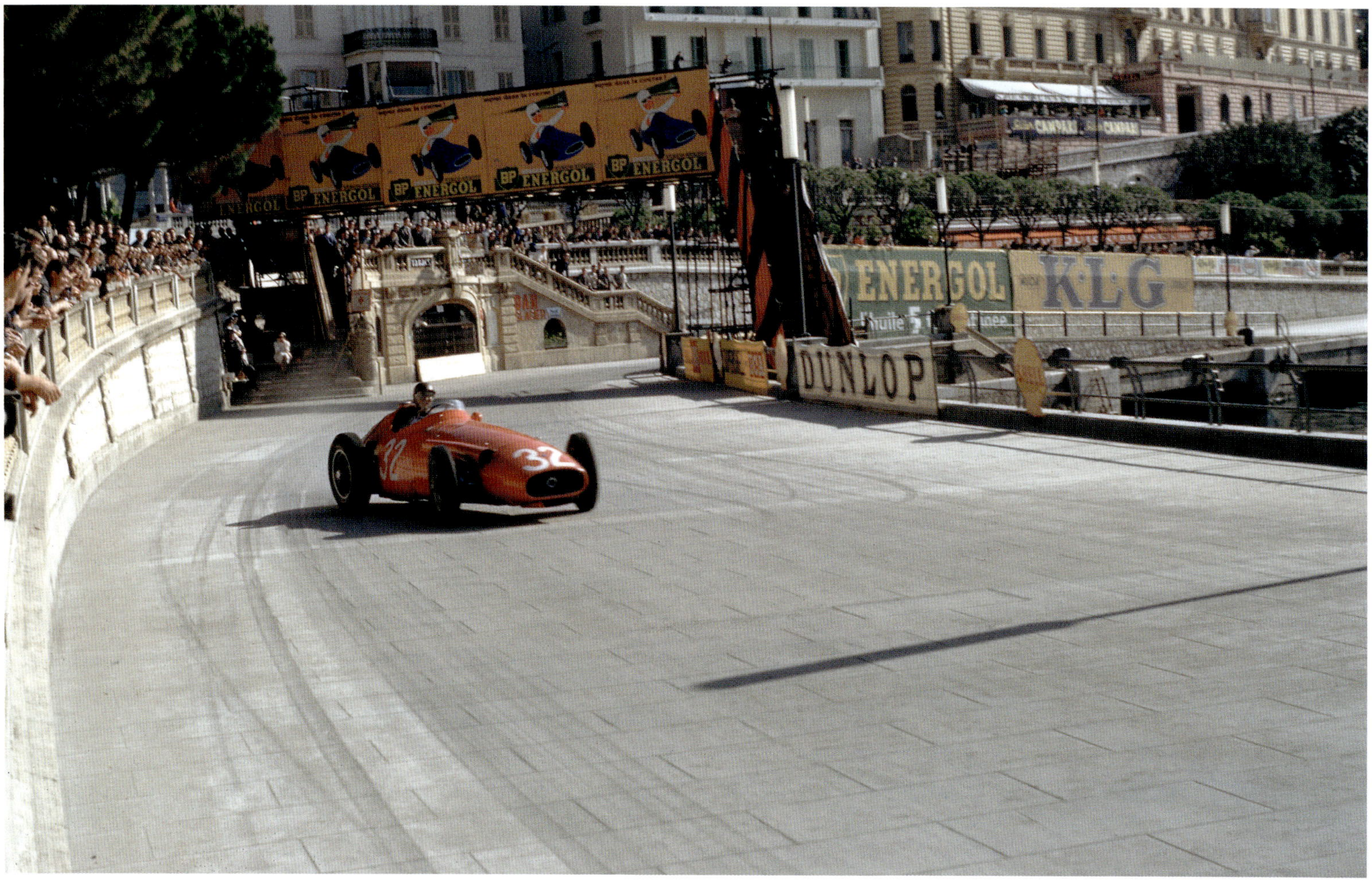
BP ENERGOL
ENERGOL
KLG
DUNLOP

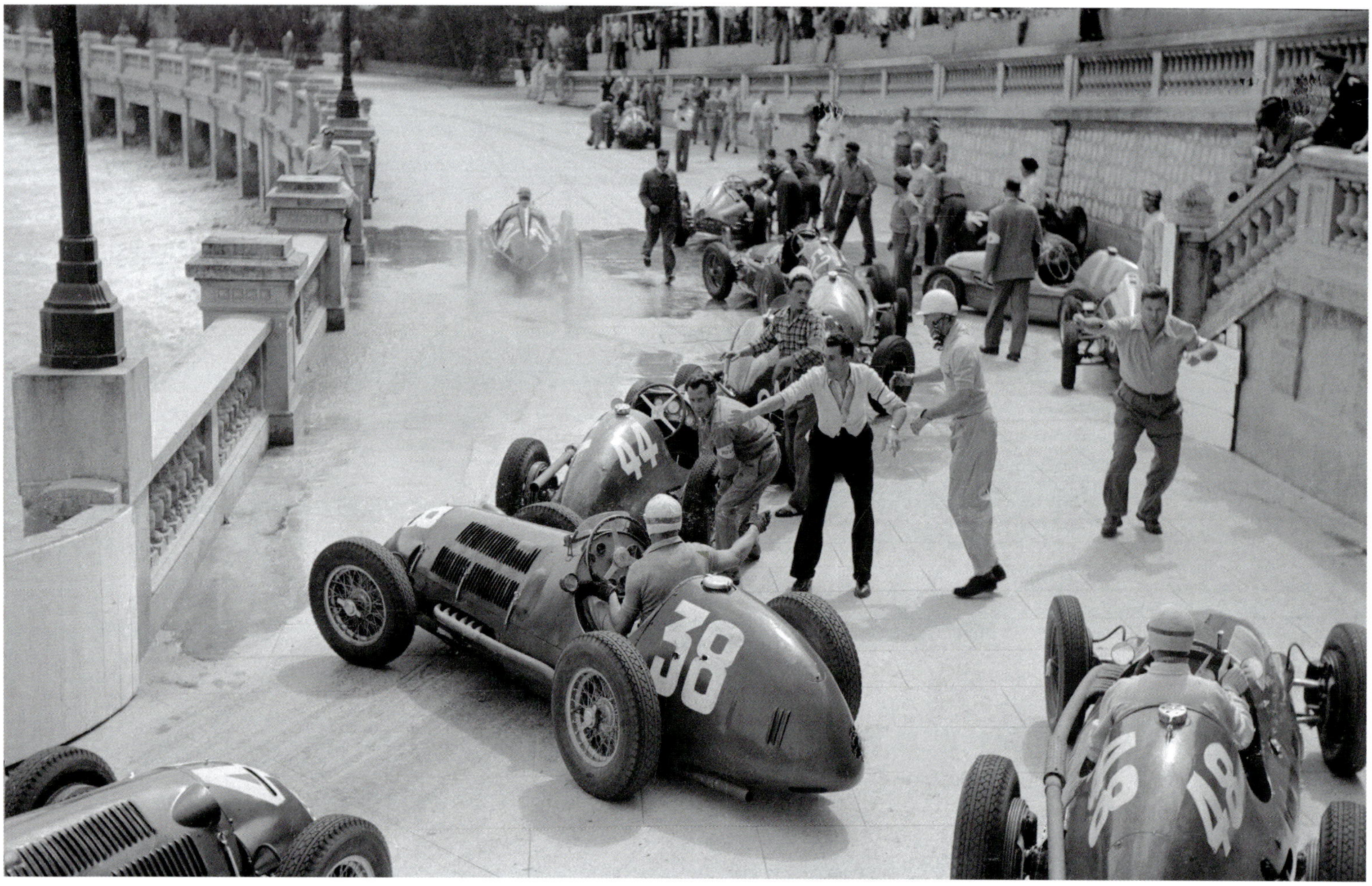

Opposite top **Juan Manuel Fangio** drifts his Maserati 250F through Tabac during the 1957 grand prix. Fangio went on to win the race.

Above **Esteban Ocon** takes considerably more speed through Tabac in his Alpine in 2023. There is no room for power-sliding the modern generation of Pirelli tyres without dire consequences.

Opposite bottom **In 1950** a wave flooded over the harbour wall on the opening lap at Tabac causing second-place Nino Farina to crash. It resulted in a multiple pile-up that blocked the track and accounted for nine cars from a field of 19.

Left **Pastor Maldonado** made contact with Max Chilton after a re-start in 2013 and went straight on into the barriers, dislodging the Tecpro and blocking the track. The race was red-flagged.

plan gained the approval of Monegasque grand prix star Louis Chiron. In the late 1920s Chiron was at the height of his powers. In 1928 he had won the Rome, Marne (at Reims), Spanish and Italian Grands Prix, driving a Bugatti. In fact his success ensured that he would miss the inaugural grand prix of 1929 – he was away competing at Indianapolis in a Delage.

The modern grand prix runs to 78 laps, but for the debut race of 14 April 1929, the distance was set at 100 laps. The entry list was by invitation only, and so the organizers were disappointed when drivers from the top teams of Alfa Romeo and Maserati declined to attend, despite the proximity to Italy. However there was a large contingent of Bugattis on display, and Mercedes sent their top driver Rudi Caracciola.

Hardcore fans of modern F1 resist the idea of reverse grids, citing it as blatant manipulation and not consistent with the history and spirit of motorsport, but in 1929 the grid placings – so important within the tight confines of Monaco – were determined by ballot. Caracciola drew 15th (of 16 starters) and was advised not to attend the casino. When the flag dropped he picked his way through the field in his Mercedes SSK to take the lead, but a four-minute pitstop for tyres and fuel dropped him back and he had to be content with third place.

After four hours of racing Englishman William Grover-Williams, racing under the sobriquet 'Willliams' finished the winner in a Bugatti 35B. The race was viewed as a tremendous success, not only did it accomplish the object of gaining the Automobile Club de Monaco a place amongst the top echelon of motor clubs, it was a financial success and returned in 1930 and in 1931 Louis Chiron won his home race.

Through the 1930s the race gained prominence and glamour, in no short measure through the evocative artwork of Georges Hamel. At a time when posters were an important advertising medium, Hamel's designs for the annual grand prix, signed 'Geo Ham' encapsulated the drama and excitement of a race through the exotic streets of the sun-drenched resort.

To acknowledge its position as one of the most important European races, the Association Internationale des Automobiles Clubs granted Monaco the status of *Grande Épreuve* in 1933. With no annual championship in place, races could be established across the continent with the title of 'Grand Prix' and top teams and privateers could pick and choose which race they attended depending on the start money and where it lay in their schedule. In the case of Mercedes, it was important that the host nation was a valuable market for their cars. The Donington Park Grands Prix of the 1930s, which both Mercedes and Auto Union attended, were not *grande épreuves*. These were the top international races: the Belgian, French, Italian, German and Spanish Grands Prix. Only four years after its inception, Monaco had joined that elite.

The 1933 race in Monaco brought a new innovation to the sport. For the first time a grand prix grid would be decided by practice times. And it was a thriller: Achille Varzi and Tazio Nuvolari, duelling through the streets, swapping the lead many times before Nuvolari's Alfa Romeo caught fire on the 99th lap of 100.

Caracciola would finally get his Monaco race win in 1936 when rain drenched the circuit. Nicknamed the 'Regenmeister', Caracciola kept his car out of the lampposts, walls, railings and other roadside hazards on the barrier-less circuit, made all the more tricky by a car depositing liberal quantities of oil on the racing line. While the Mercedes-Benz of home favourite Louis Chiron exited the race along with Luigi Fagioli, Manfred von Brauchitsch, and Bernd Rosemeyer in the Auto-Union, Caracciola brought his Mercedes-Benz home. He was in contention again the following year, duking it out with von Brauchitsch, before he had to give best to his team-mate.

It proved to be the final race before World War II; an unresolved financial dispute with the governing body over race fees put paid to the 1938 race and the dark clouds of war brought a cancellation of the 1939 event.

Motor-racing was not the first thing on people's minds once hostilities concluded. Though many of the pre-war players were waiting for the figurative green flag, one who would not see racing action again was William Grover-Williams. He had sought to replicate the adrenalin rush of racing with work for the Special Operations Executive (SOE). Parachuted into France he had set up a Resistance cell near Paris working with two other former drivers Robert Benoist and Jean-Pierre Wimille, until captured in 1943 and executed by the Germans in 1945.

In the late 1940s resources were stretched, and so the newly minted Fédération Internationale de l'Automobile (FIA) devised a formula based on the pre-war 'voiturette' class, a step back from the powerful pre-war machines typified by the Silver Arrows. Giuseppe 'Nino' Farina won the 1948 Monaco Grand Prix based on this formula. There was no race in 1949 after the passing of Prince Louis II, but in 1950 Monaco became the second race in Formula 1's debut season. Juan Manuel Fangio took pole and victory while Alfa Romeo team-mate Nino Farina, the eventual 1950 World Champion, was involved in a multiple accident and retired on Lap 1. The beneficiary was 50-year-old Louis Chiron who qualified eighth, but was able to finish in third place, 29 years after he had won the race.

In the days before large-scale sponsorship, Monaco was not as important to teams as it would become from the 1970s onwards, when it was the perfect venue to entertain current and potential clients. And so for a variety of financial and

Opposite The start of the 1962 race with Jim Clark (18) on pole, in a Lotus 25. Alongside is Graham Hill (10) in a BRM and Bruce McLaren (14) in a Cooper. McLaren won what would be a race of attrition with only four cars finishing within a lap of the leader at the chequered flag. Organizers the Automobile Club de Monaco would only allow 16 starters.

Above Today, what was once the startline is now occupied by three-story temporary pit buildings and the pit lane.

Below Three iterations of the Monaco Grand Prix poster emphasizing speed and glamour. There are many reproductions on sale today, while the originals will sell for thousands at auction. French artist Georges Hamel 'GeoHam' was responsible for the early Monaco posters, but the vision of a radiator and front wheels flashing towards the viewer was established as early as 1908 in posters for the Vanderbilt Cup Race.

Opposite Three Maserati 250Fs lined up on the quayside in 1956. Monaco has always struggled to find space for its teams. One of the reasons that F1 has been reluctant to add an 11th team to the grid is the crush of space at the sport's blue riband event. Cars were serviced on the other side of the track in the 1950s.

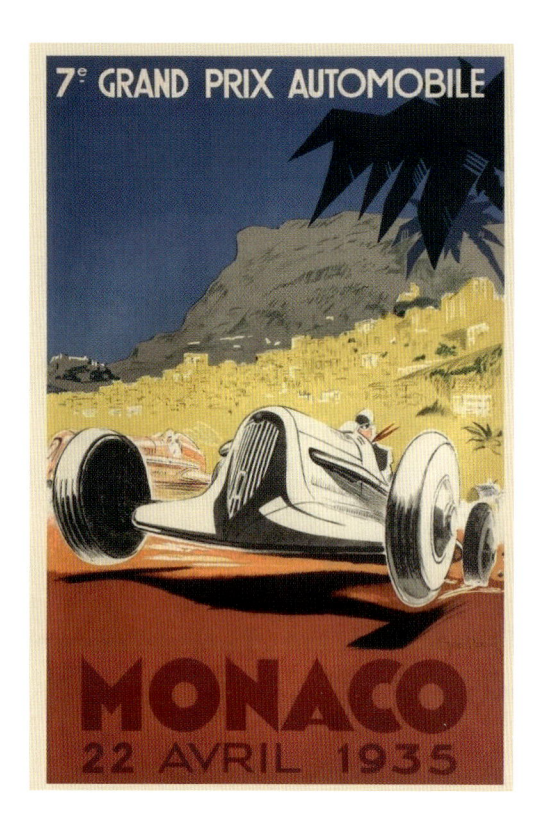

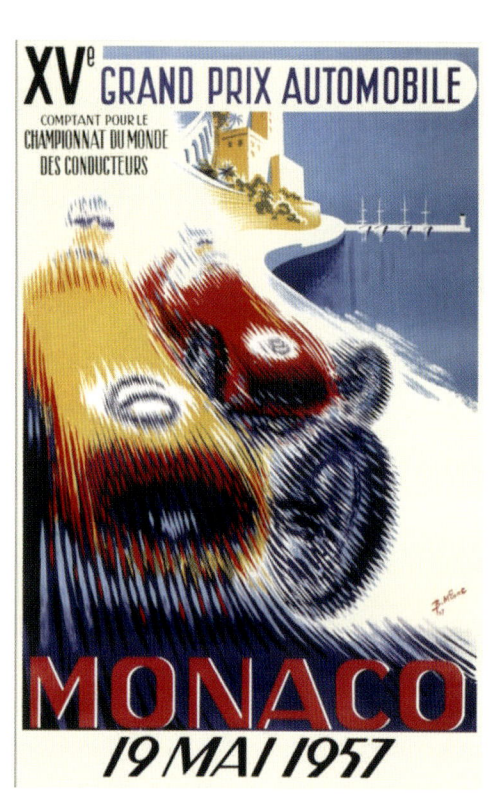

regulatory reasons it disappeared off the race calendar. One year, 1952, it was run as a sports car race but the event was overshadowed by an accident in the tunnel during practice. Luigi Fagioli, 'the old Abruzzi Robber', was a star of the 1930s and a rival to Tazio Nuvolari for the affections of the Italian public. Unlike Nuvolari he made his debut in the inaugural F1 World Championship, scoring podiums in five of the first six races at the age of 52. Fagioli lost control of his Lancia, struck a stone balustrade and was thrown out of the car. He had suffered a broken arm and leg and was unconscious for four days. Three weeks after coming to, he suffered a complete nervous failure and died.

When the Monaco Grand Prix returned in 1955 for its continuous run up till 2020, another fifty-something entertained the crowd. Fresh from winning the 1955 Monte Carlo rally for Lancia, the F1 works team handed Louis Chiron a drive in his home race. He duly brought his car home in sixth place, in what would be his final grand prix. Although he was entered in both 1956 and 1958 races, he would start neither, blowing two Maserati engines in 1956 and failing to qualify in 1958. After his retirement at the age of 58, Prince Rainier asked him to run both of the principality's prestigious motorsport events, which he did until the 1979 Monaco Grand Prix.

One of the few significant changes to the circuit occurred in 1955 – the start/finish line was moved off Boulevard Albert I and onto the quayside a few hundred metres away from the tight Gazometre hairpin. There were still no barriers of note along the harbourside when double World Champion Alberto Ascari lost control of his Lancia D50 which plunged into the harbour after the Chicane du Port. Ascari was able to swim clear with only minor facial injuries, but was killed in an impromptu test of a Ferrari sports car at Monza four days later.

Juan Manuel Fangio won the 1957 race in a front-engined Maserati, but the 1958 grand prix marked the changing order of Formula 1. Already Stirling Moss had made history by duping the rest of the field at the Argentine Grand Prix. They had assumed he would be making a pit stop. With his tyres worn down to the canvas Moss had brought his privately entered Cooper-

Climax home to score the first victory for a rear-engined car. At Monaco that year, Maurice Trintignant repeated the victory in a Cooper T45, proving the case that under normal circumstances a nimble-handling car on the streets of the principality was a much greater asset than a big lump of engine. Jack Brabham won in a Cooper the following year.

The start/finish line moved back to its permanent position on Boulevard Albert I in 1963, while organizers constantly tinkered with the position of the harbourside chicane. Moving it, narrowing it and slowing it whenever they could to reduce speeds. The consequences of an accident there were brutally brought home in 1967. Like the first corner at St. Dévote, it was the most likely place for an incident, Alberto Ascari and Australian driver Paul Hawkins having both put cars in the harbour there. In 1957, an accident at the chicane took out three Brits in close succession: Stirling Moss, Mike Hawthorn and Peter Collins, none of them rookies.

But in 1967 Lorenzo Bandini misjudged the corner, crashed among the token straw bales, rolled over in the middle of the track and his Ferrari car caught fire. The race was not stopped. Marshals took an age to rescue the badly burned driver from the wreck. Bandini clung to life for three days before succumbing to his injuries. It was a terrible reminder of the price of F1, a year earlier he had been the driver double for actor Yves Montand in John Frankenheimer's remarkable movie, *Grand Prix*. Now the cast and crew mourned what star Eva Marie Saint described as, "a really lovely man". It was Bandini who had suggested the movie crew emulate Ascari's plunge into the harbour.

By 1969 the pioneering safety efforts led by Jackie Stewart, who had endured a frightening injury at the 1966 Belgian Grand Prix, where he had to be rescued by his fellow drivers, began to pay off. For the first time a large proportion of the Monaco track was lined with Armco barriers. These were in place just in time to witness the final appearance of skyscraper wings, which were used in practice and then banned before the race.

However the most significant change to lap length came about in the early 1970s. With little room to deviate from Noghés' original plan, land reclamation from the sea allowed the building of the Rainier III Aquatic Stadium at the harbour's edge over what had once been the start/finish line. Now the route of the grand prix had to zig left, short sprint, and zig right to avoid what was more mundanely known as 'Swimming Pool'.

In 1972 the pits had moved for one year only to the straight between the chicane and Tabac, but by 1973 they had returned to their rightful position near the start/finish line. In addition to 'Piscine', the Gazometre hairpin had gone, replaced by a loop around the Rascasse restaurant then a dart uphill past the new pit lane entrance, to a corner named in honour of Antony Noghés. This was a fairly open turn to start off with but was subsequently tightened to slow cars as they approached the pit entry.

The circuit's other hairpin had survived, but the demolished station had been replaced by a brutalist concrete chunk of architecture more in keeping with Torremolinos than the Baroque splendour of the Hotel de Monaco a few hundred metres away.

In the 1960s Graham Hill was the dominant driver around the street track. Having retired from his first four attempts, he went on to notch up five wins and two podiums between 1963 and 1969. It was a race that required total precision and absolute concentration. It was estimated that a grand prix driver would change gear up to 100 times a lap – steering the car with both hands was a luxury. Only the very best won at Monaco when retirements were low. On the odd occasion, the attritional nature of a narrow and bumpy circuit, especially combined with rainfall, would throw up a remarkable result.

Jean-Pierre Beltoise won his only grand prix, for BRM, in the pouring rain of 1972, while a decade on, a late-race shower created a finish that even film scriptwriters would have rejected as implausible. Alain Prost had been leading the race for Renault after team-mate and polesitter René Arnoux had dumped his RE30 into the wall at the Swimming Pool on Lap 14. Prost, rarely comfortable in wet conditions, failed to adjust for the rain on track and crashed at the chicane. Riccardo Patrese in a Brabham inherited the lead but spun on oil at the Loews Hairpin.

That left Ferrari's Didier Pironi leading on the final lap, only to find his Ferrari stuttering to a halt in the tunnel. Next in line would have been the Alfa Romeo of Andrea de Cesaris and a maiden GP win, but the Roman ran out of fuel. Derek Daly might have clinched a first win for Ireland, but the gearbox on his Williams seized on the penultimate lap. Patrese managed to get a bump start down the hill to Portier and continued to the flag, unaware that he had won his first grand prix. In 208 starts de Cesaris never did win a race.

Two years later and Alain Prost looked like losing another Monaco Grand Prix thanks to rain. In a race delayed by wet weather he had inherited the lead from Nigel Mansell. But as the rain increased, lap times slowed, and Prost found himself being reeled in by the fast-closing Toleman of rookie Ayrton Senna. And the pair of them were being caught by the Tyrrell of Stefan Bellof.

A frantic Prost gestured to the sky as he came across the start/finish line indicating that he thought it was too wet to continue, despite the apparent ease of his pursuers. On Lap 31 he got his wish and the race was ended. It was a controversial decision by Clerk of the Course Jacky Ickx who failed to consult the stewards before stopping the race. Ickx was fined $6,000 by the FIA and his licence suspended and Senna was denied his first win – which, unsurprisingly, came in the rain of Portugal.

For the rest of the 1980s, between 1984 and 1993 it was only Prost or Senna with their name on the Monaco winner's trophy.

A major change to the chicane was introduced in 1986. Previously it had created a small break in speed as cars approached from the tunnel exit. Now drivers had to break hard for a left turn, ride the kerb as much as they dared through a right flick, then exit with as much momentum as possible on the left flick. This not only slowed the cars along the Quai des Etats-Unis, it also presented an overtaking opportunity under braking for the very brave/stupidly optimistic.

The next significant change came in 1997. The approach to the Swimming Pool had always been a tremendous place to witness an F1 car at speed close up. Television pictures rarely convey the outright pace of cars on track, and so the extensive grandstands that stretch around from Tabac provide a breathtaking vantage point to experience it. This experience got even more visceral when the turn into Swimming Pool was cut, cars now passing a spot previously occupied by a grandstand at even greater speed.

The reprofiled corner was named Virage Louis Chiron after the Automobile Club de Monaco's long-serving race director, a man who still holds the record for the oldest participant in an F1 weekend (at 58, though he failed to qualify). A statue to Chiron stands near the first turn, St. Dévote

Another important change which improved life for the teams was brought in for the 2003 season. Another 5,000 square metres had been reclaimed from the harbour, affecting the stretch from the Swimming Pool to Rascasse. This allowed the track to be moved 10 metres towards the sea. In turn this facilitated the opening of a much wider pit lane and an increase in garage

Opposite **Lorenzo Bandini (38)** in the Ferrari 156 heads through a Casino Square uncluttered by protective barriers in the 1962 Monaco Grand Prix, a race in which he would finish third.

Above In 1962 there was no separated-off pit lane at Monaco – cars were prepared at the side of the track just after the Gazometre hairpin where speeds were low. An experiment to locate them on the harbour front between the Chicane du Port and Tabac in 1972 was not a success. By 1973 the Rascasse and Antony Noghés corners had been added along with a narrow pit lane parallel to Boulevard Albert.

size for the teams. The ACM also took the opportunity to re-route the exit of the pit lane on the uphill run to Beau Rivage, whereas previously it had fed out straight into the braking zone of St Dévote. The pit lane is still cramped, with the lowest speed limit of the year, and it is the scene of chaos should it start to rain and teams double-stack their cars. But this is Monaco.

While the organizers have laudably worked on the safety of the circuit, very little has been done to provide an overtaking opportunity. Thus races are processional, especially in the modern era when reliability is strong. This places an absolute necessity on a strong qualifying performance. Likewise, once a driver has put his car into P1, there has been a temptation to cement it by underhand methods. In 2006, Michael Schumacher caused outrage by effectively parking his car on the exit of Rascasse to protect his pole position from the fast-charging Fernando Alonso. Former World Champion Keke Rosberg called it, 'the cheapest, dirtiest thing I have ever seen in F1'.

So many in the paddock thought it was ironic that in 2016, after setting the provisional pole time, Nico Rosberg, Keke's son, went straight on at Mirabeau, bringing out the yellow flags and preventing the fast-charging Lewis Hamilton from taking pole off him. Schumacher had his qualifying result removed, Rosberg took P1 and won the race. It was still a Mercedes lock-out of the front row, and a 1–2 finish, but the points swing would have won Hamilton the World Championship.

A lack of overtaking opportunity has also caused endless frustration for drivers in demonstrably faster cars from making

Opposite top Early illumination in the tunnel was primitive to say the least. This 1969 photo shows lightbulbs at the side of the track.

Opposite bottom The exit of the swimming pool complex is the most likely to catch drivers out as they turn in and touch the inside barrier with their front right tyres. There is lap time to be gained in qualifying, but as both Max Verstappen and Charles Leclerc have found out, the penalty for getting it wrong can be severe.

Right Johnny Servoz-Gavin, Chris Amon, Jackie Stewart and John Surtees line up in front of the royal box after qualifying for the 1970 grand prix.

Below In a world of increasingly heightened podiums, the Monaco royal box has been given a lift – though it still fronts the same mundane 1960s apartment blocks. Max Verstappen was on the top step in 2023, a year where Fernando Alonso was just a strategy call away from taking his first F1 victory since 2013.

progress. David Coulthard took flak in the motorsport press after his McLaren was stuck for 56 laps behind Enrique Bernoldi's Arrows, suggesting the slower driver should have let him through. Coulthard had qualified on pole, but a software glitch had prevented him launching from the grid on the parade lap, and he had been forced to start from the back.

In 1992, Nigel Mansell's dominant Williams FW14B was leading comfortably till a late-race puncture forced him into the pits and he emerged behind Ayrton Senna's McLaren on worn tyres. Despite being two seconds a lap quicker he could find no way past. Perhaps the greatest feat of 'Monaco race management' was Daniel Ricciardo's 2018 grand prix win. Leading in the Red Bull his MGU-K failed on Lap 28, yet he managed to keep the lead in front of Sebastian Vettel's Ferrari for the subsequent 50 laps, despite being considerably down on power.

In recent years, Liberty Media's expansion has added races with similar appeal to Monaco – Las Vegas has more than enough casinos to rival the pocket principality and Miami has the sun, even if their sea is glassfibre and their marina populated by boats with nothing below the waterline. It remains to be seen if Monaco can retain its vital cachet as 'the most glamorous grand prix'. Already it has abandoned its insistence to run first practice on Thursday, not Friday, falling into line with other circuits.

Soon they might need to consider using reclaimed land to provide an overtaking place, and not just the exclusive apartment blocks outside the old sea wall at Portier…

GRAND PRIX AT MONACO

In 1965 John Frankenheimer set about making what would become the greatest F1 movie, *Grand Prix*. Frankenheimer was a Ferrari owner and club racer in the States, with a single-minded attitude to film-making. To gain acceptance into the close-knit world of Formula 1 he first contacted American sports car designer Carroll Shelby, who put him in touch with Dan Gurney and America's first World Champion Phil Hill.

'The year before the movie I went to all the races and I signed these guys – Jochen Rindt, Bruce McLaren, Jo Bonnier – up for two years' exclusivity to movies. They still didn't really believe us or think of us as someone to take seriously. As a matter of fact we were a big inconvenience to them as we had track time before their practices. We also had a big big film unit in situations where we got in the way.'

Gradually more drivers came on board: Graham Hill, Lorenzo Bandini, Richie Ginther, Jack Brabham, Mike Parkes, Jo Schlesser joined the cast. There is one memorable scene of a driver briefing, where Bruce McLaren has dialogue and the majority of the faces in the room are F1 drivers.

In the days before team sponsorship, cars ran in their national colours and so Frankenheimer could use cars painted in the rosso red of Italy, but what he wanted most of all was the agreement and participation of Ferrari. Enzo was not impressed. 'He just said, "You go make your movie, it has nothing to do with

Top **Echoing the crashes of Alberto Ascari and Paul Hawkins, a replica F1 car (Frankenheimer used modified F2 and F3 cars) is fired via a hydraulic ram along with a dummy of driver 'Pete Aron'.**

Above **Former World Champion Phil Hill drives the Ford GT40 camera car as it approaches the chicane in front of a BRM driven by actor James Garner. Garner, who performed his own stunts – which included leaping out of a burning car at Brands Hatch – was highly rated as a driver by Dan Gurney.**

Opposite top **Yves Montand, who plays Ferrari driver Jean-Pierre Sarti, waits to get into his car on the start/finish straight.**

Opposite bottom **James Garner, pictured at harbourside, flew into a rage during the Monaco sequences as shopkeepers from La Condamine blocked camera shots. The race track covers two communes: Monte Carlo and La Condamine, and whereas the Monte Carlo businesses had been compensated for the disruption, the Condamine businesses had not.**

what we do ... And you can't use the word Ferrari in this picture."'

Undeterred, Frankenheimer set about shooting the movie. For Monaco he had brought along a Ford GT40 modified into a camera car and driven by Phil Hill. This was going to be a live action movie, not one supplemented by endless studio back projections. In addition he had a helicopter camera in place for practice and the race, which swooped down over the harbour to pick up cars as they exited the tunnel, headed through the chicane and along the quayside. At one point, race control warned the director that his helicopter was flying too low, such was the desire to capture the action. It carried on regardless.

'After Monaco was over I cut together a quick 30-minute roughcut of stuff I shot at Monaco, called Enzo Ferrari and asked him if he would look at it." Frankenheimer recalled. "And he said, 'well I don't have any projection equipment'. I said just tell me you'll look at it. So I shut the movie down, chartered a plane, brought a projector and projectionist to Maranello in his office. Set it up and ran the 30 minutes. When it was over, the lights came up and he embraced me. He said, "You can have the team, you can have the factory, you can have everything."'

MONTJUÏC PARK, BARCELONA, SPAIN

Barcelona Montjuïc

A GRAND PRIX IN A VIBRANT CITY CENTRE – FORMULA 1'S RETURN TO BARCELONA LOOKED LIKE IT COULD HAVE A LONG FUTURE, UNTIL SAFETY MEASURES LET IT DOWN

Few Formula 1 circuits can be reached by cable car or funicular railway, but until 1976, Montjuïc was one of them. Long after it lost its strategic significance to Barcelona, the forests on the 'mountain of the jews' were converted to parkland and in 1929 hosted an International Exposition or Worlds Fair.

Legacy buildings included the commanding Spanish-Renaissance-style, Palau Nacional, now used as the National Art Museum of Catalonia which commands fabulous views over Barcelona (and in 2000, the days of big money car launches, was the site of the Benetton B200 unveiling). There is also the old Olympic Stadium built in the hope of attracting the 1936 Olympic Games that went to Berlin.

It also became the site of an itinerant Catalan motor race known as the Penya Rhin Grand Prix. This event was held for three years in the 1920s in Vilafranca del Penedès, 60 kilometres west of Barcelona, before re-appearing at Montjuïc from 1933 to 1936 and curtailed by the onset of the Spanish Civil War.

The pioneers of the circuit were the Motorcycle Runners of Catalonia who organized a road race that started off in Parc de Montjuïc in 1932. The first four-wheel race appeared the following year on what would become a familiar circuit, encircling the grand building, but for now with the start/finish straight at the bottom of the hill. Although the first race was not an established event on the European calendar, a *grande épreuve*, it attracted the participation of Tazio Nuvolari in an Alfa-Romeo 8C run by

Opposite Clay Regazzoni in the Ferrari brakes for the downhill Vias right-hander during practice for the 1975 Spanish Grand Prix.

Left The magnificent Cartographic and Geological Institute of Barcelona is just one of many fine buildings in Montjuïc Park. Ironically, the grand prix circuit is beloved by learner drivers who get valuable road experience on little used city streets.

Below Left Mark Donohue's Penske-Ford tackles the fast-flowing downhill section of track from Teatro Griego to Vias.

Below The building to the left on Passeig de Santa Madrona is part of El Teatre Lliure one of Catalunya's most serious playhouses.

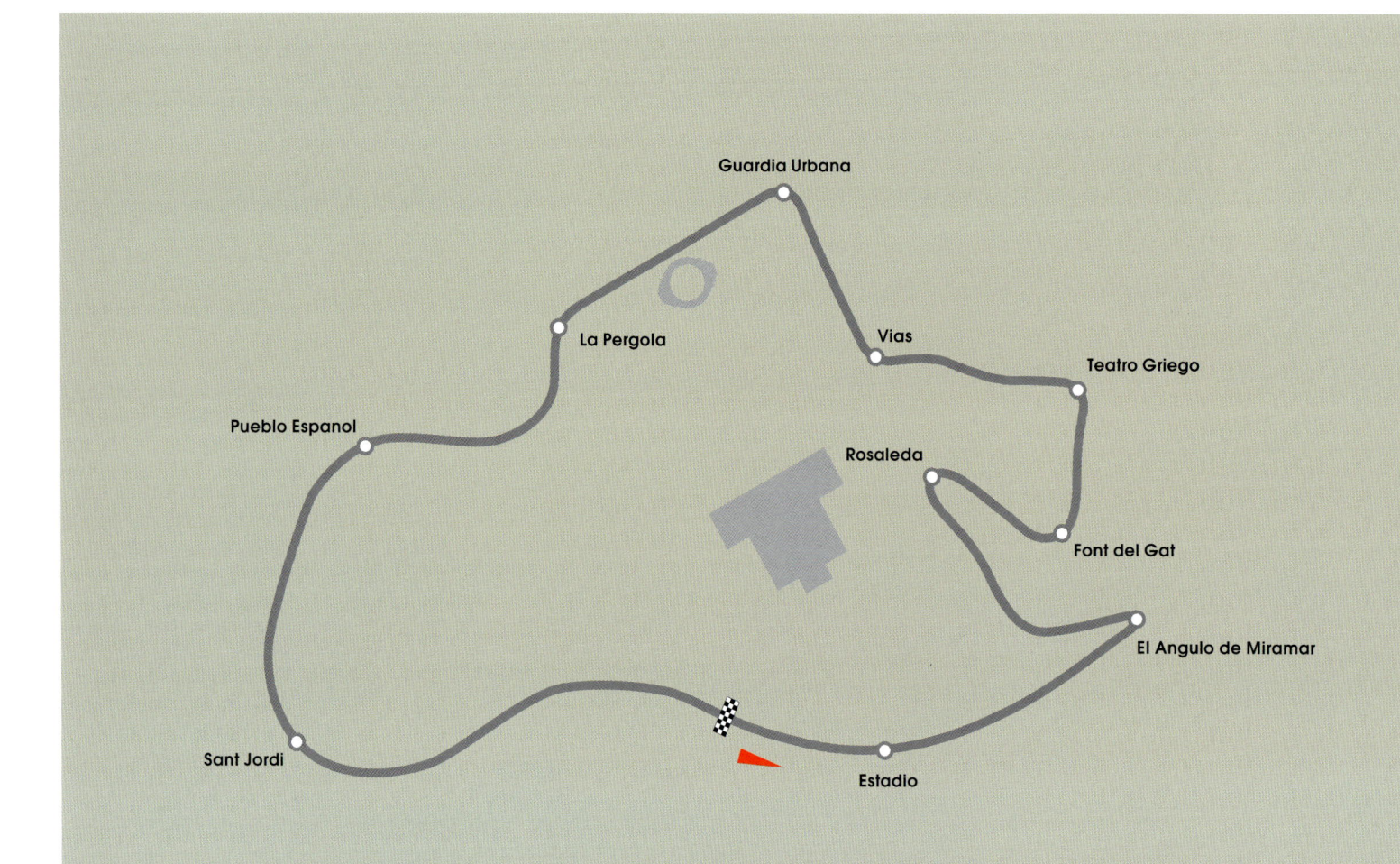

MONTJUÏC PARK

Length: 3.791 km (2.356 miles)
Lap Record: 1:23.800 (Ronnie Peterson, Lotus 72E, 1973)
Opened: 1933
First F1 Grand Prix: 1969
Number of F1 Grands Prix hosted: 4
Number of laps: 75
Circuit Designer: Real Automóvil Club de Cataluña (RACC)
Race winning fact: Jackie Stewart won the race twice, both in World Championship-winning years – 1969 (with Matra) and 1971 (with Tyrrell).

Jackie Stewart racked up the most wins over the four races run through Barcelona's beautiful hillside park. Despite having two very tight corners – El Angulo de Miramar and Rosaleda, and the reasonably slow Font del Gat, Ronnie Peterson's lap record was in excess of 100mph. With such a fast-flowing circuit it was no surprise that the drivers were anxious to see the trackside barriers properly secured.

Scuderia Ferrari, which led from the start until engine problems forced a lengthy pit delay.

The race, run over a variety of road surfaces which included asphalt and cobblestones, intersected occasionally by tramlines, was won by Achille Varzi in an Alfa the following year; by Luigi Fagioli in a Mercedes in 1935 and finally by Nuvolari for Alfa in 1936. Although the Penya Rhin GP departed to Barcelona's outskirts, Pedralbes, in the late 1940s and early 1950s, Montjuïc would host touring car races including the Nuvolari Cup. Spanish car manufacturer SEAT helped promote a sports car race and gradually the speed and sophistication of the racing machinery on display around Montjuïc increased, with GT racers and Formula 3 events.

Finally, in 1966, the circuit hosted the Gran Premio de Barcelona, a Formula 2 race that attracted the top F1 drivers of the day. Jim Clark, Jackie Stewart, Graham Hill and Jack Brabham had made the short dash across the Pyrenées from the F2 race in Pau to compete. They would return in 1967 and 1968, Brabham winning the first rain-sodden event, Clark the second and Stewart the third. By 1969 the circuit boasted its first F1 grand prix and Montjuïc was on the map.

It was partly thanks to Jarama's ham-fisted attempt to put on a race in 1968, but mostly down to politics that attention turned to Barcelona. There has long been competition for sporting prominence between Madrid and the Catalan capital, perhaps exemplified by the enmity between football teams

Top **Tony Brise in a Williams-Ford near the top of the hill in Montjuïc at the almost 180-degree Rosaleda corner during the 1975 grand prix.**

Above **A learner driver emerges from the road previously blocked by straw bales in the 1975 photo (with the stone steps beyond visible in each). Beyond are the domes of the National Museum of Art of Catalonia, the location of the Benetton launch in January 2000, the days when teams spent a lot of money unveiling their cars.**

Real Madrid and Barcelona. And thus, like Britain and France, Spain alternated their races between the two top circuits: one a modern, twisty, purpose-built facility, the other boasting motorsport heritage, a beautiful city backdrop, but inherently more dangerous.

The location of the pits and starting grid for four-wheel races had been moved to behind the Palau Nacional to the Avenida de l'Estadi for the F2 races, with the crumbling old Olympic Stadium acting as the paddock. Its debut race proved to be the final hurrah for the high aerofoil rear wings, first introduced on CanAm cars. The unsightly wings created valuable downforce, but were held aloft on slim, stress-vulnerable struts, and in the 1969 race the aerodynamic load became more than they could bear. As Graham Hill's Lotus crested the rise beyond the pits, the struts buckled and the wing collapsed with the sudden loss of rear downforce sending him into the barriers. He was unhurt in the crash but had no time to warn team-mate and race leader Jochen Rindt whose rear wing failed on Lap 20. This time the Lotus smashed into the barriers and Hill's abandoned car, flipping it over. With 55 laps of fuel still on board, Hill managed to turn off the electrics on the car and help Rindt struggle free, blood streaming from a cut on his face. It was effectively the end of the high rear wing era. Although they appeared in Monaco for practice, by race day they were consigned to history.

The adoption of slick tyres from the 1970 season onwards, together with an advance in the slippery art of aerodynamics, advanced F1 speeds in the 1970s. The follow-up races in 1971

Top An unharmed Graham Hill exits his car after it had gone light over the bump in front of the Olympic Stadium and collapsed the rear wing, sending him into the barriers. He was unable to warn team-mate Jochen Rindt in time whose Lotus 49B suffered a similar fate and crashed into the wreckage of Hill's car.

Above Where Hill and Rindt crashed is the highest point on the circuit, an area made famous by the city views from the Olympic Park during the 1992 Games.

and 1973 were run without major incident – the race in 1971 won again by Jackie Stewart in a Tyrrell-Ford and in 1973 by Emerson Fittipaldi in a Lotus-Ford. That 1973 race featured the singular appearance on the podium of American driver George Follmer in a Shadow-Ford, who became the oldest F1 rookie at 39 (barring the 1950s).

However it was the 1975 race that spelled the end of Montjuïc. Without the widespread use of catch-fencing as seen at circuits like Monaco and Indy, it was down to a double layer of Armco barrier to stop cars from leaving the circuit and crashing into spectators. A track inspection before practice showed that many of the barriers had not been bolted in place properly or their mounting posts secured. Organizers were slow to react and with the job still unfinished on Saturday morning the teams' mechanics joined in the task.

Still there was unrest. Although the more dangerous sections had been checked, drivers threatened to boycott the race and in response the organizers threatened the teams with legal action for potential breach of contract and were prepared to impound the cars. That threat was all the more real with teams encamped within the old Olympic Stadium, the gate of which could easily be locked. A legal dispute 14 days before the Monaco Grand Prix was not to be entertained.

A compromise was found where drivers were given the opportunity to drive for three laps and then retire. World Champion Emerson Fittipaldi and Williams-Ford driver Arturo Merzario were soon on their way to the airport, but others saw the opportunity of a strong result and raced on. The field was immediately diminished by a first lap tangle between Vittorio Brambilla and Mario Andretti that punted Niki Lauda's Ferrari into team-mate Clay Regazzoni. Patrick Depailler retired with suspension damage and James Hunt took the lead in a Hesketh then spun into the barriers on oil leaving the unlikely Rolf Stommelen, who'd qualified in P9, leading the race.

But on Lap 26 it all went horribly wrong. At close to the same point where Graham Hill had lost his skyscraper wing in 1969, Stommelen's Hill-Ford lost his own rear wing as the car went light over the crest of the hill at 160mph. The car clipped the Brabham of Carlos Pace and became airborne, riding over the barriers and smashing into a lamppost.

Race Control failed to realize the enormity of what had happened for four laps, after which it was red-flagged. Stommelen survived the accident with a broken leg, a broken wrist, and two cracked ribs, but a fireman, a spectator and two photo-journalists were killed instantly by the impact. It was the first race to be awarded half points, and the only win of Jochen Mass's career. It also marked the first (and only) points scored by a woman driver, Lella Lombardi in the March-Ford, who was in sixth place when the race was stopped. The bitter irony of it all was that it had been a car failure not a safety barrier failure that had caused the loss of life, but the Spanish Grand Prix would not return to Barcelona until 1991 with the debut of the Circuit de Catalunya.

Top March team boss Max Mosley (second left) along with his driver Vittorio Brambilla, and Lotus boss Colin Chapman along with his driver Ronnie Peterson, stride purposefully back to the pits having inspected the barriers out on the course. The race endured a tragic accident with Rolf Stommelen injured and five spectators killed, though not from a failure of the Armco.

Above Today there is no reminder of the park's grand prix past, but curious F1 fans can still trace the exact route the cars took in 1975, which is spectacular. Barcelona has lost the grand prix to great rivals Madrid, but given the safety measures now imposed on modern F1 venues, Madrid would struggle to beat the epic challenge that Montjuïc represents.

ÎLE NOTRE-DAME, MONTRÉAL, CANADA

Circuit Gilles Villeneuve

NAMED AFTER CANADA'S GREATEST FORMULA 1 DRIVER, THE CIRCUIT HAS A TENDENCY TO THROW UP SOME UNEXPECTED RESULTS

Île Notre-Dame in Montréal was created by dumping 15 million tons of rock into the Saint Lawrence River in the early 1960s. It's a unique setting for an F1 race. The artificial island was originally created with the excavations from the new metro system in anticipation of providing a site for Expo 67, the world trade exhibition which would celebrate Canada's centennial.

Nearly all of the Expo 67 pavilions were demolished or dismantled in 1975 to create a rowing basin for Montréal's 1976 Summer Olympics. The elaborate, modernist French pavilion remained and was converted into a casino, while much of the British Pavilion was eventually shipped back to Scotland and reconstructed at the University of Stirling.

In the late 1970s Canadian motorsport was looking for a new home for its grand prix after the perennially rainy Mosport, near Toronto, proved inadequate. The Île Notre-Dame circuit was hurried into readiness for the 1978 race and home fans witnessed a historic victory, Gilles Villeneuve bringing his Ferrari 312T3 home in front of Jody Scheckter driving a Canadian car, the Walter Wolf-entered Wolf-Ford.

Prospects of a future Canadian World Champion were cut agonisingly short when the popular Québecois was killed in final qualifying for the 1982 Belgian Grand Prix at Zolder. He had been engaged in a furious battle with Ferrari team-mate Didier Pironi, who was embroiled in more tragedy at the Canadian GP a month later. Starting from pole position Pironi stalled just as

Opposite The striking French pavilion and the more prosaic British tower were two of the Expo 67 legacy buildings still on site when the grand prix rolled into town in 1978.

Below The two Ferraris of Carlos Sainz and Charles Leclerc slip through the final chicane with the French pavilion beyond now turned into a casino.

Bottom left After Jean-Pierre Jarier's Lotus retired, Gilles Villeneuve inherited the lead and delighted Canadian F1 fans with his debut victory (as well as sponsors Labatt, by spraying a large bottle of beer from the podium).

Bottom right Ferrari designer Mauro Forghieri (left) and team manager Antonio Tomaini (centre) grill a subdued Gilles Villeneuve before the fateful practice sessions at Zolder in 1982.

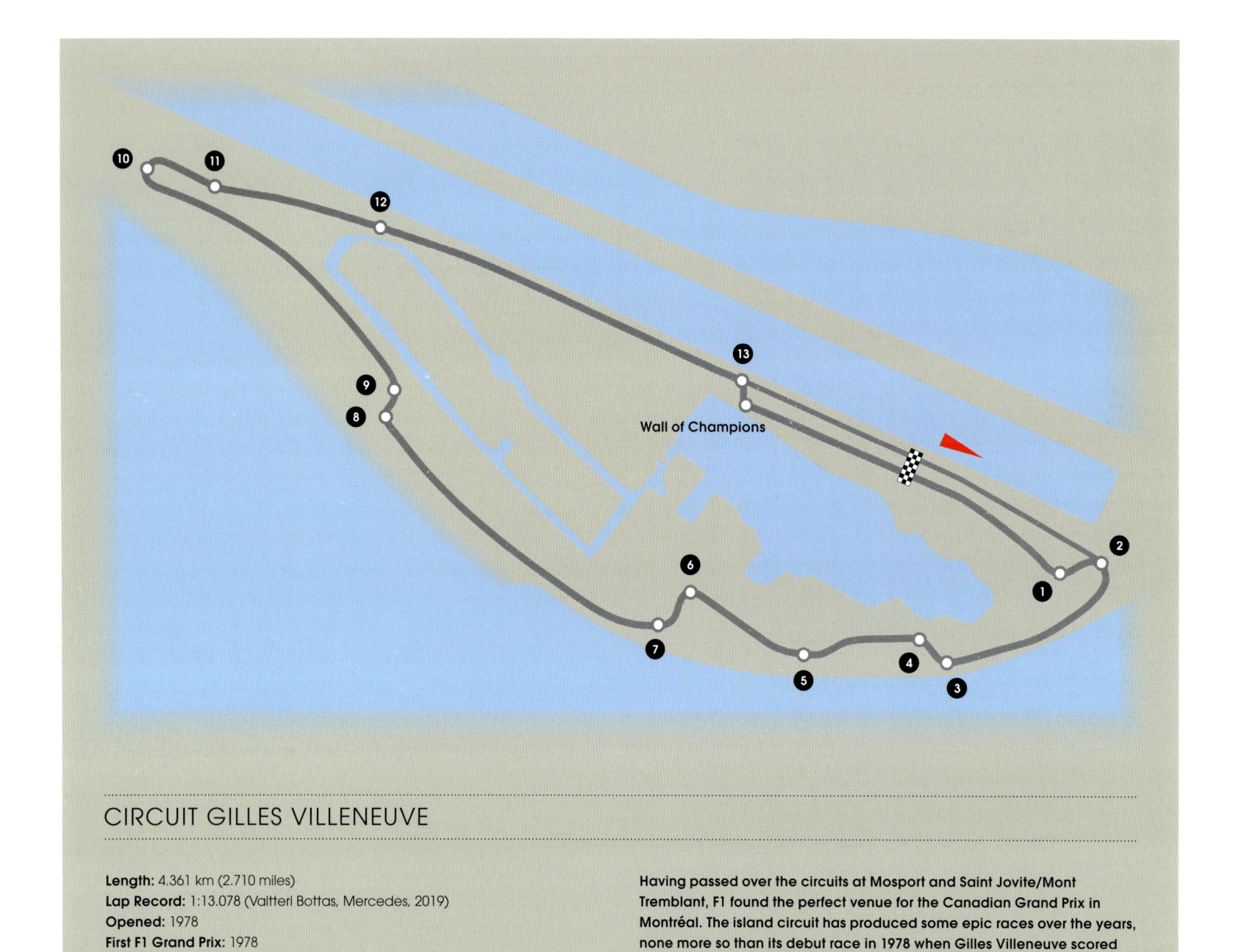

CIRCUIT GILLES VILLENEUVE

Length: 4.361 km (2.710 miles)
Lap Record: 1:13.078 (Valtteri Bottas, Mercedes, 2019)
Opened: 1978
First F1 Grand Prix: 1978
Number of F1 Grands Prix hosted: 42
Number of laps: 70
Circuit Designer: Roger Peart
Race winning fact: Max Verstappen's win at the 2024 Canadian Grand Prix was the 60th of his career, and his third consecutive victory at the Circuit Gilles Villeneuve.

Having passed over the circuits at Mosport and Saint Jovite/Mont Tremblant, F1 found the perfect venue for the Canadian Grand Prix in Montréal. The island circuit has produced some epic races over the years, none more so than its debut race in 1978 when Gilles Villeneuve scored his first F1 victory for Ferrari, overtaking Jody Scheckter (in a Canadian-backed Wolf-Ford). They would be Ferrari team-mates the following year.

the lights switched to green and while most of the field got past without major impacts, the unsighted rookie Ricardo Paletti, starting from the back of the grid in an Osella, piled into the back of the Frenchman's Ferrari. The Italian suffered massive chest trauma and died later that day. It would be the last F1 race fatality until the grand prix weekend of 1994 that claimed both Roland Ratzenberger and Ayrton Senna.

In September of 1982 the circuit was renamed in honour of Gilles Villeneuve with an inscription 'Salut Gilles' embedded in the tarmac by the start/finish chequered stripe.

For one reason or another Canadian Grands Prix have rarely been contiguous, with interruptions for hosting fee disputes, Covid and, in 1987, a sponsorship row between Canadian

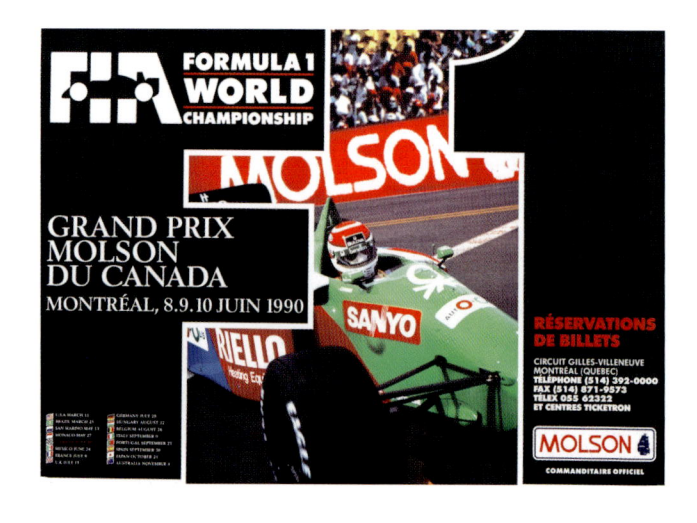

Above Alan Jones in a Williams FW06 flashes past the pits after taking the hairpin. Beyond, Niki Lauda in the Brabham BT46 is about to retire. Beyond them both is the Buckminster Fuller-designed geodesic dome that enshrouded the US pavilion at Expo 67.

Left Rain is a frequent visitor to the Canadian Grand Prix. Lando Norris's McLaren exits the hairpin with the Montréal Biosphere, dedicated to the environment in Montréal, visible beyond.

Opposite The two leading Canadian beer brands, Molson and Labatt, have sponsored the race in the past.

142

Opposite top Cars approach the hairpin in 1978. A line of promotional balloons mark the position of the original pit complex to the left. Beyond is the tower of the British Pavilion.

Opposite bottom Spectator seating has increased tremendously in the intervening years and the big screen allows both drivers and fans to keep abreast of developments in the race.

Left In 2023 the Canadian Grand Prix celebrated 50 years of the Safety Car, first introduced unofficially at Mosport, Ontario, in 1973. However the yellow Porsche 914 used during that race failed to pick up the leader and it took a great deal of post-race calculation to work out the full result.

Below Jacques Villeneuve exits his BAR-Supertec at speed having dumped it into the 'Wall of Champions' during the 1999 race.

brewers Molson and Labatt. The absence of a race allowed organizers to move the rudimentary pits and start/finish line from just past the hairpin to their current position.

There have been a variety of minor tweaks to corners over the years, not least the final chicane leading onto the start/finish straight which has been tightened to make it a bigger braking event and hence aid overtaking; this combined with a straightening out of the Casino Straight.

The final turn has a minimum run-off, lined by the 'Wall of Champions' that in 1999 claimed the machinery of three World Champions – Damon Hill, Jacques Villeneuve and Michael Schumacher. Fittingly, the slogan on the barrier reads 'Welcome to Québec'.

Drivers and spectators alike enjoy the Montréal track and the vibe in the city during the grand prix weekend. There are two traditions of the weekend not seen elsewhere across the Formula 1 season. One has been suspended since Covid and may not reappear now that teams are faced with a 24-race calendar. This is the impromptu raft race where mechanics compete with makeshift rafts on the Olympic rowing basin next door.

The second is a regular appearance on track of an animal Kimi Räikkönen struggled to describe to his mechanics. "Okay, there's that animal running around in the middle of the track at Turn 6. I don't know what they're called." For every grand prix on Île Notre-Dame, it's Groundhog Day.

MONZA, ITALY

Autodromo Nazionale

MONZA IS ONE OF THE ORIGINAL CIRCUITS FROM THE 1950 SEASON, A UNIQUE VENUE WITH PASSIONATE FANS SUPPORTING A CAR NOT A DRIVER

If France had been the cradle of motorsport, holding the first grand prix of 1906 in Le Mans, it was Italy that sought ascendancy in the years following World War I. The Automobile Club of Milan chose a site in the royal park which could be used for both testing and racing.

Even in the early 1920s, conservationists had their influence and brought construction to a halt, protesting over the number of ancient trees that would be felled to make way for the circuit. Hasty modifications to the plan involved using roads already in place through the park, thus limiting the number of trees that would be taken down.

The months-long delay ensured a frantic, large-scale building project to meet the deadline of the Italian Grand Prix on 0 September. It even involved laying temporary rail tracks through the park to transport the large quantities of concrete needed for the north and south curves. The road course would be all-tarmac, the oval or speed course (*pista di alta velocita*) had wide, banked concrete curves and shared one straight, the start/finish straight, with the road course. This gave organizers the flexibility to runs races on the road or speed courses, or combine the two, with one lap of each and the crossover on the main straight – as employed for the 1955 Italian Grand Prix.

After 110 days everything was in place, the road course, the shallow-banked oval, grandstands, service roads – the circuit would never see such a rapid building programme again. Everything was in place for the Grand Prix of Italy, 1922.

Monza is known by many names, its official name Autodromo Nazionale may well have been intended as a political slight to Rome, but it is apt. The national expectation of Ferrari to do well at Monza comes into sharp and sometimes excruciating focus every year. It is also known as the 'pista magica', 'the temple of speed' and 'the cathedral of motorsport'.

Cathedral is apt too, for the circuit in the royal park is the guardian of many lost souls, the ghosts of drivers, marshals and spectators killed in racing and testing accidents. As veteran F1 journalist Joe Saward described it: 'The list is frighteningly long and tragically distinguished.'

In 1928 Emilio Materassi lost control of his Talbot on the main straight as he passed the slower car of Giulio Foresti, ploughing through the barriers and into the crowd. The accident claimed the life of Materassi and 27 spectators. It would remain the worst in motor-racing till surpassed by Le Mans in 1955. Though there

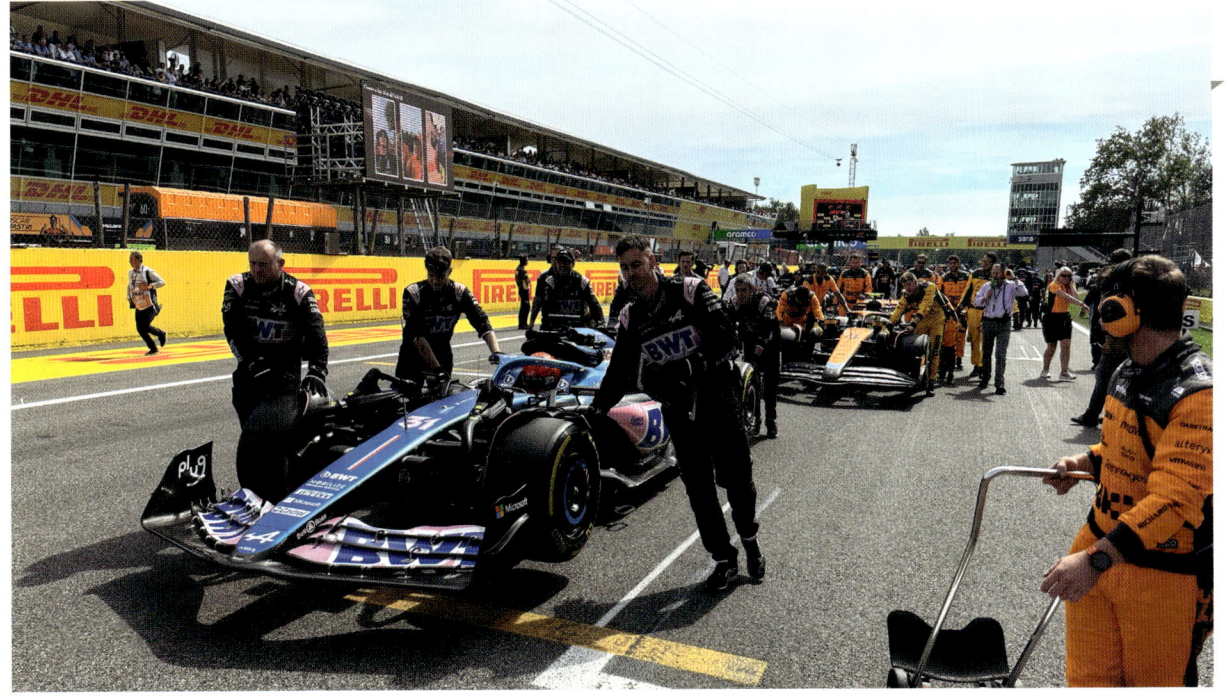

Opposite The world as it should be: Two Ferraris on the front row for the Italian Grand Prix at Monza. One of the classic scoreboard towers overlooks the grid.

Above The grid, seconds before the start of the 1951 race. It would be won by Alberto Ascari in a Ferrari.

Left Cars are wheeled into position before the 2023 race, accompanied by Martin Brundle (pink shirt) delivering another grid walk for Sky TV. In the distance, the tower has lost its scoreboard and now is the perfect platform to witness the podium celebrations.

AUTODROMO NATIONALE

Length: 5.793 km (3.600 miles)
Lap Record: 1:21.046, Rubens Barrichello, Ferrari F2004, 2004
Opened: 1922
First F1 Grand Prix: 1950
Number of F1 Grands Prix hosted: 74
Number of laps: 53
Circuit Designer: Alfredo Rosselli
Race winning fact: Ayrton Senna (1990) only won a single Italian GP, equal with Juan-Pablo Montoya (2005), both for McLaren.

Monza has always been known as the Temple of Speed and is regularly the fastest grand prix on the calendar. Fittingly, the fastest F1 lap was recorded here, in qualifying for the 2020 Italian Grand Prix, when Lewis Hamilton claimed pole with a 1:18.887 lap, which equated to 264.362kmh (164.267mph) in his Mercedes W11. Hamilton's time eclipsed the mark set by Kimi Räikkönen in 2018 by a slender 0.232 seconds.

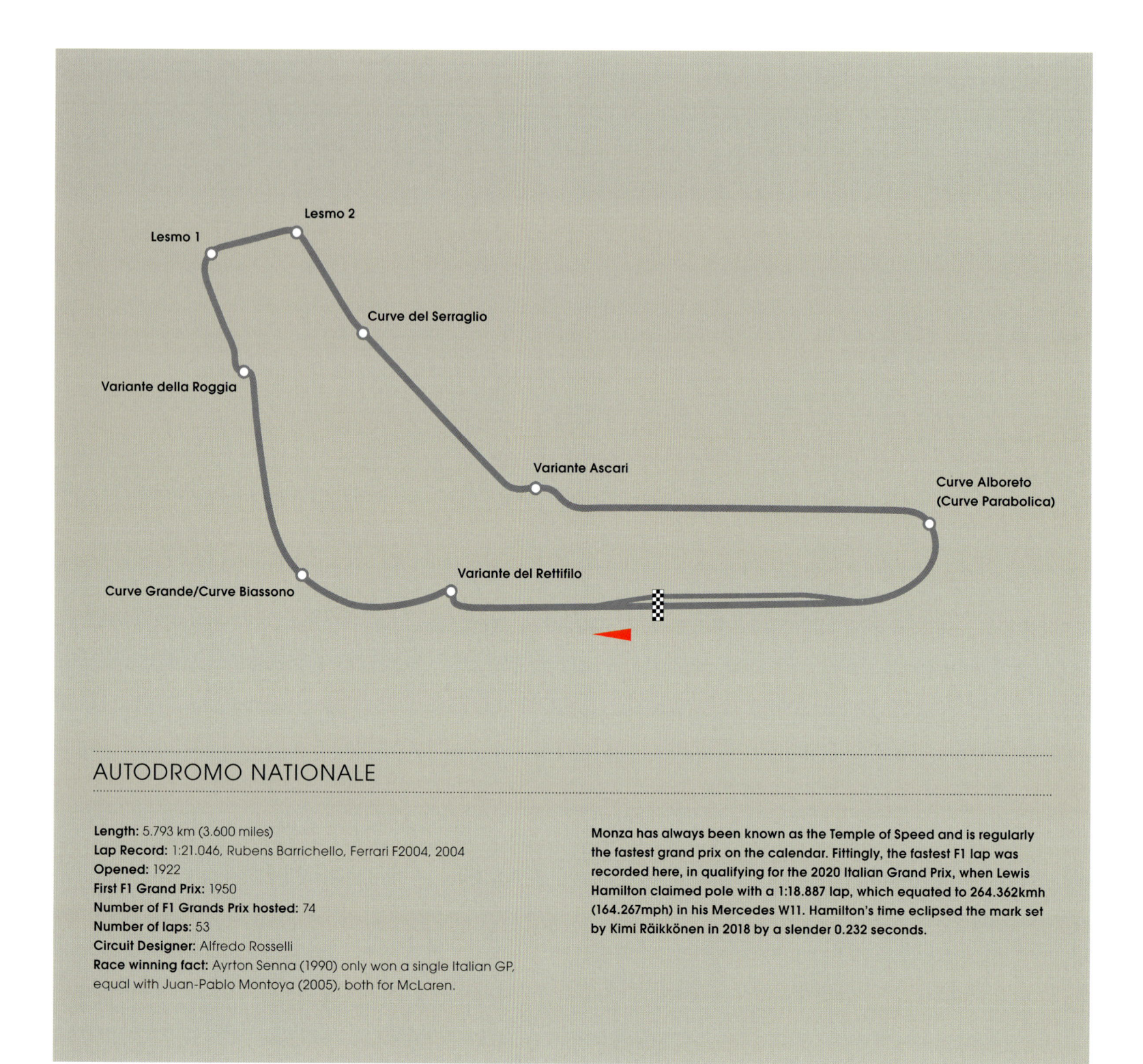

were inevitable spectator incidents on Italy's great road races – the Mille Miglia, Coppa Acerbo and Targa Florio – circuit racing was supposed to be safer.

It was Vincenzo Florio, founder of the great Sicilian road race, who suggested a safer alternative, bypassing the North Curve and returning to the back straight, close to where the exit of the Ascari Chicane is today.

The jeopardy of suffering a blown tyre or any mechanical issue on the high-speed banking was brought home on 10 October 1933, a date that would become known as Black Sunday. Three drivers died on the South Curve, an Alfa Romeo and Maserati slid off on oil left by another competitor, while the Bugatti of Polish Count Stanisłas Czaykowski, overturned and caught fire, the driver trapped in his burning car. The high-speed curves would not be used again before World War II intervened.

Just as its famous counterpart in France, Le Mans, was wrecked by its German occupiers, so Monza fared badly in World War II, but this time under the Allies. A post-war military parade with tanks and other armoured vehicles tore up the track surface and many of the buildings were converted to store army surplus. In 1948 the Automobile Club of Milan enacted a refurbishment plan to restore once more the *magica* to the *pista*.

Part of the great scheme was to rebuild the contentious banked curves, this time on concrete pillars and with a

Above left The poster for John Frankenheimer's 1966 F1 movie featured the Monza banking and James Garner in a Chris Amon-inspired helmet design. Despite the bumps, a great deal of in-car footage was shot on the concrete track that hadn't hosted an official grand prix since 1961.

Above A poster for the 12th Italian Grand Prix in 1934 by Plinio Codognato makes it clear it will be a battle between the racing white of Germany against the rosso red of Italy.

Left A scene from the movie where a car leaves the oval track above, close to where the grand prix circuit passes underneath, between the second Lesmo and Ascari.

Right **Italian racing driver Eugenio Castellotti photographed out on the banking ahead of the 1955 Italian Grand Prix. It was the first time the combined oval and road circuit had been used since 1933 and the newly installed concrete banking was around 10° steeper.**

Below **Castellotti soaks up the applause as he walks with his Ferrari 'Squalo' to the grid before the 1955 race. He finished third behind the Mercedes of Fangio and Taruffi, and third overall in the World Championship. He would lose his life testing a Ferrari at Modena in early 1957.**

Opposite top **A promotional photo for team sponsors Shell in 2015 shows exactly how steep the 30° Monza banking looks. Sebastian Vettel and Kimi Räikkönen were on driving duties in 2015 with a youthful-looking team principal Mauricio Arrivabene at centre. Arrivabene survived in the role until January 2019.**

Opposite bottom **Two examples of the banking from 2011. The uppermost image shows the early part of the oval near the Variante del Rettifilo (also visible in the picture on page 154).**

much steeper inclination at 30 degrees. There were also two matching, modernist glass-walled towers built at either end of the start/finish straight facing towards the pits and pit lane. These classic examples of post-war International architecture remain to this day, while the concrete banking was in use for less than a decade.

The initial four runnings of the Formula 1 Italian Grand Prix took place solely on the road course. In the early 1950s Italian cars and/or Italian drivers led the way. Nino Farina took the first race in an Alfa Romeo, Alberto Ascari the second two in a Ferrari, while Juan Manuel Fangio won the 1953 event in a Maserati. Indeed, Fangio was lucky to compete that year at all having driven through the night to compete for Maserati in the 1952 Monza race before crashing badly, suffering concussion and a broken vertebra in his neck when he was thrown from the car.

When the combined road and oval course was used in 1955, Fangio made it a trio of victories, having won the previous year for the dominant Mercedes marque. With the F1 team exiting the sport at the end of the 1955 season in the wake of the Le Mans tragedy, it was left to Stirling Moss in a Maserati to take victory over the combined course in 1956. But there was a problem. By necessity, large areas of concrete need expansion gaps to stop the surface from buckling, as experienced by every motorist using concrete sections of motorway. At speeds of 150mph this was playing havoc with suspensions and driveshafts of F1 machinery. The combined course was dropped… and then, largely at the behest of Ferrari, reinstated for the 1960 and 1961 grands prix because it favoured engine power, after the impudent *garagista* Cooper had won the 1959 race on the road course.

The British teams boycotted the 1960 race, citing safety reasons, and so Phil Hill scored a fairly hollow victory for Ferrari in what would be a historic first and last. It was the last time a rear-engined car would win an F1 race. It was also the first time an American driver had won an F1 grand prix. A year later he would be the first American to win an F1 World Championship.

In 1961 the *garagistas* were back for the last non-fictional F1 race using the concrete curves. It proved to be a tragic finale, though one that did not involve the banking. Wolfgang von Trips was leading the championship for Ferrari, driving the beautiful 'shark-nose' 156. Team-mate Phil Hill was his main rival. The Italian Grand Prix was the final race of the season. With the prospect of a guaranteed Ferrari World Champion and with von Trips starting from pole, Monza was heaving with *tifosi* ready to celebrate.

But von Trips was slow off the line and lost positions on the opening lap, the No.4 Ferrari getting submerged into the pack. Monza has always been a slipstreaming race and heading down the back straight towards Parabolica Jim Clark pulled out of the Ferrari's tow to make a pass just as von Trips moved over. The German's car clipped the front wheel of Clark's Lotus and it crashed into the banking and along a fence lined with spectators on the outside of the track. Von Trips was flung onto the track like a rag doll, killed by the impact. Fifteen spectators died with many catastrophically injured.

Although it was used in sports car races – such as the 1000 Kilometres of Monza – until 1969, the last use of the combined circuit for F1 machinery was in 1966. The conclusion of John Frankenheimer's *Grand Prix* movie took place with cars hurtling around the evocative Monza banking, some with large Panaflex movie cameras threatening to rattle loose. Although it is no longer used for races, it has survived proposals to have it demolished and made a brief appearance in the 2021 World Rally Championship. It is fenced off to keep curious *tifosi* at bay.

As the speed of F1 cars increased through the 1960s, and with the disappearance of foot-to-the-floor circuits like Reims and the original Spa, so Monza became the acknowledged 'fastest race on the calendar'. In 1970 it also claimed the life of the only man to become a posthumous World Champion. A likely brake failure on Jochen Rindt's Lotus 72 in practice sent it hurtling straight on into the barriers at Parabolica, destroying the front of the car. There is a heartbreaking photo of model wife Nina Rindt in the Lotus garage, stopwatch and lapchart in hand, waiting for her husband to come through.

In 1971 slipstreaming reached its zenith with the closest finish of all time in the fastest (and quickest) race of all time. There have been close finishes throughout the history of F1 – at Reims, in Austria, at Jerez and Jarama, with cars using the slipstream down the final straight to pull alongside the leader at the flag. The 1971 Italian Grand Prix involved five cars, which were separated at the line by 0.61 of a second. Peter Gethin in a BRM edged Ronnie Peterson's March by 0.1 seconds. The winner

Opposite One of the most heartbreaking photos in Formula 1. Nina Rindt, wife of Jochen, waits on the pitwall stopwatch in hand, for her husband to complete another lap. Rindt has just suffered a failure on his Lotus 72 sending him hurtling into the barriers on the outside of Parabolica with fatal consequences.

Below Four cars head into the Variante del Rettifilo during the 1971 Italian Grand Prix - the slipstreaming grand prix. From left to right Ronnie Peterson in a March, François Cevert in a Tyrrell, Mike Hailwood in a Surtees and Jo Siffert in a BRM. Despite the clear differences in chassis aerodynamics the racing is close. They have all been following each other down the main straight and are about to shuffle the order going into the braking zone.

Bottom Peter Gethin's BRM crosses the line first in 1971 followed by Peterson, Cevert, Hailwood and Howden Ganley, the first five cars covered by 0.61 seconds.

clocked up an average speed in excess of 241km/h (150mph). The road course had become the *pista velocita*.

Mindful of its tragic past, chicanes were added in 1972 to reduce speed, the first as cars approached the Curve Grande – a left/right chicane in its first incarnation known as Variante del Rettifilo, the second after cars dipped down under the bridge which carried the north banking. This was the critical Vialone curve, through which drivers needed to carry speed for a slingshot onto the back straight. It was renamed for Alberto Ascari who had perished at the corner while testing his reactions in a Ferrari sports car, four days after plunging into Monaco harbour.

In 1976, a chicane was added between the Curve Grande and the two Lesmo corners, the Variante della Roggia. All three

Left In 1988 the first chicane, the Variante del Rettifilo, was a left turn followed by a right. Stand-in Williams driver Jean-Louis Schlesser fails to realize that he is about to be lapped by Ayrton Senna and ruins McLaren's 100% winning season by clattering into him.

Below Spectators flood onto the track and make their way towards the podium to celebrate Carlos Sainz's third place after the 2023 Italian Grand Prix. The Rettifilo has long been a right turn followed by a left and the source of contentious overtaking moves.

chicanes have subsequently been reprofiled and in the case of the Variante del Rettifilo changed from a left/right to a right/left. When McLaren looked like becoming the first team to win every grand prix in a season during their dominant 1988 campaign it all fell apart at the left/right Rettifilo. Senna came up to lap Williams's substitute driver Jean-Louis Schlesser, who simply failed to see him and drove into the side of the MP4/4.

In 2021 when an uncharacteristically slow pit stop by the Red Bull team dropped Max Verstappen behind Lewis Hamilton, the Dutchman made a rash overtaking move in the right/left Rettifilo, which ended up with the RB17 launched on top of the Mercedes with the Red Bull's front tyre striking Hamilton's helmet and the Halo device preventing any serious injury.

Despite the chicanes, Monza remains a temple of speed, the fastest race of the season, with the highest percentage of full throttle. It has continued to provide moments of high drama. It was Celtic manager Jock Stein who said that, 'football is nothing without the fans', and Monza's unique atmosphere could not be generated without the *tifosi*, passionate Ferrari fans for whom a podium is the very minimum expected from Scuderia Ferrari.

In 1976 they were astonished to see the return of Niki Lauda, only six weeks after he had been given the last rites from his incendiary Nürburgring crash. With his skin grafts still raw and the driver visibly under stress, he climbed into his Ferrari 312T2 to continue the season-long battle with James Hunt. It was surely the most heroic fourth place ever recorded at the Autodromo

Left The back straight from the Ascari chicane to Parabolica very much as it would look four years later, when Wolfgang von Trips' Ferrari tangled with Jim Clark's Lotus sending the car up the bank on the right and into the crowd. In the 1957 race Stewart Lewis-Evans (managed by Bernie Ecclestone) put his car on pole, but it was the Vanwall of team-mate Stirling Moss which won the race.

Below left Today, spectators are protected by a triple layer of Armco and extensive catch-fencing. Here, Carlos Sainz holds off Max Verstappen during the first stint of the 2023 grand prix, but the Ferrari had to give best to the Red Bull RB19's superior tyre degradation.

and his treatment by the Italian media after he ultimately pulled out of the season finale at Mount Fuji was shameful.

Two years later a multiple crash on the opening lap of the Italian Grand Prix left Lotus driver Ronnie Peterson with severe leg injuries. Unlike times past, the race was stopped and Peterson taken to hospital, seemingly in the clear. But it was there that complications set in, the Swede lapsed into a coma and died, to the shock and disbelief of the paddock who had assumed the popular driver was out of danger.

James Hunt never forgave Riccardo Patrese who he believed caused the accident that took Peterson's life and his subsequent BBC commentaries were often laced with disparaging references to the Italian.

In 1988 it looked like the Scuderia would receive yet another drubbing from the unstoppable McLaren MP4/4 that had swept all before it with Prost and Senna locking out the front row. It was less than a month since Enzo Ferrari's death and it looked like there would be no cause for celebration for the *tifosi* – until Alan Prost's engine let go and Senna came up to lap Jean-Louis Schlesser... Gerhard Berger led home Michele Alboreto for an exultant Ferrari 1–2.

Fast forward to 2008 and another landmark win for an Italian team, but this time the rebadged Minardi team, now running as Toro Rosso, but still based in Faenza. Helmut Marko's German prodigy Sebastian Vettel put his car on pole and drove away from the field in unseasonably rainy conditions. As the

153

154

Opposite The pit lane at Monza goes quiet on the Saturday of the 1970 Italian Grand Prix. News is filtering through that World Championship leader Jochen Rindt has been injured after his car hit the barriers at Parabolica.

Below Charles Leclerc and Max Verstappen's cars make a return to the Monza pits after Friday practice in 2022.

Opposite bottom left Stirling Moss prepares to drift his Maserati 250F across the cobbles of Parabolica in 1954.

Opposite bottom right No drifting at all from Pierre Gasly's Alpine at the recently renamed Parabolica. From 2021 it was officially renamed Curve Alboreto after Michele Alboreto, who drove for Scuderia Ferrari between 1984 and 1988.

track dried out no-one could catch him and Vettel took his maiden victory at a record-breaking age of 21 years 73 days in addition to giving Minardi/Toro Rosso their first win (with a 2007-spec engine!)

Charles Leclerc managed to score a victory for Ferrari in 2019, but had to settle for a second place in 2022 on the occasion of the team's 75th anniversary as a constructor. In 2023 it was Carlos Sainz on the podium at Monza, having to give best to the all-conquering RB19 in the hands of Max Verstappen. It was the Dutchman's tenth consecutive grand prix win, breaking the record Alberto Ascari had set in his Ferrari 500 way back in 1953. Sainz would put an end to that record-run the following race in Singapore, just as Verstappen had ruined the Monza party.

In 2024, it looked like being a nailed-on McLaren 1–2 with Lando Norris and Oscar Piastri occupying the front-row on the difficult-to-pass circuit. But starting from third on the grid, while all around him made two stops on the newly resurfaced track, Charles Leclerc managed to make his one-stop strategy work to give Fred Vasseur's team a much-needed victory.

NUREMBERG, MIDDLE FRANCONIA, GERMANY

Norisring

FORMULA 1 HAS NEVER RACED HERE, BUT THE CIRCUIT HAS PLAYED A SIGNIFICANT PART IN MOTORSPORT HISTORY

In the history of motor-racing there have been many disparate locations for circuits – former swamps, casino car parks, airfields, and country house estates. But nothing quite matches the former site of the Nazi party's Nuremberg rally ground.

The Zeppelin Field at Nuremberg – named after a Zeppelin landing on the meadows in 1909 – was planned to be the site of a giant complex of buildings to celebrate the achievements of the Third Reich. Although the rally grounds were completed in time for the 1935 and 1936 rallies, including the Albert Speer-designed main grandstand or Steintribune with its 'fuhrer podium', the world's largest sports arena and Congress Hall were never finished.

At war's end the 'Great Road', a *paradestrasse* for Nazi stormtroopers two kilometres long and built of black and grey granite found better employment as part of a new motorcycle racing circuit, endorsed by the US occupants. The Steintribune was transformed into a motorsport grandstand. But what to call this new track? 'The Nurembergring' was obviously going to cause problems with the Nürburgring – and so officials adopted 'Noris', the seventeenth century name for the city and called it the Norisring.

By the 1960s it was racing on four wheels that had taken over, with touring cars and sports cars entertaining the crowds. In 1971 Pedro Rodríguez interrupted his F1 season to drive a Ferrari 512M of Herbert Müller, his friend and teammate at the Targa Florio

Opposite **The wrecked Steintribune in 1945 with jeeps from the occupying American forces.**

Left **The neoclassical wings may be gone, but the central tribune survives at the Norisring. Where once Hitler's stormtroopers paraded is now the start/finish straight for DTM races. There can be no more bizarre grandstand in motorsport.**

Below **Pedro Rodríguez, one of the brothers for which the Mexico City circuit is named, about to start his final race at the Norisring.**

that year. Trackside photographers reported his right front tyre coming away from the rim under heavy braking for the sharp S-Kurve as early as the tenth lap. Two laps later the tyre came off completely. The Ferrari cannoned into the wall before catching fire, claiming the life of Mexico's most successful F1 driver.

The hugely successful DTM has been a regular visitor to the Norisring, along with support series, such as European Formula 3. And it was the 2014 Norisring round of the Euro F3 series that helped shape the history of Formula 1. Max Verstappen arrived for the three rounds off the back of winning all three previous races at Spa. He was racing for Fritz Van Amersfoort, not the strongest F3 team, against Esteban Ocon in the Prema team, which was.

Helmut Marko was monitoring Verstappen's progress closely. It was the rain that fell on Sunday which marked out the Dutchman's advantage over the rest of the field. "The moment I thought he was really special was at the Norisring," Marko revealed, "it was more wet than dry and he was over two seconds per lap faster than anyone else." Max won all three races, making it six in succession. Nobody had done that before in Euro F3 and he was still only 16 and in his first season of single-seaters. Knowing that Mercedes were already talking to the Verstappens Marko moved quickly and offered Max the Toro Rosso drive the following week. The rest is history.

NÜRBURG, RHINELAND-PALATINATE, GERMANY

Nürburgring

STIRLING MOSS LOVED IT, JACKIE STEWART HATED IT, BUT WITH A GRAND PRIX OF JUST 14 LAPS IT WAS NEVER GOING TO SURVIVE IN THE MODERN ERA

In 1930s America, Franklin D. Roosevelt was famous for creating the Works Progress Administration (WPA) setting unemployed citizens to work during the Great Depression. Germany's equivalent came a lot earlier, in the 1920s, following defeat after World War I, and helped build what many consider the greatest motor-racing track.

The Nürburgring circuit had first been proposed after the hideous imperial embarrassment of being defeated by Italian racing machinery, Fiats no less, for the Kaiserpreis held on a track near Frankfurt in 1907. An irritated Kaiser Wilhelm wanted to know why German cars had not won. There was no suitable dedicated circuit to test German machinery, was the answer he received.

Plans were soon formulated to rectify that with the Eifel Mountains providing a varied range of inclines, curves and straights for the proposed project. Based near the town of Adenau, the circuit was yet to be started when the kaiser's imperial ambitions turned towards defeating Europe on a far greater scale.

In the wake of World War I and the political and economic chaos of the early 1920s, Dr Otto Creutz of the Allgemeiner Deutscher Automobile Club (ADAC) saw an opportunity for job creation, not only in building the track, but by re-emphasizing the advantages it could provide for German motor manufacturing. Backed by the mayor of Cologne (and post-war Chancellor) Konrad Adenauer – a bitter opponent of the Nazis in the 1930s – work on the site began in September 1925.

Unlike the majority of the European grand prix venues, Hans Weidenbrück designed a circuit that did not venture onto public roads. Using the natural contours of the land in the Eifel Forest, and in some cases taking over pre-existing roads, there were two distinct parts: a northern circuit or Nordschleife at more than 22 kms/14 miles with 174 corners, and a southern circuit, the Südschleife, at almost 8 kms/5 miles in length. The two shared a start/finish straight and could be combined to form a circuit that stretched to close on 29 kms/18 miles. In an early version of today's *Touristenfahrten* where drivers take their own machinery out on track, motorists could pay a toll to use the road at weekends.

With such a large distance to cover and line-of-sight between marshalling posts not possible in some cases, the

Opposite With narrow cars and a wide track it was quite possible to have a front row of four cars in 1967. Grids were set by the organizing clubs and could be 4-3-4 or 3-2-3 or even 4-4-4. It was only in the 1973 season that the standardised 2-2-2 grid was adopted. Jim Clark (3) is on pole for this race.

Above The new Nürburgring was on hand to offer a race on the reconvened 2020 calendar after Covid 19 wrecked the original schedule. It was run as the Eifel Grand Prix with limited spectators.

Right Tazio Nuvolari at the wheel of his Alf Romeo during the 1935 German Grand Prix.

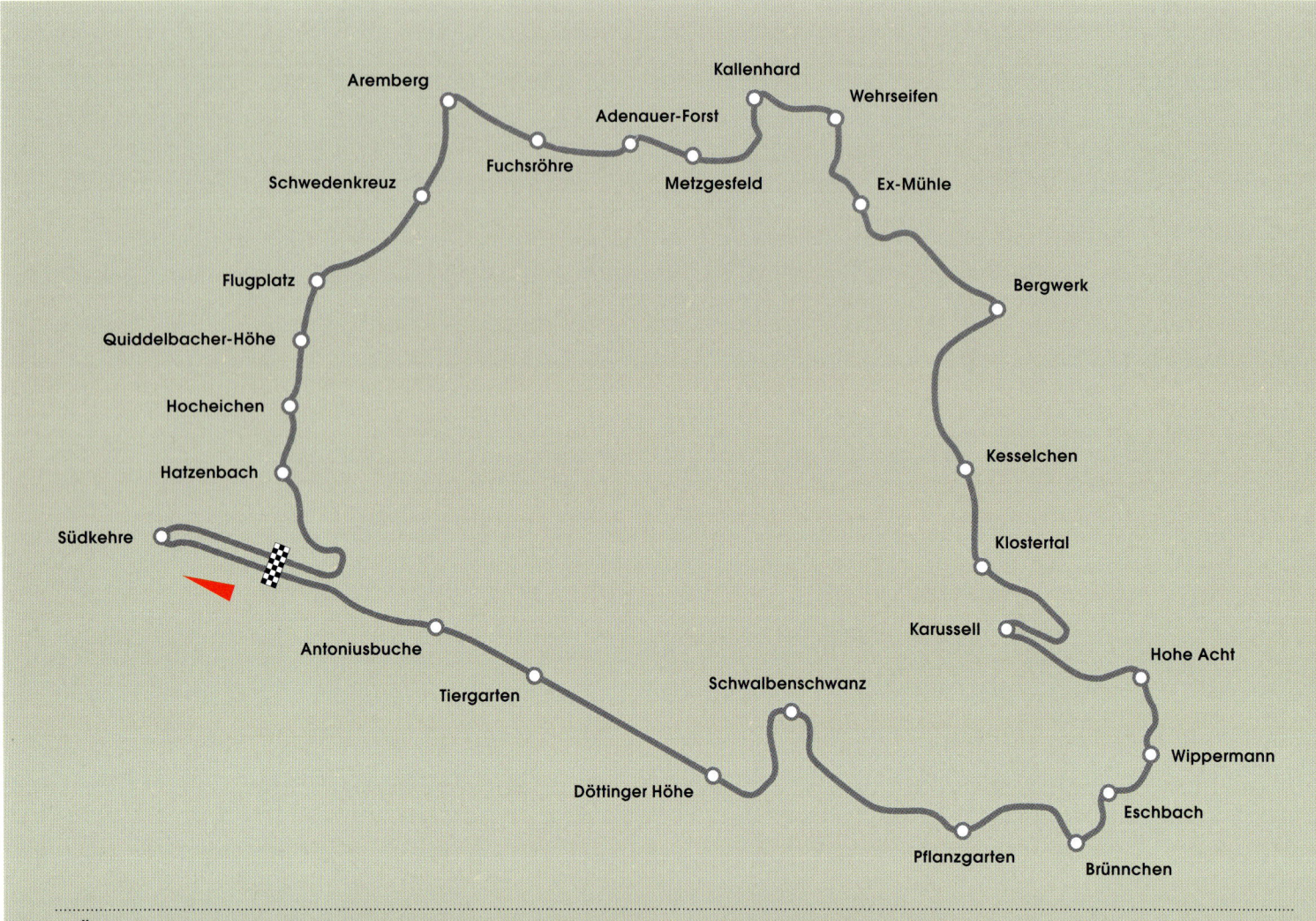

NÜRBURGRING NORDSCHLEIFE

Length: 22.835 km (14.189 miles)
Lap Record: 7:06.4 (Clay Regazzoni, Ferrari 312T, 1975)
Opened: 1926
First F1 Grand Prix: 1951
Number of F1 Grands Prix hosted: 22
Number of laps: 14 (originally 20)
Circuit Designer: Hans Weidenbrück
Race winning fact: Juan Manuel Fangio and Jackie Stewart both feared the Nordschleife, yet both won there three times, Fangio in 1954, 1956 and 1957, Stewart in 1968, 1971 and 1973.

The Nürburgring Nordschleife vies for many titles including the 'World's Greatest Race Track' and also the 'World's Most Dangerous Race Track'. Jackie Stewart's description of it as the 'Green Hell' has been fully embraced by the modern track operators as a marketing tool. German motor manufacturers still eye up the potential of beating the unrestricted lap record, re-set in 2018 by Timo Bernhard in a Porsche 919 Hybrid Evo at 5:19.546 – a staggering 145.3mph.

organizers installed telephone connections between 10 of the marshals' huts. The first great race to use the full combined course was the German Grand Prix of 1927, won by Otto Merz in a Mercedes S. Merz completed 18 laps of the newly named Nürburgring in 25 seconds short of five hours. The fastest lap was put in by runner-up Christian Werner, at 15 minutes, 54 seconds.

Like most Western economies, Germany also suffered in the Great Depression, with the German Grand Prix cancelled in 1930 and 1933. For the 1931 event, organizers switched to the Nordschleife. There would be no return to the combined track.

With state sponsorship of racing activities promoted by the Nazi government in the 1930s, Mercedes-Benz and Auto Union began to dominate races at the Nürburgring, AVUS and across Europe. The Silver Arrows swept the newly introduced European Championship from 1935 to 1939, but one significant race victory escaped them. At the 1935 German Grand Prix, Italian maestro Tazio Nuvolari in the Alfa Romeo pulled off a remarkable race victory at the Nürburgring in front of Daimler-Benz's Third Reich sponsors.

Driving an outdated and underpowered Alfa Romeo Tipo B for Enzo Ferrari's team, the atrocious weather conditions had levelled the playing field against the state-of-the-art German cars. Even so, the nine-strong entry was expected to win handsomely against the assorted Alfas, Maseratis, ERAs and a single Bugatti. Nuvolari's start was poor, but in difficult conditions he overhauled the cars in front and with the Silver

Below An early photo of the newly opened Nürburgring in 1928. The track looped back behind the pits and disappeared off into the country.

Right The line-up of Scuderia Ferrari cars ahead of the 1953 German Grand Prix. World Champion Alberto Ascari stares into the camera lens from his Ferrari 500. Beyond him Mike Hawthorn sits in the No.4 car. Hawthorn had become the first Briton to win an F1 grand prix that year when he took a win at Reims.

Arrows pitting earlier Nuvolari took the lead. But then his own pit stop was botched thanks to a refuelling delay. He set off on a charge from sixth place. The 300,000 spectators watched the Italian pick off the Mercedes and Auto Unions to regain second place, and heading into the final lap he was 35 seconds off leader Manfred von Brauchitsch in a Mercedes W25. Lap times of the Nordschleife were close to 11 minutes, but von Brauchitsch had leant hard on his tyres early in the stint and they were fading.

Straining their ears to hear the engine note of the approaching car, the crowd in the grandstand of the Sporthotel were shocked to see Nuvolari roar past the chequered flag, two minutes and fourteen seconds in front of second place Hans Stuck in an Auto Union for what was dubbed 'the impossible victory'. Von Brauchitsch could manage only fifth place, finishing more than six minutes behind. There were eight Silver Arrows in the top nine places, but it was an Alfa Romeo that had won.

As with all European race circuits, World War II caused a cessation of racing hostilities and the buildings, including the massive Sporthotel in the grandstand opposite the pits, put to a variety of unexpected uses. The Südschleife was recommissioned first in 1947, followed by work on the Nordschleife in 1949.

The Nürburgring was back as an international venue hosting the German Grand Prix in 1951, Alberto Ascari scoring another win for Scuderia Ferrari, but this time the team had supplied their driver with one of Enzo's cars, a 4.5-litre Ferrari 375.

In the hard-up years of the 1950s grids for the German GP were often bolstered by Formula 2 machinery, as spectators would only get to see the cars come round 20 times in all. For road racers like Juan Manuel Fangio, who had cut their teeth on epic 2,000-mile and 6,000-mile events like the Carrera Panamericana and the Gran Premio del Norte, which he described as a "terrible ordeal", the absence of barriers, abundance of trees and lack of marshals was a familiar set of hazards. But as these road races, such as the Mille Miglia, were branded too dangerous and fell off the calendar, so attention turned to race circuits.

Fangio had emulated Nuvolari in 1957 with an epic chase of the two Ferraris of Mike Hawthorn and Peter Collins who were fuelled for the entire race. Fangio chose to run light on softer tyres and refuel halfway through – except at the pitstop, the mechanic changing his rear left wheel let the wheel nut roll under the car and it took thirty seconds to find it. Fangio set off after the Ferraris in his Maserati 250F and broke and re-broke the lap record nine times before closing and passing the two Brits, coming home with a three-second advantage. This one was billed as 'the race of the century'.

It was Fangio's final race win: 'I have never driven that quickly before in my life and I don't think I will ever be able to do it again,' were his telling post-race comments. In his autobiography *My Twenty Years of Racing* he wrote: 'Nürburgring was my favourite track. I fell totally in love with

Opposite top Mike Spence (2) in the Lotus 33 approaches the 180-degree Südkehre during the 1965 grand prix. The 15-lap race would be won by Lotus team-mate Jim Clark.

Above Action from the 2020 Eifel Grand Prix, at one of the early corners of Hermann Tilke's resurrected Nürburgring circuit, in the approximate position of the Nordschleife's old Südkehre.

Opposite bottom Juan Manuel Fangio puts his Maserati 250F 'in the ditch' of the famous Karussel corner during the 1957 German Grand Prix.

Left Sebastian Vettel in a Red Bull RB7 leads David Coulthard in an RB8 through the Karussel during a celebration of Red Bull motorsport held at the Nürburgring in 2023.

Left Jackie Stewart on his way to a crushing victory in 1968, finishing four minutes ahead of second place Graham Hill and almost six minutes in front of polesitter Jacky Ickx.

Below The 1968 German Grand Prix was started by a man waving the national flag. Ironically, the Nürburgring had introduced a far more efficient lights system as early as 1935 but it had been discontinued. Jacky Ickx (9) had set pole with a lap time of 9:04.

Bottom Despite his misgivings before the 1976 grand prix, Niki Lauda was not holding back in practice. His Ferrari 312T leaves the ground at Flugplatz. It would be a suspension breakage that caused his fiery accident during the race.

it and I believe that on that day in 1957 I finally managed to master it. It was as if I had screwed all the secrets out of it and got to know it once and for all... For two days I couldn't sleep, still making those leaps in the dark on those curves where I had never before had the courage to push things so far." A year later Peter Collins was killed at the Nürburgring when his Ferrari ran wide at the Pflanzgarten, flipping the car and throwing the driver into a tree.

As the 1960s dawned, drivers began to question the safety record of the Nordschleife, often led by Jackie Stewart who christened it 'the Green Hell' a name which stuck. Despite the pontification from traditionalists such as journalist Denis Jenkinson, who believed losing drivers was an occupational

Right A contemplative Niki Lauda sits with a relaxed Clay Regazzoni and Ferrari team manager Daniele Audetto before the 1976 German Grand Prix. Audetto had taken over from Luca di Montezemolo in 1976, and, like future Ferrari team boss Jean Todt, was a former rally co-driver.

hazard, Stewart stuck to his message. It wasn't as though he was slow around the Nürburgring either, he won the race in 1968, 1971 and 1973. The 1968 race was the drive of his life, in a race beset by fog and rain. Just months after losing best friend Jimmy Clark at a rain-sodden Hockenheim, Stewart took his sixth-place-starting Matra to a lead of nine seconds on the opening lap. On the second he stretched out his lead over Graham Hill to 34 seconds in atrocious conditions. He won the race by more than four minutes.

The bumpy condition of the track led to breakages, and breakages often ended up causing accidents. It was a race that needed five times the number of marshals and its sheer length meant that medical help was slow to arrive in an era when races weren't stopped for catastrophic accidents. The drivers organized a successful boycott of the race in 1970, and the circuit owners were forced to make changes. By 1971 it was back on the calendar, thanks to verge widening, tree felling, the addition of more Armco and the removal of jumps at Kesselchen and Brünnchen, but its days were numbered.

Niki Lauda's fiery accident on the second lap of the 1976 race, well-documented in Ron Howard's movie *Rush*, highlighted the shortcomings. Lauda lost control, hit an earth bank, his Ferrari 312 burst into flames and was hit by the following cars of Brett Lunger and Harald Ertl. Guy Edwards stopped to help them, but the drivers struggled to pull Lauda from the car until joined by Arturo Merzario. Ex-Ferrari driver Merzario was familiar with the Klippan belts the team used and despite the intense heat and reduced visibility was able to get Lauda's seatbelts undone.

Formula 1 would not return to the Nordschleife. The inherent risk was one thing, but its sheer length made the race difficult to televise, especially when Bernie Ecclestone was trying to maximize TV revenues through his role in FOCA (Formula One Constructors Organization). From 1977 the German GP would take place at Hockenheim.

In 1984 a new, shortened version of the Südschleife was opened, which shared the start/finish straight of the Nordschleife. Constructed within the boundaries of the 1920s circuit it was deemed a poor imitation of its predecessors, but unlike its predecessors didn't kill drivers on a regular basis. With the upsurge in German interest created by Michael Schumacher's 1994 World Championship the new Nürburgring was able to host an additional F1 race from 1995, billed as either the European Grand Prix or the Luxembourg Grand Prix.

By now, Jackie Stewart's son Paul Stewart had graduated from running an F3000 team to Formula 1, with father Jackie in a close advisory role. It was fitting that the team's only grand prix victory, a surprise win for Johnny Herbert in the 1999 European GP, should come at the Nürburgring. Naturally it was in the wet.

Serial mismanagement of the facility has seen the modern Formula 1 circuit taken over by the regional authorities and neither the stellar success of Sebastian Vettel or alternating the German Grand Prix with Hockenheim has generated enough home interest to keep the race on Liberty Media's cash-friendly F1 schedule of races. But unlike any other pre-war racing circuit, the track still exists, and punters can take their own vehicles out for a lap of the Green Hell and imagine what it was like to race at 150mph with closer trees, no run-offs and a complete absence of Armco barriers.

SPIELBERG, AUSTRIA

Red Bull Ring

IT STARTED LIFE AS THE ÖSTERREICHRING, WAS RESURRECTED AS THE A1-RING AND REACHED NEW FANS AS THE RED BULL RING

The Österreichring was the complete antithesis of Spielberg's original F1 track – Zeltweg airfield was flat, bumpy, and boring, and shook cars to pieces on its bumpy parallel runways. Its days were clearly numbered after a single chaotic grand prix in 1964 was won by Lorenzo Bandini, with most cars retiring through vibration-related faults. In the hills above the Mur Valley, the enthusiastic Austrian organizers created the Österreichring which had everything that drivers loved – elevation changes, fast-flowing, challenging corners taken in third, fourth and fifth gears, all through majestic Tyrolean scenery.

Opened in 1969 the circuit roared off up the hill, over the brow to the blind entry of the Hella Licht Kurve before disappearing behind a ridge of trees, climbing up to the top of the circuit where it turned right at the sweeping Dr. Tiroch-Kurve, before swooping downhill, through a kink, to the fearsome Bosch-Kurve, with a barrier hard against the outside of the track. Then it was a long, gently tightening 180-degree turn, known with typical Austrian humour as 'Schikane', up through the trees, over the hill and down to the final Parabolica-like Rindt Kurve before heading for the start/finish. With its complete absence of slow corners it was a very fast track.

The debut Formula 1 grand prix of 1970 had all the portents of a home race victory for World Championship leader Jochen Rindt after he put his dominant Lotus 72 on pole position. But in the race his Cosworth V8 engine packed up on Lap 21.

Opposite The start of the 1977 Austrian Grand Prix and Niki Lauda (11) leads James Hunt (1) in the McLaren and Ferrari team-mate Carlos Reutemann (12). The race would be won by Alan Jones driving a Shadow-Ford.

Above Max Verstappen turns sharp right after the start of the 2023 grand prix, whereas the first turn for his predecessors was over the crest of the hill.

Left Jacky Ickx and Clay Regazzoni, both in Ferrari 312Bs, exit the Bosch Kurve in 1970. Ickx won the grand prix to the delight of the army of travelling fans who carried him off after the race.

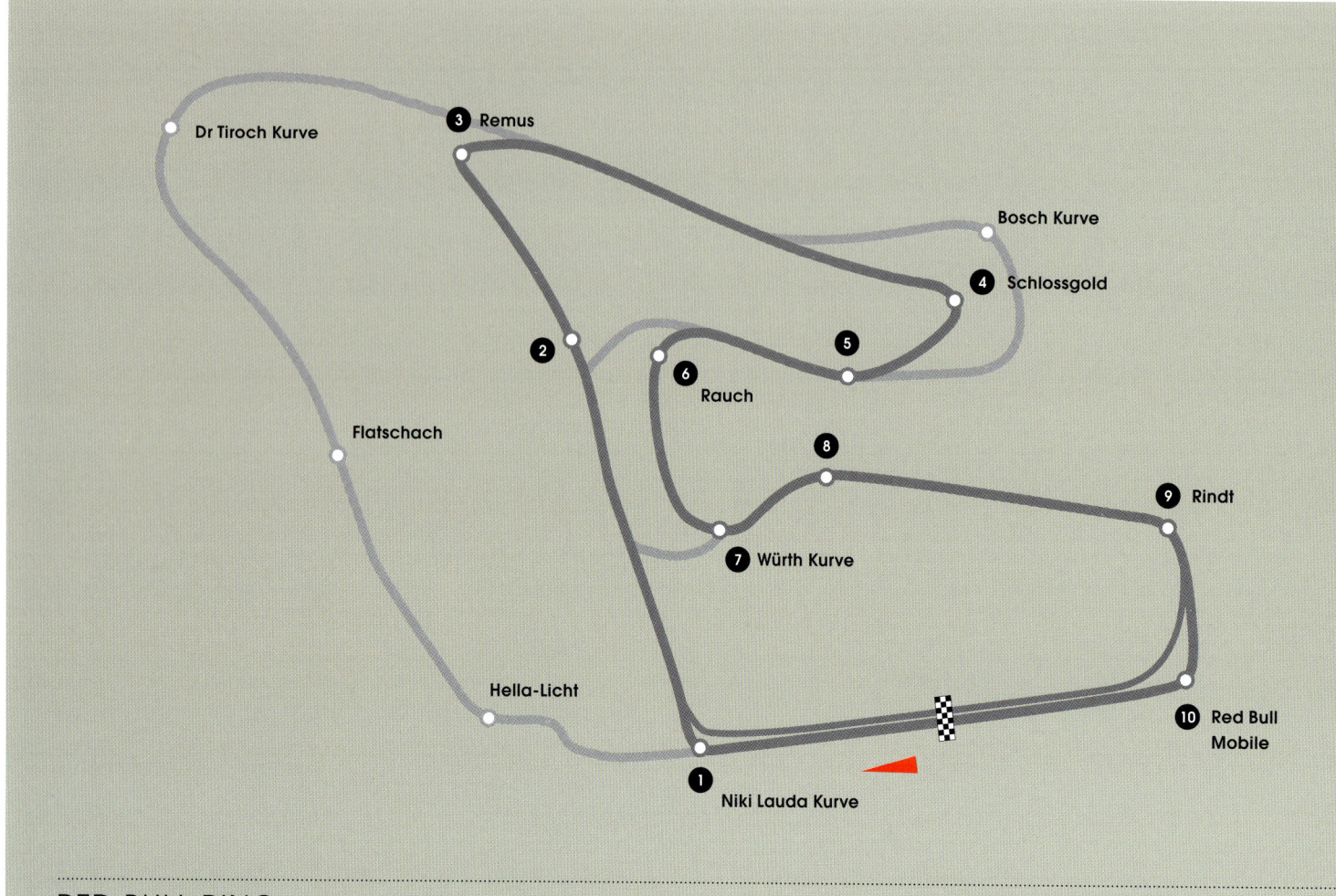

RED BULL RING

Length: 4.318 km (2.683 miles)
Lap Record: 1:05.619 (Carlos Sainz Jr., McLaren MCL35, 2020)
Opened: 1969
First F1 Grand Prix: 1970
Number of F1 Grands Prix hosted: Österreichring (1970–1987) 18 races, A1-Ring (1997–2003) 7 races, Red Bull Ring (2014–2024) 12 races
Number of laps: 71
Designer: Hans Mesmer, the Austrian Automobile Club (ÖAMTC)
Redesigner: Hermann Tilke (1997)
Race winning fact: Much to the Austrian crowd's dismay, Jacky Ickx won the first grand prix in 1970. Jochen Rindt had taken pole, but suffered engine failure on Lap 21.

The Red Bull organization has done an impressive job rehabilitating the circuit after Hermann Tilke shortened the Österreichring in the mid-1990s to make it compatible with modern F1. The A1-Ring hosted seven GPs between 1997 and 2003, but then fell silent, much to the neighbours' joy. After the proposed New York metropolitan area grand prix fell through, Red Bull seized the opportunity for a re-instated Austrian Grand Prix which returned on 22 June 2014. In 2020, the hastily reworked F1 season started with successive races at the Red Bull Ring, with the Austrian Grand Prix followed a week later by the Styrian Grand Prix.

Tragically, it would be his final race start, next up was Monza.

The race ran successfully through to 1987, sometimes throwing up unexpected results, none more so than in 1975. 'The Monza Gorilla', Vittorio Brambilla, a driver prone to wrecking chassis, won his only grand prix, a rain-sodden race which was stopped on Lap 29. Brambilla punched the air with delight as he crossed the line and promptly crashed the car. It was the March team's first ever win in Formula 1, but most of the other teams thought it would be re-started after the rain had abated. March boss Max Mosley quickly pointed out that it could not be re-started after the chequered flag had been waved and the team kept their result.

In the early 1970s, it was the Italian fans that flooded over the border to make it an additional *tifosi*-supported race, but in 1976 they stayed home, as the Ferrari team skipped the grand prix following Niki Lauda's fiery crash at the Nürburgring. That left the door open for John Watson to score the Penske team's only F1 win. A year later Alan Jones scored the Shadow team's only grand prix victory starting from 14th place in a rain-affected race. Lauda was second that day, the closest any Austrian would come to winning their home race until 1984, when Niki won it in his World Championship year.

Before its removal from the grand prix calendar the Österreichring underwent few but significant changes. Bright American prospect Mark Donohue crashed at Hella Licht during the 30-minute pre-grand prix warm-up in 1975. It's thought a tyre failure sent him into the catch fencing and over the Armco,

Top left Alain Prost's Renault heads a queue of cars in parc ferme after qualifying for the 1983 Austrian Grand Prix. Beyond is the original, sweeping final turn.

Above Looking down on the circuit, in its previous guise as the Österreichring the track disappeared behind the ridge of trees beyond Turn 1 and rejoined at the top of the circuit. The final two corners have been squared off to allow more run-off and the building of a grandstand.

Top right Ayrton Senna tackles the Bosch Kurve during the 1986 race, by which time the circuit had built a large grandstand in the forest. Though it is further back from the modified track it is still packed to the rafters with Dutch fans on race day.

Right Vittorio Brambilla in the March on the way to his only win, at the 1975 Austrian Grand Prix. Despite crashing and bending his front wing, the Italian was able to embark on a victory lap.

Right **Patrick Tambay leads Ferrari team-mate René Arnoux through the improbably named, sweeping Texaco Shikane in 1983.**

Opposite **The modern circuit has cut inside the old Shikane in a tighter version of the old loop. Charles Leclerc leads Ferrari team-mate Carlos Sainz through Power Horse in 2023.**

Below **Alain Prost in the McLaren leads Nigel Mansell's Williams through the Hella Licht chicane in 1985.**

Bottom **Carnage at the back of the field in 1997 after Nigel Mansell's slow getaway caused problems further back down the grid.**

killing a marshal. A dazed Donohue walked away from the car, but died the following day from a brain haemorrhage. It was suspected that his helmet might have struck one of the catch fencing support posts. Reacting to the accident, organizers installed a chicane to slow cars through the turn, and wire catch-fencing was gradually phased out through the late 1970s. There was little that could be done to the Bosch Kurve, but the piece of track that took the race off the F1 calendar was far more mundane. The start/finish straight was simply too narrow and the 1987 grand prix reinforced this. At the first start Martin Brundle crashed his Zakspeed, causing collateral damage to two Tyrrells and a Ligier. Red flag.

On the second attempt Nigel Mansell in the Williams was slow away with clutch problems – the front runners got past, but the rear of the field concertinaed up until Eddie Cheever and Riccardo Patrese touched and then half the grid was involved in a low-speed pile-up. The 1980s was a time of spare cars, and two hours later with much repair work done, a full grid of 26 cars made it off the line and up to the Hella Licht chicane. Ironically, Nigel Mansell won the race and celebrated with a hefty bang on his head from an overhead gantry in the post-race parade. The Österreichring was dropped from the F1 calendar, despite widening the main straight by three metres.

A decade later and Austrian telecoms company A1 helped resurrect the circuit with a new, shortened and considerably safer version. Mindful of neighbours who weren't keen to have the hills alive with the sound of V8s, the circuit now turned right before it disappeared over the ridge with a long drag up the hill to Remus corner (the site of many overtakes in the modern era), before rejoining the old track. From there to the finish, Tilke tightened virtually every corner by bringing them inside their old counterparts. It made for a more compact circuit with slower corners and more overtaking opportunities, but purists mourned the loss of the Bosch Kurve.

F1 returned in 1997 for seven years, but struggled financially. One of the events, the 2002 race, was distinguished by the crowd venting its frustration at Michael Schumacher and Ferrari team orders. It was only race six of a 17-race season, Schumacher had won four of the preceding five races, yet Ferrari obliged his teammate Rubens Barrichello to slow down and hand the win to the German. On the podium, the heckles and whistles became too much and Schumi handed the top step to Barrichello.

Bernie Ecclestone pulled the plug on the 2004 race because of the Austrian government's stance on tobacco advertising, and Formula 1's addiction to the cash. But in its demise lay its salvation. The circuit was bought by Austrian drinks magnate Dieter Mateschitz with grand plans for a new pit complex, racing school, hotel, auto museum, all paid for with Red Bull money. There were even plans to revive the untouched parts of the old Österreichring to the west. Angry neighbours agitated and Austria's environmental authorities blocked the proposals. Mateschitz reacted by mothballing the site for six years.

In those six years Red Bull Racing started gaining ascendancy in Formula 1. Mateschitz bought the Minardi team, rebadged it as Toro Rosso, and the team scored its first win at the 2008 Italian Grand Prix with Sebastian Vettel. In 2009 Red Bull were the runners up in the constructors' championship and in 2010 took both top trophies. A re-invigorated Mateschitz set about 'Projeckt Spielberg', supporting the local economy by developments within the circuit, leaving to one side the contentious revival of the old circuit.

Relaunched as the Red Bull Ring in May 2011 it was soon hosting the Historic F1 Championship and the DTM. Formula 1 returned in 2014 and soon the annual invasion by the red hordes of Ferrari fans had been replaced by Max Verstappen's Oranj Army, who quite literally turned the grandstands orange. Verstappen has always gone well in Austria, even in his European F3 days, but in 2019 having wrecked his car in practice and been swamped at the start, put in the drive of a future World Champion. Chasing back through the field he caught Ferrari's Charles Leclerc on Lap 69 of 71 and passed him for the win. It was Honda's first victory since their troubled return to F1 in 2015, the first since Jenson Button's Hungaroring win in 2006 and left the Japanese engineers in tears.

With the grand prix re-instated, and hybrid engines being considerably quieter than their antecedents, investigations were made in 2016 about reviving the surviving parts of the old track. There would be a chicane around the site of the Hella Licht Kurve and another at the top of the hill by Remus Kurve. Nothing came of it, and with the passing of Dieter Mateschitz in 2022 the existing facility is a good enough reminder of his vision for a home race.

PAU, PYRENÉES-ATLANTIQUES, FRANCE

Circuit de Pau-Ville

THE PAU GRAND PRIX SERVED AS THE PERFECT SHAKEDOWN TEST FOR THE IMPORTANT RACE IN MONACO

The French Grand Prix held at Le Mans in 1906 and won by Ferenc Sziz in a Renault, has been hailed as 'the first grand prix'. Strictly speaking, the first motor race to carry that name was the Grand Prix de Pau in 1901. Winding its way around three hundred kilometres of the Pyrenées it was won by champion tandem cyclist/record-setting aviator Maurice Farman in a Panhard.

The race was shortened and brought closer to Pau in later years and in 1930, the French Grand Prix was run on a circuit close to the town. But it was in the early 1930s, after the tremendous success of the Monaco Grand Prix, that organizers saw an opportunity to bring the race into the centre of town where it remains today. Like Monte Carlo, it has hardly changed in 90 years.

While F1 cars have been forced to adapt to Monaco, with Pau, as speeds have increased, so the different tiers of racing on Pau's streets have come and gone. In the post-war period it hosted non-championship Formula 1 and F2 races. In 1972 it became a round of the European F2 championship which morphed into F3000 from 1985, and lasted until F3000 became a support race for F1 grands prix. Since then it has attracted F3 and the Formula 3 Euro Series.

Because it has hosted F1 feeder series for so many years, like the Macau GP in China, the list of race winners reads like a *Who's Who* of the sport. Indeed, such is its role in establishing the stars of the future, Stefano Domenicali, who was running the FIA Single Seater Commission in 2016, banned Nelson Piquet Jr. from

Opposite The 1953 Pau Grand Prix was won by Alberto Ascari and featured many F1 stars including Mike Hawthorn, Harry Schell, Jean Behra, Maurice Trintignant, Nino Farina and Louis Rosier.

Top Max Verstappen (30) lies second to Australian Mitch Gilbert in a round of the 2014 European Formula 3 Championship at Pau. Unlike bitter rival Esteban Ocon, Verstappen did not win a round at Pau – although it was his first and only single-seater season before joining Toro Rosso.

Above and Right Rudolf Caracciola's Mercedes-Benz W154 in the pits during the 1938 race. Pau was prestigious enough for Mercedes to use wins there as publicity in the motorsport press.

making a one-off Euro F3 series appearance at Pau. Nothing to do with 'Crashgate of 2008', Domenicali reckoned that allowing the 30-year-old reigning Formula E champion to compete was against the spirit of the championship, "as one of the primary steps on the ladder to F1".

The role-call of winners of the Pau GP who have appeared on the F1 grid include Juan Manuel Fangio (1949, 1950), Alberto Ascari (1953), Jean Behra (1954, 1955, 1957), Jim Clark (1961, 1963, 1964, 1965), Maurice Trintignant (1962) Jackie Stewart (1968), Jochen Rindt (1969, 1970) and Peter Gethin (1971, 1972). After it became an official Formula 2 race there were wins for François Cevert, Patrick Depailler and René Arnoux and in the F3000 era, Jean Alesi and Juan Pablo Montoya. When European F3 came to town in 2014 Esteban Ocon won a race, but Max Verstappen crashed out.

The most popular non-French winner of the race never made it into F1, but did make it onto the F1 Channel 4 commentary team. After his double leg amputation following an F4 accident at Donington Park in 2017, Billy Monger returned to racing in specially adapted cars. In 2019 the Pau Grand Prix was part of the Euroformula Open series and in a wet race Monger's Carlin team switched him onto wet tyres early. From last place he had moved up to third when Motopark team-mates Liam Lawson and Julian Hanses collided and Billy held on for victory, with Yuki Tsunoda in third place.

Moving forward, with a lack of municipal funding, the grand prix took a sabbatical in 2024 while France focused on the Olympic Games and intends to return on a biennial basis.

Opposite top François Cevert competes in a Tecno-Cosworth during the 1969 race, held in April. The precarious skyscraper wings would only last in F1 and F2 until the Monaco Grand Prix in May after which they were consigned to history.

Opposite bottom Jochen Rindt showed his prowess once again on the tight confines of the Pau circuit in 1969, winning in Lotus F2 machinery from Jean-Pierre Beltoise and Piers Courage.

Left In 1953 Alberto Ascari (left) won for the second year running in a Ferrari; popular American privateer Harry Schell (centre) was third in a Gordini and Mike Hawthorn second in another Ferrari 500.

Below Alexander Albon (races uphill towards the Pont Oscar. The Toro Rosso, Red Bull and Williams driver competed in the European F3 season in 2015.

175

Right In its original configuration, the circuit at Le Castellet was introduced as: 'a circuit with the latest safety features which will allow the cars to reach the highest speeds with maximum safety'. The circuit ran in a clockwise direction, with the top loop cut out from 1987.

Opposite Today, the addition of high-abrasion, multi-coloured asphalt has made the circuit look like an exercise in land art. Despite the teams loving the venue and the convenience of an airport next door, the spectator access has proven problematic.

Below A grand prix run through striking Provençal scenery – in this instance the 1978 French Grand Prix, with Mario Andretti and Ronnie Peterson in the Lotus 79 ahead of James Hunt in a McLaren.

LE CASTELLET, VAR, FRANCE

Circuit Paul Ricard

TEAMS LOVED GOING TO THE EXCLUSIVE CIRCUIT WITH ITS OWN AIRPORT, BUT THE LOCAL ROADS RESTRICTED EASY ACCESS

With Reims slipping off the F1 calendar and both Rouen and Clermont-Ferrand heavily dependent on public roads, French drinks magnate and inventor of pastis, Paul Ricard, decided to build his own private race circuit in the south of France. Ricard used sport to promote his brand in much the same way as Red Bull do today, and his idea was to create a world-class facility next to his own airport.

Planned in 1969 and opened in 1970, the circuit was a short drive inland from the Mediterranean, between Marseille and Toulon. Typical of private projects funded by multi-millionaires it was constructed to the highest standards with a three-storey air-conditioned pit building and a large landscaped paddock. Combined with very wide run-off areas it was more in line with circuit developments adopted in the twenty-first century.

Matra drivers Jean-Pierre Beltoise and Henri Pescarolo gave their input to the design, which included the 1.8-km (1.1-mile) Mistral Straight, the longest in F1 once the circuit gained the French Grand Prix in 1971. With its oceans of space for cars leaving the track it was seen as a good, safe testing track, available with three different configurations. Teams enjoyed visiting because it had an airport next door and unlike Anderstorp was located in vineyard-rich Provence.

Charade held on to the race for 1972 after which the French Grand Prix alternated between Paul Ricard and Dijon until hosting it alone from 1985 to 1990, when French politics dictated that Magny-Cours should take over this prestigious event.

Right **Jackie Stewart dominated the 1971 French Grand Prix at Paul Ricard in his Tyrrell 003. The circuit buildings were impressive, well ahead of their time and it was only French politics that denied a longer spell hosting the national race.**

Opposite top **Mauricio Gugelmin made the sports pages the world over when his Leyton House March locked its brakes and collided with Nigel Mansell's Ferrari at the start of the 1989 grand prix. A shaken Gugelmin was able to take the re-start from the pit lane.**

Opposite bottom **Two images from 2022 – a photo showing the proximity of the airport, and Carlos Sainz leads Ferrari teammate Charles Leclerc in practice for the race. It proved to be a turning point in the season with Leclerc spinning out under pressure from Max Verstappen and the Dutchman taking the momentum to win his second world title.**

Its role as a safe test track was tragically undermined in 1986 when one of the most popular drivers on the grid lost his life in a testing accident. Elio de Angelis was taking the high-speed esses when the rear wing on his Brabham-BMW detached, sending the car cartwheeling over the barriers, whereupon it caught fire. The closest marshal was dressed in shorts and a T-shirt and had a single fire extinguisher. De Angelis had only suffered a broken collarbone, but due to the lengthy delay in getting him out of the car he died from smoke inhalation.

Changes were deemed necessary. Previously the grand prix had run to the full 5.81-km (3.61-mile) length, but now drivers turned right before they got to the Verrière curves and made a short-cut to the Mistral Straight, joining almost halfway down.

The shortened version had been available since the debut of the track in 1970, as seen in the aerial photograph.

French president François Mitterand spent part of his political career representing the Nevers region, 160 miles south of Paris, and put his weight behind a plan to revamp the old Winfield Racing School circuit at Magny-Cours. Thus in 1990 the French GP headed north for 18 years, to a circuit loved by Michael Schumacher (he won eight times) and much to the teams' collective dismay at abandoning Ricard.

Motorsport continued at Le Castellet until 1999 when the circuit was bought by one of Bernie Ecclestone's companies. Racing finished and Paul Ricard became exclusively a test track. The closure allowed a large amount of corner reprofiling to be done along with extra connections made around the circuit. Ultimately this would create 169 different track configurations, depending on what kind of corner combinations were needed. Bernie was even in charge of the weather – a circuit variant boasted a sprinkler system that could create the conditions for wet running. However the business model suffered a blow in 2009 when the FIA banned in-season testing.

One of the biggest changes to the flow of the circuit was the introduction of a chicane to break up the Mistral straight. The biggest *visual* change was the replacement of gravel run-offs with coloured, red and blue, highly abrasive asphalt. Add in the new, advanced Tecpro safety barriers and Ricard had become a Centre of Excellence in motorsport. The Toyota team, anxious to get a foothold in the glamorous world of F1, set up a permanent test team there before its disastrous championship debut.

However the ban on F1 testing, along with manufacturers exiting F1 at speed in 2008–9 brought a change of philosophy at Ricard. Regular racing returned and with Magny-Cours long off the calendar, the French GP resumed at Le Castellet in 2018 using the full-length circuit with Mistral chicane. The race was extremely popular – too popular – the numbers brought chaos to roads that were unused to absorbing such a massive influx of spectators. In 2019 and 2021 a limit on crowd numbers eased the problem, but Liberty Media are looking for race day crowds of 100,000, an untenable figure for the site. After the contract lapsed in 2022, the French Grand Prix disappeared.

PESCARA, ABRUZZO, ITALY

Circuito di Pescara

THE GREAT DRIVERS FROM HISTORY HAVE WON AT PESCARA FROM ENZO FERRARI TO STIRLING MOSS

Opposite Vanwall boss Tony Vandervell, wearing a straw hat, stands next to Stewart Lewis-Evans' car ahead of the Pescara Grand Prix in 1957.

Below left Today, there is little trace of what author Richard Williams described as 'The Last Road Race' in his 2004 book chronicling the 1957 grand prix. At one point the old startline was marked across the road a little further down the Via Adriatica Nord, but it has since disappeared.

Below centre The first Coppa Acerbo was staged in 1924 and won by Enzo Ferrari in an Alfa Romeo. He promptly retired as a driver.

Bottom An original poster from the event revels that it was the 25th running on the course through the Abruzzo Hills.

The Pescara circuit has long ceased to be. It held just a single F1 race in 1957, but still commands the description 'legendary'. It has the distinction of being the longest circuit the World Championship has ever raced on, longer than the Nürburgring Nordschleife. It is also the circuit where Enzo Ferrari made his fourth and final grand prix appearance in 1924. And it was the setting for one of motor-racing's greatest displays of sportsmanship.

Situated on Italy's Adriatic coast, on a broad parallel with Rome, from 1924 it hosted the famous road race, the Coppa Acerbo. Enzo Ferrari won the first staging in an Alfa Romeo and promptly retired to set up his own racing team. The course took cars up into the Abruzzo Hills through the villages of Spoltore, Villa St Maria and Capelle before thundering back to the coast along the 'flying kilometre', part of the 25.83-km (16.05-mile) triangle. A 90-degree turn at the coast sent cars screaming back through the streets of Pescara, along the Via Nazionale Adriatica Nord to the start/finish.

Because of the speeds cars were reaching as they passed the pits, organizers introduced a new concept in motor-racing, the 'bus-stop chicane', before they got there. Because the race was run through a grid of city streets, by necessity this involved four right-angle turns before rejoining the Via Nazionale and a significant reduction in speed.

In the early 1930s the race was won by a familiar list of Italian race winners: Achille Varzi, Giuseppe Campari, Tazio Nuvolari and Luigi Fagioli, followed by the German domination of the late 1930s with Bernd Rosemeyer and Rudolph Caracciola. After the war, the name of the race changed, as all links with the fascist originator Tito Acerbo were dropped. It would now be the Circuito di Pescara.

There was never a possibility of replacing the Italian Grand Prix, but in 1957 the Belgian and Dutch Grands Prix were cancelled at short notice after the organizers reduced the teams' start money and the FIA was looking round for a replacement.

It was a sensitive time for motor-racing in Italy following the deaths of spectators and Spanish driver Alfonso de Portago in the Mille Miglia. The Italian government had banned racing on public roads, but gave Pescara a special dispensation. Enzo Ferrari, who had been implicated in the Mille Miglia disaster,

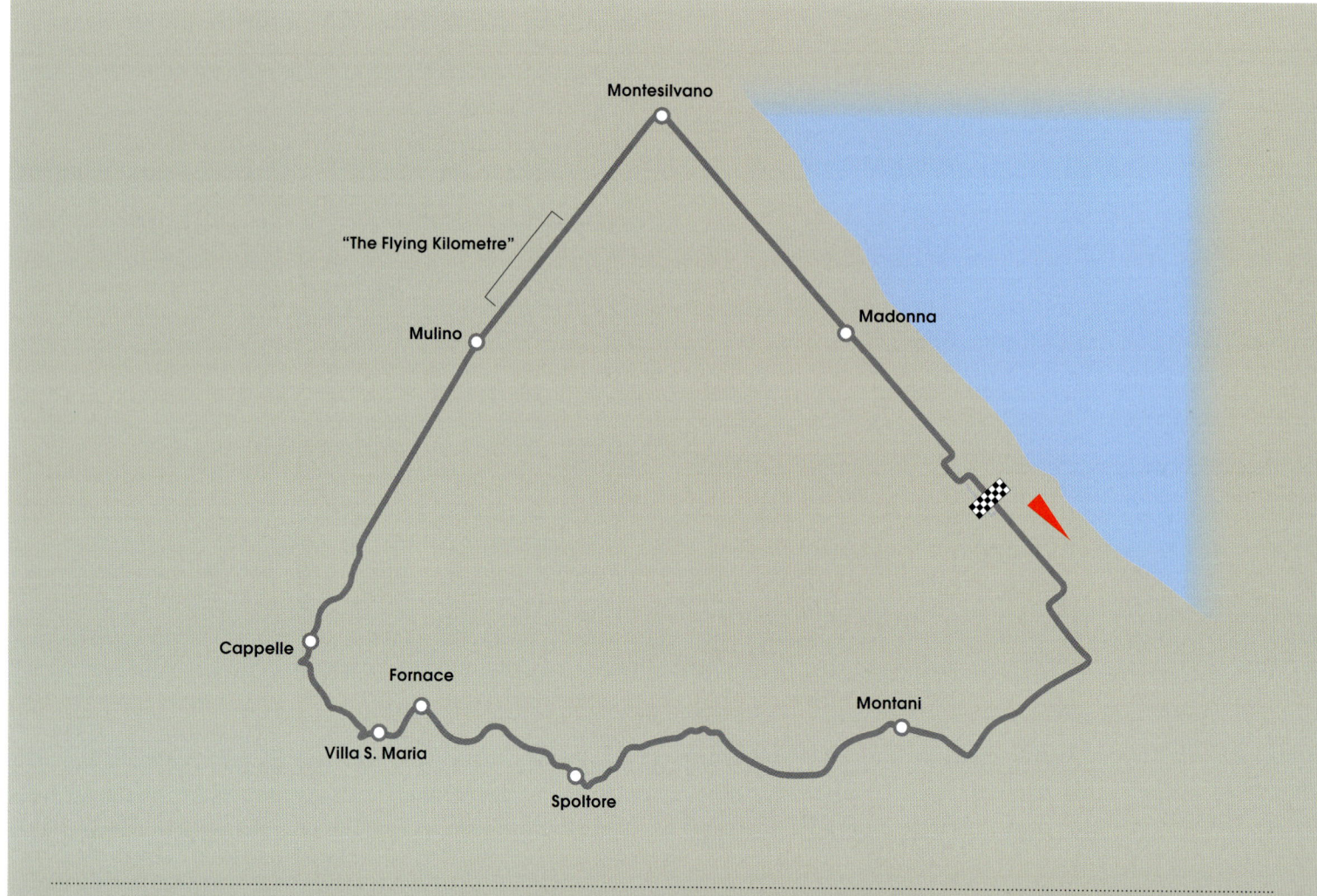

CIRCUITO DI PESCARA

Length: 25.801 km (16.032 miles)
Lap Record: 9:44.6 (Stirling Moss, Vanwall, 1957)
Opened: 1924
First F1 Grand Prix: 1957
Number of F1 Grands Prix hosted: 1
Number of laps: 18
Designer: The route was planned by Vincenzo Florio, the man responsible for organizing the Targa Florio in Sicily.
Race winning fact: The Pescara Grand Prix was followed by the Italian Grand Prix at Monza – the first time two F1 races were held in the same country – Stirling Moss won them both.

Covering the same course as the Coppa Acerbo, the one-off grand prix at Pescara had more in common with Sicily's Targa Florio road race than a conventional circuit grand prix. Thus it will always hold the record for the longest F1 circuit and Juan Manuel Fangio's pole time of 9:44.6 will remain the longest pole lap (although at the Nürburgring that year he took P1 with a 9:25). His time represents a speed of 167.29kmh (104mph).

---

declined to send his cars. However after persistent requests by star driver Luigi Musso, he was given a Ferrari 801 on the understanding it was not a team entry.

Sixteen cars lined up at the start with Juan Manuel Fangio on pole. He had good knowledge of the course and had won a non-championship race at Pescara in 1950, almost against his wishes. He and Luigi Fagioli had both been driving for Alfa Romeo that year. Fagioli was leading on the last lap when a front spring broke on the Alfa, collapsing the bodywork against the wheel. Fangio, who was in second place, pulled up behind him. "I'm out," Fagioli told the Argentinian.

Fangio was having none of it and told him to continue, he would follow. They still had a gap to third place Louis Rosier. So

Opposite top Stuart Lewis-Evans leans on the rear fairing of his Vanwall prior to the race. Of the three Vanwalls entered, Moss won, Lewis-Evans finished in fifth place, while Tony Brooks' car retired after a single lap with engine problems.

Opposite left Fangio winds his way up towards the hill villages of Spoltore and Capelle in his Maserati. The roads have changed little in the intervening years.

Opposite right Giorgio Scarlatti waits to climb aboard his officially entered Maserati 250F. In addition to the Pescara GP, the course hosted sports car races and in 1961 Scarlatti and Lorenzo Bandini won the 4 Hours of Pescara in a Ferrari 250 Testa Rossa.

183

184

Opposite top Two Alfa Romeos, the second a 312 driven by Nino Farina (28), pass through the hill village of Spoltore in close succession. This 1938 edition of the 'Acerbo Cup' was won by Rudolph Caracciola in the surviving Mercedes W154 – two other W154s and all three Auto Unions failed to finish.

Opposite bottom Jean Behra early in the 1957 race in his Maserati 250F. Behra had qualified fourth fastest but had to retire the car after three laps with an oil leak.

Below left The village of Spoltore as it looks today. The post-war circuit was identical to the pre-war version.

Below right Juan Manuel Fangio (left) congratulates the victorious Stirling Moss in 1957. In his autobiography he recalled: 'The duel was long and exciting, but Stirling Moss, the contemporary driver I admired most, won at an average of more than 95mph. I had to be content with second place.'

Fagioli started the engine, his car bouncing up and down 'as if he had a camel instead of a car' as they toured slowly towards the finish. In his autobiography, *My Twenty Years of Racing* Fangio wrote. 'We came down from the Capelle pass together, continued on the Monte Silvano Straight. We kept looking back nervously all the time, afraid to see Rosier's Talbot … The warped wheel finally locked entirely but, win or lose, it was better to go on … It was Fagioli who first caught sight of Rosier's Talbot coming up at full speed. "Get going," he yelled.'

Fangio then accelerated past his ailing team-mate to take the win, while Rosier passed Fagioli 150 metres from the line.

In 1957 Fangio recorded a lap time of 9:44 in qualifying in his Maserati 250F. The Argentinian was ten seconds clear of Stirling Moss driving a Vanwall, who in turn was six seconds quicker than Luigi Musso. Slowest of all was Jack Brabham in the rear-engined Cooper, almost two minutes adrift, the 1.5-litre Climax engine totally unsuited to such a power circuit.

On race day it was Moss in the Vanwall who beat his former team-mate Fangio by three minutes, lapping the Vanwall of Stuart Lewis-Evans on the way. Luigi Musso's outing in the Ferrari came to nought on the ninth lap when an oil leak forced him to retire the car.

Seven of the 16 cars were running at the finish, including seventh place Jack Brabham, who was driving along the Via Nazionale on the final lap when he realized his spluttering Cooper had run out of fuel. Seeing a petrol station, he coasted to a halt on the forecourt. The petrol pump attendant immediately spotted his predicament, topped the car up and Jack finished the race in seventh place, albeit three laps down.

Formula 1 did not return to Pescara and racing only lasted until 1961, the final race for sports cars won by Lorenzo Bandini and Giorgio Scarlatti. It was simply too risky.

The history of racing at the Adriatic venue was the subject of a 2015 documentary *Acerbo Cup* and included a reminiscence of a pre-war race. In 1935 Tazio Nuvolari, driving an Alfa Romeo, had stopped at the side of the road to check his faltering engine and was immediately surrounded by curious village children keen to see what the great man was up to. Before getting back in the car he hugged each of them and wished them well. As the interviewee, now in her 80s, confides, 'This is a memory I will always keep in my heart.'

GUEUX, REIMS, FRANCE

Reims-Gueux

THE CLASSIC GRAND PRIX BUILDINGS AT REIMS HAVE BEEN PRESERVED TO GIVE A REAL FLAVOUR OF RACING IN TIMES PAST

The circuit at Reims was first used in the 1920s when the Grand Prix de la Marne moved to a road course west of the city using roads linking the villages of Thillois and Gueux, and a long stretch of the Route Nationale between Soissons and Reims.

With the start/finish on the long downhill stretch of the D27 from Thillois, the 1926 course sprinted downhill before entering the village of Gueux and, after a sharp right-hander, headed out of town up the Avenue de la Gare towards the village of Muizon. Sketching out a rough triangle, with long straights and few corners, it was a fast circuit measuring 7.816 kms (4.857 miles).

Thanks to the increasing popularity of the circuit – the 12-Hours of Reims sports car race was established in 1927 – the Automobile Club de France was persuaded to transfer the French Grand Prix from Linas-Montlhéry to champagne country for the 1932 event. Tazio Nuvolari won for Alfa Romeo. It returned to Paris for most of the 1930s, but Reims hosted two more grands prix in 1938 and 1939, characteristically dominated by the silver arrows of Mercedes and Auto Union.

Racing resumed in 1947 with a Grand Prix de Reims and soon it was hosting the French Grand Prix again, although this time in rotation with the circuit at Rouen-Les Essarts, which became a grand prix circuit in 1952. With speeds increasing, the organizers decided to bypass the village of Gueux, building the link roads Bretelle Sud and Bretelle Nord, which took the course across farmland north of the village instead of up Avenue de la Gare.

Opposite The grid is set for the start of the 1966 French Grand Prix at the Reims-Gueux circuit. Lorenzo Bandini was on pole for Ferrari, but it was a race for the Brabham-Repcos of Jack Brabham and Denny Hulme who finished first and third. The pit building and garages are beyond the start line to the right.

Below The grand prix buildings were left to nature after the racing stopped, with trees engulfing the grandstands. It is thanks to the herculean efforts of Les Amis du Circuit de Gueux, working with the local authority, that they have preserved an important part of France's historic racing past.

Bottom Rudolph Caracciola is escorted from the garages to the grid before the 1938 French GP. He would finish second behind team-mate Manfred von Brauchitsch.

The course swept west through open country, around Virage de la Hovette to Muizon, the hairpin where the track joined the Route National. The long straight blast uphill to the Thillois corner now rivalled Le Mans' Mulsanne Straight for an unadulterated stretch of full throttle. Then it was a right turn at the junction of the N31 and D27 before another long blast down the pit straight towards the impressive pit buildings. This significant alteration to the track lengthened it to 8.301 kms (5.158 miles).

With so much flat-out running it is no surprise that grands prix at Reims turned into slipstreaming affairs as exemplified in the 1953 race. Mike Hawthorn's Ferrari was involved in a race-long dice with the Maseratis of Juan Manuel Fangio and Froilán González, closely followed by the Ferrari of Alberto Ascari.

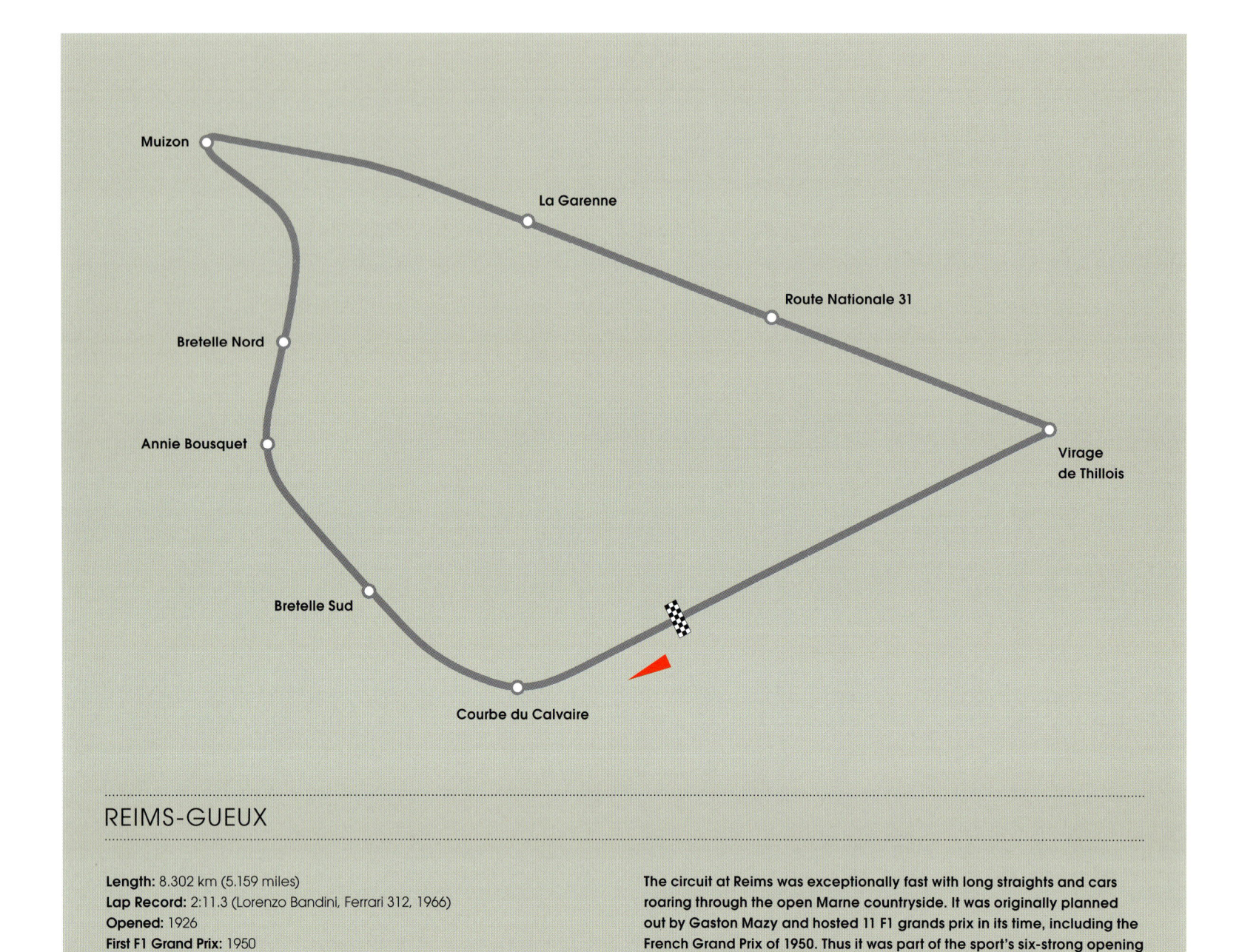

REIMS-GUEUX

Length: 8.302 km (5.159 miles)
Lap Record: 2:11.3 (Lorenzo Bandini, Ferrari 312, 1966)
Opened: 1926
First F1 Grand Prix: 1950
Last F1 Grand Prix: 1966
Number of F1 Grands Prix hosted: 11
Number of laps: 48
Race winning fact: Giancarlo Baghetti remains the only F1 driver to win his debut grand prix, (other than the inaugural race) which he did at Reims in 1961 driving a Ferrari 156. It was no fluke. Weeks earlier he had won the non-championship Syracuse Grand Prix.

The circuit at Reims was exceptionally fast with long straights and cars roaring through the open Marne countryside. It was originally planned out by Gaston Mazy and hosted 11 F1 grands prix in its time, including the French Grand Prix of 1950. Thus it was part of the sport's six-strong opening season – and only Bremgarten in Switzerland and Reims-Gueux are no longer part of the World Championship.

After almost three hours, all four cars thundered down the hill to the finish line together with Hawthorn edging ahead at the chequered flag to become the first British driver to win an F1 grand prix.

He won again in 1958 his World Championship-winning year, but the victory was saddened by the death of his team-mate Luigi Musso. While chasing Hawthorn, his Ferrari ran wide at the 150mph right-hand Gueux curve just after the start, flipping the car and killing Musso instantly. Reims had already witnessed tragedy in 1956 when the Franco-German sports car racer, Annie Bousquet entered her Porsche 550 Spyder for the 12 Hours of Reims. She had driven 500 kms overnight from the Porsche factory and insisted on taking the first stint. Her left front wheel

Opposite top In the original configuration of the circuit, cars drove into the village of Gueux before turning right and heading out towards La Garenne. In the early 1950s, the village was bypassed and the route shifted to join the Route Nationale further out at the Muizon hairpin.

Opposite left Annie Bousquet at the wheel of a Porsche 550 Spyder photographed in July 1956. In response to her death at Reims, the Automobile Club de l'Ouest, organizers of Le Mans, banned women from competing in the 24 Hours race until 1971, despite a long tradition of female drivers taking part.

Opposite right A corner on the circuit was named in tribute to Annie Bousquet. There is also a small roadside cross on the stretch of road approaching Muizon, further on from Annie Bousquet corner.

189

Top Apart from staging the French Grand Prix eleven times from 1950, the Automobile Club de Champagne was also famous for organizing the 12 Hours of Reims sports car races. The building above dates to the 1930s.

Above Thanks to preservation efforts, the original control building once slated for demolition remains. It is the pit buildings and garages beyond that have disappeared. The extent of these can be judged from Bernard Cahier's photograph taken from the Dunlop Bridge opposite.

Right A promotional poster from 1961 poignantly referencing two prominent drivers who lost their lives – Jean Behra at AVUS in 1959 and Chris Bristow at the Belgian Grand Prix of 1960.

Left The French Grand Prix of 1959 and Tony Brooks' Ferrari leads the harrying Cooper-Climax of Jack Brabham, and Ferrari teammate Phil Hill in front of packed grandstands.

Bottom Lorenzo Bandini leads the 1966 French Grand Prix from John Surtees in a Cooper-Maserati. Neither would finish, the victory going to Jack Brabham in a Brabham-Repco. The photograph shows the lengthy straight from Virage de Thillois down past the pit buildings.

Below Until Les Amis du Circuit de Gueux got to work, the grandstands had become obscured by trees, but today they are free of foliage and the comparison between Then and Now is obvious.

Top **The portly figure of Mercedes team manager Alfred Neubauer shepherds photographers out of the way of his driver Juan Manuel Fangio (bottom left) as the Silver Arrows make a return to the French Grand Prix in 1954.**

Above **More grandstands were added in the intervening years. Although visitors are free to wander around the old pit buildings, it takes a certain amount of 'parkour' skills to get into the grandstands.**

left the track on the approach to Muizon on the 17th lap, the car flipped and she broke her neck in the impact. Race organizers subsequently named a corner in her memory and there is a poignant roadside memorial close to where her car left the road.

The F1 grand prix lasted until 1966, when Jack Brabham won in a Brabham BT19. The circuit ran into financial difficulties and faced competition from other circuits for an international race. Added to that it was a circuit of its time, suited more to engine builders than spectators. The 12 Hours of Reims lasted one more year, won by Guy Ligier and Jo Schlesser, and there were motorcycle races until its ultimate closure in 1972.

The old grandstands and pit buildings stood abandoned for years afterwards, but when the local commune moved to have them demolished, Les Amis du Circuit de Gueux (a non-profit organization) stepped in to halt what they saw as cultural vandalism. The first pit garages had already gone, but they saved an impressive variety of buildings that draw motorsports fans from around the world to revel in times past.

Left Tony Brooks (24) leads into the slow Muizon corner, followed by Jack Brabham (8), Phil Hill (26) Masten Gregory (10) is putting a move on the BRM of Stirling Moss (2).

Below left Today the road has been converted to a farmer's field. The position of the camera is where it stops at a dead end, just after the cars in 12th and 13th places in the 1959 photo.

Bottom left Reims being the centre of the champagne exporting business, 50 bottles were offered for the driver on pole position. Stirling Moss ensured he got the fastest start to his qualifying lap possible by going off the road at Virage de Thillois on the preceding lap in order to get a better run down the main straight. The familiar hunched figure of Froilán González, takes the conventional line through Virage de Thillois in 1953.

Bottom right La Garenne restaurant is still in business today at what is a busy roundabout on the RN31 into Reims.

ORIVAL, ROUEN, FRANCE

Rouen-les-Essarts

THE CIRCUIT AT ROUEN RESEMBLED SPA-FRANCORCHAMPS, DEMANDING THE DRIVERS' FULL ATTENTION IN THE FLAT-OUT DOWNHILL KINKS TO THE HAIRPIN

The circuit near the village of Orival, to the southwest of Rouen, was not for the faint-hearted. Opened by the Automobile Club de Normand in 1950, within two years they had constructed new pits and a grandstand on the fast D938 road which plunged down the hill from Les Essarts towards Orival on the river Seine. Before the track got to the village there was a cobblestone hairpin, the Virage du Nouveau Monde, where the circuit turned abruptly uphill on the other side of the valley, following the D132.

In many ways it was like the Spa-Francorchamps circuit in Belgium where two public roads used for the grand prix converged at La Source hairpin. On the way down to La Source there is the famous flat-out Blanchimont curve – Rouen's equivalent was the Virage des Six Frères which was equally, if not more fearsome. It was one of four high-speed curves that drivers tried to take flat out on the way downhill to the hairpin.

After the turn there was a long, steep, uphill stretch through the Essarts Forest, before the track plateaued out at the top of the hill. The circuit then turned right onto the N138 at Virage du Gresil for a flat straight, before turning right again at Virage de la Scierie onto the D938 and back to the start/finish.

Rouen-les-Essarts hosted the French Grand prix five times in 1952, 1957, 1962, 1964 and 1968. The first race delivered a Ferrari lock-out of the podium places with Alberto Ascari leading home Giuseppe Farina and Piero Taruffi. Five years later it was a masterclass from 'Old Man' (as *Motor Sport* described him) Juan

Opposite Jean Behra (4) jumps the start at the 1957 French Grand Prix in his Maserati 250F. Alongside him are Juan Manuel Fangio (2) also in a Maserati and Luigi Musso (10) driving a Ferrari.

Left There are few traces at roadside of the old circuit, though the distant radio antenna links both photos. The straw bales beyond the grid in the vintage photo opposite mark the place where an underpass connects the two sides of the circuit.

Below Vanwall driver Roy Salvadori and Tony Vandervell (straw hat) stand over Stuart Lewis-Evans' Vanwall in the pits during practice for the 1957 French Grand Prix.

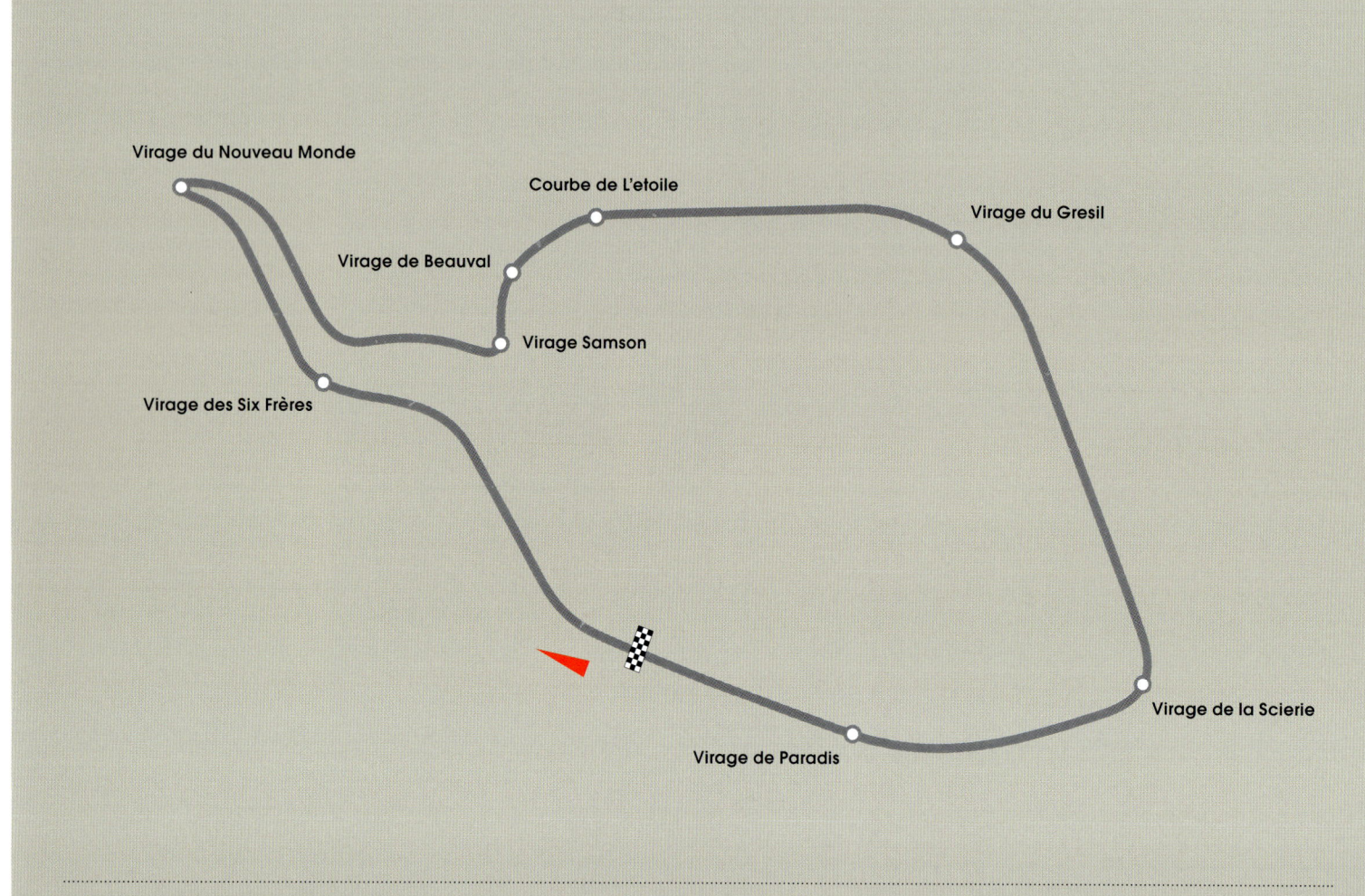

ROUEN-LES-ESSARTS

Length: 6.542 km (4.065 miles)
Lap Record: 2:11.4 (Jack Brabham, Brabham BT7, 1964)
Opened: 1950
First F1 Grand Prix: 1952
Last F1 Grand Prix: 1968
Number of F1 Grands Prix hosted: 5
Number of laps: 60
Designer: Jean Mermoz
Race winning fact: Jacky Ickx drove an outstanding race to win in the wet-dry race of 1968, finishing almost two minutes ahead of second place John Surtees.

The circuit at Rouen hosted five F1 French grands prix between 1952 and 1968. The downhill sprint towards the village of Orival on the River Seine required drivers to go flat through Virage des Six Frères before the hairpin at Nouveau Monde and a return up the hill at an incline that was 9% in places – hence a strong engine and a strong nerve were required. It was no surprise that two-time Rouen winner, Dan Gurney, also claimed a victory at Spa.

Manuel Fangio in a Maserati, showing the way to the young Ferrari upstarts of Musso, Collins and Hawthorn. American Dan Gurney, who coincidentally also won at Spa, took the victories in 1962 and 1964.

The 1968 race was remembered less for its winner, Jacky Ickx, than the accident that befell Honda driver Jo Schlesser on the second lap of the race. Schlesser lost control of his Honda RA302 at the difficult Six Frères corner, his car overturned and caught fire. Laden with fuel and with a high degree of weight-saving magnesium used in the car, the fire burnt intensely before Schlesser could be extricated. The race was not stopped. Shockingly, five years later, the same fate befell Roger Williamson at Zandvoort with the race not stopped, demonstrating the staggering intransigence of the sport's governing body.

Formula 1 did not return to Rouen, but it continued to host junior formulae. The circuit had to be modified and shortened in 1972 by the arrival of an autoroute that pushed through the top end of the circuit. It still ran Formula 2 races until 1978 and Formula 3 races as late as 1993, along with rounds of the French touring car championship. The sheer complication of organizing a race that involved the closure of two well-used public roads (the arrival of the autoroute had pushed the circuit off the third, the N138) and further safety concerns.

In 1973, promising Scottish F2 driver Gerry Birrell was killed at the Six Frères corner when a front tyre failed on his Chevron B25

Below The first turn at the 1957 race and the fast-starting Jean Behra streaks away from Musso and Fangio with Peter Collins (12) in a Ferrari to his right. Behra would ultimately finish in sixth place, eight laps behind.

Bottom left Jochen Rindt's Brabham BT26 in practice before the final grand prix at Rouen in 1968.

Bottom right Today trees of the Essarts Forest cloak the side of the track as it sweeps downhill towards Virage des Six Frères. Like the Masta Kink at Spa-Francorchamps, this corner had a reputation all its own, and after the deaths of drivers, including Jo Schlesser, a chicane was added. In 2024 a granite memorial to the lost 'pilotes' was added in the layby that now represents the original line of the corner.

in practice. Birrell, who had been in talks for a potential Tyrrell F1 drive in 1974, hit a poorly secured crash barrier at something like 150mph. Similar to Romain Grosjean's accident in Bahrain, the rail was lifted by the force of the impact and the Chevron passed beneath it. Organizers responded by introducing a chicane at Six Frères, which today is visible to the left of the road going downhill as a layby.

After the circuit's closure in 1994 the local authorities ignored the example set by Reims and in 1999 tore down the grandstands, the pit boxes and bulldozed the new section of road added through the Forêt des Essarts, made necessary when the autoroute arrived. Today, there are still small vestiges of the former circuit that can be discovered walking around the route, and a drive down the D938 from the old start line at the top of the hill gives an indication of just how perilous it might have been to pilot an F1 car at 160mph through that section. And in 1968 parts of the race were run in the wet...

Top **Peter Collins, on his way to third place in the 1957 French Grand Prix, rounds the Virage du Nouveau Monde hairpin at the bottom of the hill.**

Above left **Trees cover the banking now, but the original cobblestones can be seen through the eroded tarmac.**

Left **Dan Gurney in the Porsche 804 turns in to the hairpin, over the cobblestones, during the 1962 race. It was Gurney's first grand prix win and he repeated the feat at Rouen two years later, for his second.**

Left The Nouveau Monde hairpin viewed at a distance during the 1957 race. The set of concrete steps noted in this book's Introduction is just beyond the turn leading to an enormous gallery ranged on the hillside.

Below Graham Hill waits for mechanics to fix his Lotus during practice for the 1968 grand prix. Team boss Colin Chapman is to the right leaning against the pitwall. It was a wet race on the Sunday and Hill stopped at the corner before the hairpin with a broken halfshaft. Jo Siffert, in another Lotus, stopped and borrowed Hill's visor as his had broken.

Above Looking down on Silverstone circuit in 1965, with Woodcote corner at the bottom of the photo and vehicles parked behind the 'new' pits on the straight before Copse. Apart from providing extra parking, the old runway between Becketts and Woodcote formed part of the National Circuit.

Opposite Silverstone has undergone a metamorphosis unlike any other circuit of its vintage. A section of the old National Circuit straight is now the Wellington Straight.

SILVERSTONE, NORTHAMPTONSHIRE, ENGLAND

Silverstone

BERNIE ECCLESTONE'S REMORSELESS BULLYING OF SILVERSTONE FINALLY GOT THE BRITISH GRAND PRIX THE CIRCUIT IT DESERVED

Silverstone was the place where the F1 World Championship was waved off the line in May 1950. Only six circuits were used that first year and the Northamptonshire track is one of the four still remaining, along with Spa, Monaco and Monza. Apart from a few chicanes, Monza and Monaco are still the same, and Spa, while much shorter, is the same track from the start/finish line all the way up to the top of the hill at Les Combes. Silverstone has the Hangar Straight and the old pits straight to Copse, but almost every corner has been changed.

After World War II, Britain was left with a number of surplus airfields which were readily taken up by motorsport clubs anxious to exhaust their petrol rations. RAF Snetterton Heath had hosted the USAAF and Martin B-26 Marauders, RAF Thruxton was the base for USAAF fighter groups, mostly P-47 Thunderbolts, while RAF Silverstone was a night training base for Wellington bombers. All three continue to hold motor races.

After the war, the Royal Automobile Club (RAC) were searching for a venue where they could put on an international grand prix, and discovered that the Frazer Nash Club were organizing races on the roads of RAF Silverstone, as were the Bentley Drivers Club. It was also being used to store Sunbeam and Hillman cars before export.

By 1948 the RAC had obtained a lease from the Ministry of Defence and racing began in earnest with the RAC Grand Prix won by Luigi Villoresi in a Maserati. The course used some of the

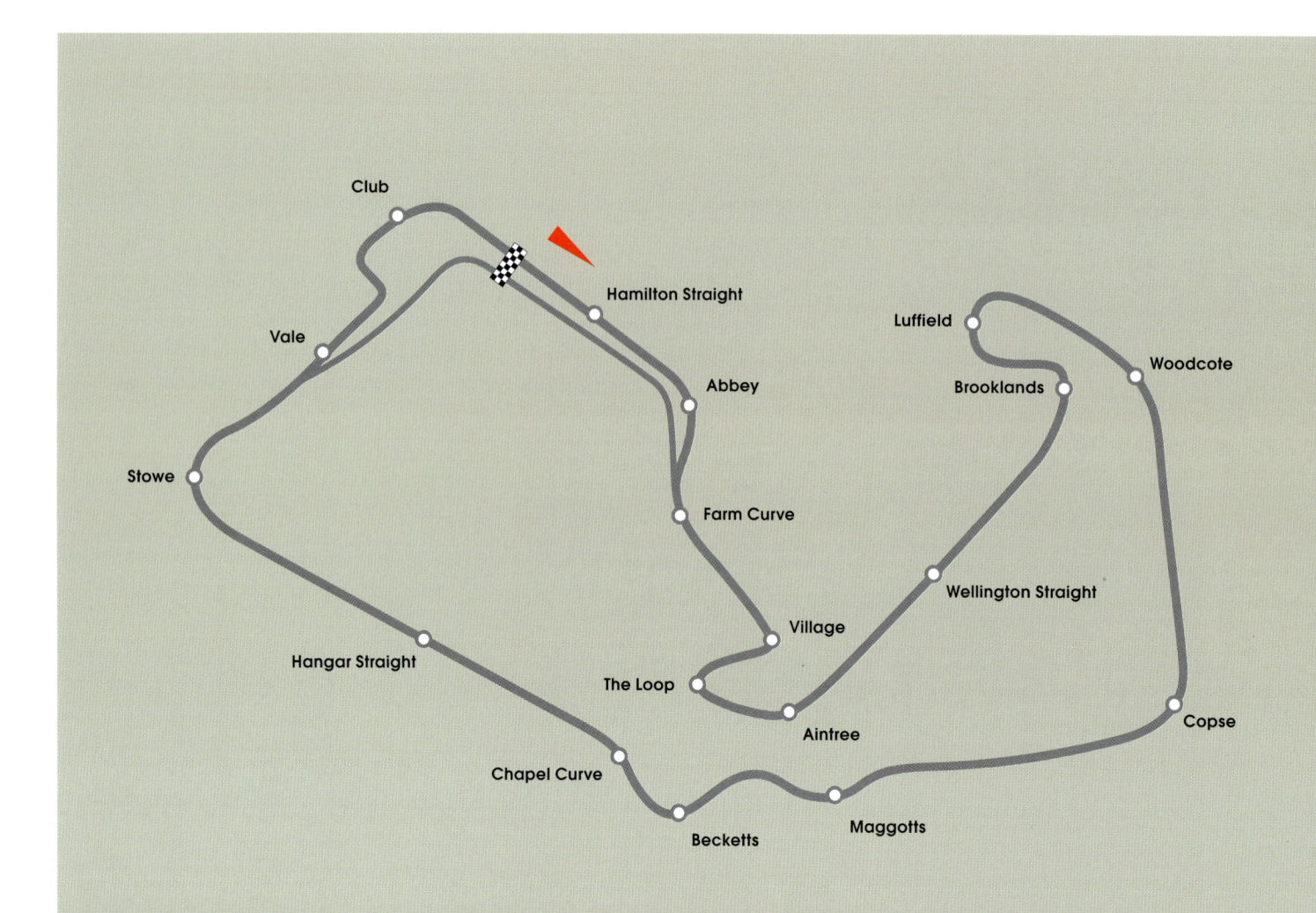

SILVERSTONE

Length: 5.891 km (3.661 miles)
Lap Record: 1:27.097 (Max Verstappen, Red Bull RB16, 2020)
Opened: 1948
First F1 Grand Prix: 1950
Number of F1 Grands Prix hosted: 59
Number of laps: 52
Designer: Edward R. W. "Eddie" Brown and the British Racing Drivers Club
Redesigner: Hermann Tilke (2011)
Race winning fact: Lewis Hamilton won his seventh British Grand Prix in 2020, six seconds ahead of Max Verstappen, having driven half the last lap with a puncture.

Given its flat topography and an absence of residential neighbours, the British Racing Drivers Club (BRDC), owners of Silverstone, have had virtual free reign to change the circuit over the years. The current configuration has been in place since 2011 and the quality of the racing has been unmatched. Drivers particularly appreciate the fast esses of Maggotts and Becketts – getting it right is important to carry speed through Chapel Curve and onto the Hangar Straight.

---

perimeter roads, but the striking difference between the 1948 course and the 1950 version was that at corners such as Stowe and Copse, drivers would take a sharp turn and head infield down the runways to the centre of the airfield, before making another sharp turn and heading down another runway to the perimeter road again. By 1950, it had reverted to the 'classical Silverstone shape' as seen in the aerial photograph from 1965.

The inaugural F1 race was won by Alfa Romeo driver Giuseppi 'Nino' Farina in front of a 150,000-strong crowd that included King George VI. It would pave the way for 'The Gentleman of Turin' to become the sport's first World Champion.

In 1952, there was the first significant change, the pits and paddock, which had previously been located on the Farm Straight were moved to between Woodcote and Copse Corner. To put enough distance between the start line and the first corner, Copse, the grid was arrayed around the bend of Woodcote. This was the Silverstone layout which lasted through to 1990, save for the niceties of a pit lane in 1964 and the addition of a chicane and then Luffield corner to slow cars through Woodcote.

The chicane proved necessary after the 1973 grand prix, following a multiple car accident on the main straight. On the second lap Jody Scheckter, trying to pass Denny Hulme on the outside at Woodcote, ran wide and then slewed across the track. The Yardley-McLaren ricocheted against the pitwall into the path of a packed midfield which could not avoid

Left The Royal Automobile Club were heavily involved in the running of the first official F1 grand prix at Silverstone in 1950. Officially it was known as 'The Royal Automobile Club Grand Prix d'Europe Incorporating The British Grand Prix'. Here Giuseppe (Nino) Farina is feted by the crowd, with a boom microphone hovering above, a precursor to the Netflix coverage almost 70 years later.

Below Copse Corner as it looked in 1953 for the Daily Express Trophy.

the unfolding accident at the speed drivers carried through Woodcote. Nine cars were involved in the resulting melee, Scheckter was unhurt, but Andrea de Adamich had to be cut from his car with career-ending ankle injuries. It would be 1998 before a greater accident afflicted F1 – when McLaren's David Coulthard tussled with Eddie Irvine on the downhill run to Eau Rouge at Spa and spun in front of the field, causing the retirement of 11 cars.

The British Racing Drivers Club (BRDC) had taken over the lease of Silverstone from the RAC in 1952 and gradually took control of all aspects of the running of the circuit. However, unlike at Monza they weren't able to secure the home grand prix on a regular basis. The race alternated with the colossal grandstands of Aintree between 1955 and 1962, and the close-to-London Brands Hatch between 1963 and 1986. Neither had the capacity to expand, while Silverstone, finally bought from the Ministry of Defence in 1971, had many acres of flat, adaptable land and far fewer neighbours to complain.

The 1991 changes were some of the biggest yet. At the start of the lap, Copse corner led onto a Suzuka-like, high-speed esses running from Maggotts, through Becketts and Chapel Curve onto the Hangar Straight. Stowe Corner was tightened from a dramatically fast sweeper into which Nigel Mansell had sold Nelson Piquet the most memorable dummy to overtake him in the 1987 grand prix. Instead of a direct run to Club corner, cars now dipped into the Vale which led to a slow left-right

Above **The start of the 1953 British Grand Prix with Fangio (23) taking the line for Copse pursued by Froilán González (24) and Onofre Marimon (26).**

Right **Tony Brooks exited his car before it went up in flames on the Hangar Straight after its throttle stuck open during the 1956 grand prix. Harry Schell passes by in a Vanwall. The aircraft hangar that gave the straight its name is beyond.**

Opposite top **The start/finish straight and main pit buildings are no longer located between Woodcote and Copse, but have moved to a position between Club and Abbey.**

Opposite bottom **Fernando Alonso's Aston Martin turns in to Stowe Corner from the Hangar Straight during the 2023 race.**

LAS VEGAS
aramco
aramco
aramco
aramco
aramco
aramco

PIRELLI
P ZERO
P ZERO
P ZERO
P ZERO

before accelerating out through Club. The lap was finished off by a new complex of corners: Bridge, Priory and Brooklands all aimed at slowing cars down before Luffield and Woodcote. Drivers broadly approved of the changes, particularly the Maggotts/Becketts/Chapel section which would get a carbon copy in Austin in 2012.

What they most certainly did was slow the lap time. Keke Rosberg had been the first F1 driver to average over 160mph in qualifying for the 1985 British Grand Prix, despite a slow rear puncture; crossing the line with a 1:05.591. By contrast, in 1991 Nigel Mansell took pole by 0.6 seconds from Ayrton Senna with a 1:20.939, more than 15 seconds slower.

In 1999, Michael Schumacher suffered the most serious injury of his career when he tried to outbrake Ferrari team-mate Eddie Irvine into Stowe corner and went head-on into the tyre barriers, his speed barely abated by the gravel trap in a 49g deceleration. Schumacher broke his leg, leaving Irvine to fight it out with Mika Häkkinen for Ferrari's first championship since 1979. It was ironic, that come the end of the season, Irvine fell short because of points he'd been obliged to give up to Michael under rigid Ferrari team orders earlier in the year.

From the mid-1990s all the way through to the end of Max Mosley's FIA presidency in 2009, he and Bernie Ecclestone were at loggerheads with Silverstone owners, the BRDC, over their lack of investment in the circuit, but in 2000 Mosley took advantage of FIA scheduling to undermine them. Instead of the traditional July date, the grand prix was set for 23 April, Easter

206

Below Woodcote has had many configurations over the years, originally being slowed with a chicane when cars approached from the Farm Straight. Now it is part of a complex of low-speed corners from Brooklands through Luffield which represent a real overtaking opportunity.

Bottom Ayrton Senna gets a lift back to the pits on the sidepod of Nigel Mansell's Williams-Renault, after 'Red Five' was victorious in the 1991 British Grand Prix.

Opposite top James Hunt (1) is slow off the line from pole in the 1977 race allowing Brabham driver John Watson through into the lead by Copse corner. The grid was arranged around Woodcote corner to allow sufficient distance between the start/finish line and Turn 1.

Opposite bottom Keke Rosberg prepares to go out in his Williams-Honda and set a new benchmark for qualifying pace in 1985.

Sunday, with all the attendant risks of Spring weather. Mosley produced a number of spurious reasons for the change, but few believed him.

Come race weekend, the constant April showers had turned the car parks to quagmires, slowing the entry of vehicles. This backed up the approach roads, creating five-hour waits for some, with many fans missing the race, unable to get in on time. Mosley was unrepentant for the misery he'd caused blaming the British Racing Drivers Club with a typical barb: 'They knew that they had 100,000 people coming and they know that it can rain. Maybe if they put some metal stuff down on the field rather than building a palatial club house they would have avoided losing money.'

Still frustrated at the lack of progress, Bernie Ecclestone sold the rights to the British Grand Prix to an investor looking to run the race at Donington Park. In July 2008 he struck a 17-year deal with Donington Ventures Leisure to host the race from 2010. When the Lehman Brothers bank collapsed two months later, accelerating the global financial crisis, and with the UK economy in freefall, nobody really wanted to invest in a motor-racing debenture scheme – the deal was effectively dead. Bernie was forced to renew negotiations with Silverstone.

The result, though, was a dramatic transformation. With guaranteed crowds in the Hamilton/Button era – after Lewis's debut Canadian GP win in 2007 circuit director Ian Phillips revealed: 'We haven't seen this level of interest since Mansell-mania in the late 80s and early 90s' – the investment was found to make Bernie happy. Leading stadium designer Populous created the futuristic Wing building, containing the new pits and media centre, on the straight between Club and Abbey. The old pits would remain for support races and national series. Instead of turning left at Abbey, the circuit headed right towards the infield for some slow, wide turns that would allow cars to run side by side onto the new Wellington Straight, before some more wide, slow turns through Brooklands, Luffield and Woodcote which have constantly generated wheel-to-wheel action in races since.

In the titanic title fight of 2021, Hamilton and Verstappen went wheel to wheel through the opening section of the grand prix culminating in Lewis's dive down the inside at Copse. An overhead camera showed that Hamilton momentarily had his front wing alongside the Red Bull's rear axle in the braking zone, but Verstappen failed to cede the space, the cars touched, resulting in Max's 51g impact with the barriers. This time, the ridged gravel and Tecpro barrier did their job and Verstappen walked away, leaving team boss Christian Horner to launch an ill-considered tirade from the pitwall.

In 2023 Silverstone attracted a record crowd of 480,000 across the grand prix weekend, making it no surprise that the grand prix contract was extended until 2034. Back in 2008 Bernie had said: 'It's Donington or nothing.' Today it is definitely a case of: It's Silverstone or nothing.

Opposite The 'palatial' clubhouse of the British Racing Drivers Club (BRDC), owners of Silverstone, which overlooks Brooklands and Luffield. Wind can be an important factor at Silverstone and former driver Mark Webber would always keep an eye on wind direction by looking at the flag on the BRDC's roof.

Left The impressive £27m Wing building was designed and built by stadium specialists Populous in 2011.

Below Silverstone now has two trackside hotels. The 197-bed Hilton Garden Inn Silverstone opened in 2022 and faces the Wing building. For those who prefer the track near Copse on the opposite side, the Escapade Hotel opened in 2024.

Above **Luigi Villoresi turns in to La Source hairpin in his Ferrari 500, in the 1953 Grand Prix of Belgium.**

Opposite **By 2022, the 'new' start/finish straight had been in use for almost 40 years. Carlos Sainz heads into La Source unchallenged in 2022 as many of the front-runners had taken engine-related grid penalties.**

Right **Another view of La Source hairpin, this time featuring the self-entered Maserati 250F of Stirling Moss in 1954. The Great War memorial is at the left edge of frame.**

STAVELOT, WALLONIA, BELGIUM 🇧🇪

Circuit de Spa-Francorchamps

TODAY IT IS THE DRIVERS' FAVOURITE CIRCUIT, BUT IN THE PAST IT HAD A REPUTATION FOR UNBRIDLED DANGER

When the Spa-Francorchamps circuit was conceived in the 1920s, the original length of 14.98 kms (9.31 miles) was not considered excessive. The Targa Florio route in Sicily was vast in comparison, while the Coppa Acerbo, run at Pescara with similar 'flying kilometre' straights, was on a lap of almost 25 kms.

It was a fast flowing course, roughly triangular in shape, run entirely on public roads. Starting below La Source, the circuit headed down over the Eau Rouge river, up the hill past Raidillon and out into the countryside of Malmedy, before taking a turn downhill at great speed through the Masta Kink, turning right at Stavelot and then another long drag down to the finish line which was beyond La Source hairpin.

The only significant difference to today's opening section was that cars didn't race flat out through Eau Rouge – instead they made a sudden left turn at the bottom of the hill, directly after the bridge, by the site of an old custom's post, *Virage de Ancienne Douane*, then a hairpin took them back towards Raidillon. This small loop was abandoned in 1939, but photos from the 1950s and 60s still show where the road diverts after the bridge.

After Formula 1 was established in 1950, the original full-length Spa course was used for the Belgian Grand Prix, one of only six that year. Shell produced a black and white promotional film of the 1955 event that captures in perfect detail the full bucolic nature of the challenge at that time on

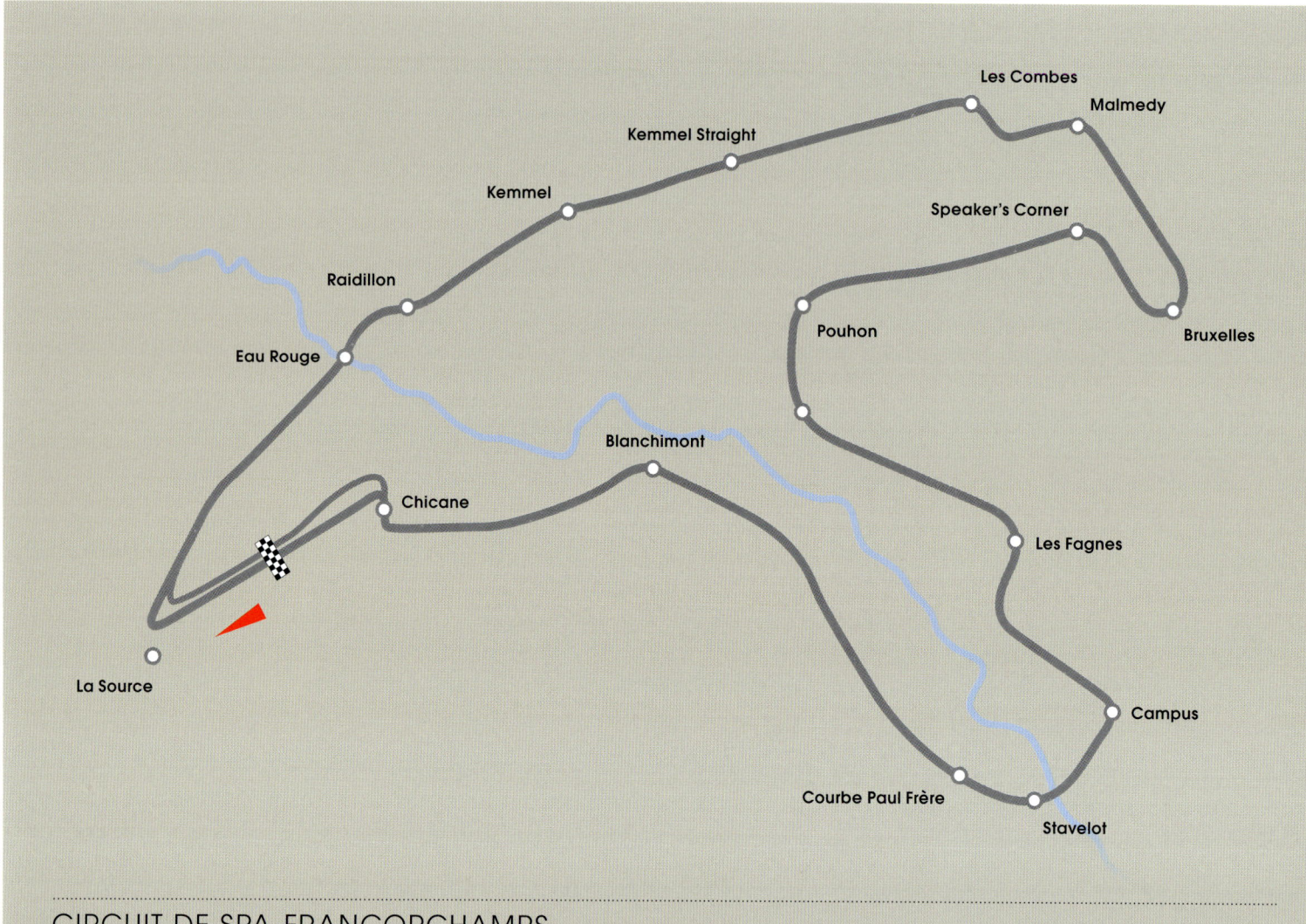

CIRCUIT DE SPA-FRANCORCHAMPS

Length: 7.004 km (4.352 miles)
Lap Record: 1:44.701 (Sergio Pérez, Red Bull RB20, 2024)
Opened: 1925
First F1 Grand Prix: 1950
Number of F1 Grands Prix hosted: 57
Number of laps: 44
Designer: Gaston Delanney
Redesigner: John Hugenholtz (1979)
Race winning fact: Jordan scored their first win, and only 1–2 finish, in a rain-soaked 1998 race, when Damon Hill and Ralf Schumacher took the honours.

The 1979 adaptation of the old Spa-Francorchamps circuit has been highly successful, playing host to thrilling races in the last 40 years. Apart from the Kemmel Straight which facilitates overtaking, and the challenging corners of Raidillon, Pouhon and Blanchimont, the unpredictable weather in the Ardennes Forest can often bring rain. With a lap time of close to two minutes this calls for exacting strategy decisions.

---

roads lined with trees, farmyards, and fields fenced with barbed wire. Stirling Moss, Jean Behra, Nino Farina and Juan Manuel Fangio drift their cars through the notorious Masta Kink to take maximum speed for the long downhill stretch to the Stavelot bend before gunning the cars downhill to La Source.

Spa already had a reputation for danger, claiming the life of pre-war Mercedes driver Richard Seaman in 1939, but the 1960 Belgian Grand Prix produced the blackest day in F1, only matched by the Imola weekend of 1994. Two British drivers were killed within fifteen minutes of each other. The first was a freak accident, Alan Stacey, driving for Team Lotus, was killed after being hit in the face by a bird and losing control of his car. The second was bright prospect Chris Bristow driving a Cooper in the same team as Tony Brooks. Battling on the road with Willy Mairesse his car left the road at the tricky Burnenville corner and he was decapitated by a wire fence. Stirling Moss had been badly injured at the same corner the day before, with an *Evening Standard* photo showing lurid skid marks across the road.

Like the Nürburgring, there was little more protection than the occasional straw bale placed against a stone parapet and nothing to stop cars from entering the scenery, a danger that was amplified in wet races. And that area of the Ardennes, as evidenced by the 2021 grand prix, is frequently wet. The rain-sodden 1966 race was covered by John Frankenheimer's *Grand Prix* cameras, which included helicopter shots tracking cars through the Masta Kink. The rain was so heavy that four cars went off at the Burnenville corner first time around. Half the field of 16 cars failed to complete the opening lap. Bob Bondurant and Graham Hill, both driving for BRM, spun off at the Masta Kink and were needed to come to the rescue of fellow BRM driver Jackie Stewart, who hit a telegraph pole and ended upside down in a ditch, injured, trapped and bathed with a race load of fuel. Using a spectator's tool kit they finally got the steering wheel off after 25 minutes. The opening lap perils form part of an eight-minute section of the *Grand Prix* film with a green BRM teetering at the edge of the track at Masta.

The accident galvanized Stewart's drive for safety in Formula 1. The circuit may have been lethal, but the medical facilities

Top Jim Hall of the USA takes the daunting Burnenville corner in the 1963 Belgian Grand Prix. In 1960, two drivers were killed within fifteen minutes of each other at Burnenville, part of the original Spa-Francorchamps circuit.

Above The start of the 1967 Belgian Grand Prix from a grid opposite the old pits, on the hill running down to Eau Rouge. Today the buildings are used for support races, with their own pit lane emerging onto the track beyond Raidillon.

Esso
FORD
PREMIER en BELGIQUE
BP
Gulf
DUNLOP
Shell
AUDI
FERODO
Shell
Shell

Opposite top Having negotiated Eau Rouge, cars head up the hill towards Raidillon at the start of the 1967 race. Spectators would have to wait three and a half minutes for the cars to return.

Above With its position on the F1 calendar under threat, the Belgian GP organizers have improved spectator facilities, including a vast grandstand looking down at Eau Rouge.

Opposite bottom The arches of the bridge over the Eau Rouge river are still visible as Fangio stretches out his lead in the 1955 race.

Left With increased speeds in the modern era, run-offs have been widened and Eau Rouge is taken flat. However, running three abreast into one of F1's most famous corners is not advised.

exacerbated the situation. After Stewart's accident he was taken back to the circuit's filthy 'medical room', left on the floor on a stretcher before an ambulance picked him up to take him to a hospital in Liège, whereupon the driver got lost. It is a far cry from the modern day, when practice cannot start unless the medical helicopter is able to fly.

Stewart's opposition to Spa culminated in a boycott of the 1969 race. Representing the Grand Prix Drivers' Association he visited the track and set out the improvements needed to make it safe. When the track owners declined to make them, the British, French and Italian teams withdrew from the race and the drivers were castigated in the motorsport press, led by chief zealot Denis Jenkinson.

Although some barriers were erected for the 1970 race, for which Stewart put his Tyrrell on pole, it would be the last time the long circuit was used in F1. The race transferred to Nivelles for 1972 and then to Zolder in 1973.

But Spa was not finished with F1. In 1979, a new section of track was built to link the two public roads, cutting out the fearsome Burnenville and Masta, instead turning right at the top of the hill at Malmedy after Les Combes, and flowing downhill through a series of challenging turns, Pouhon and Fagnes, before rejoining the circuit above Blanchimont.

When F1 made a return in 1983 drivers found an awkward 'bus stop' chicane between Blanchimont and La Source and new pit buildings opposite a new pit straight, now positioned

Opposite top left **Eddie Irvine in the Ferrari pushes David Coulthard's McLaren out wide at La Source hairpin at the start of the 1998 grand prix. Further down the road Coulthard lost control, spinning in front of virtually the whole field, causing the biggest multiple accident in F1 history. In the days when spare cars were permissible it was considerably easier to reconvene the starting grid.**

Opposite bottom **Nino Farina rounds La Source hairpin in his Ferrari 553 during the 1954 Belgian Grand Prix.**

Opposite top right **Fernando Alonso's McLaren is launched over the top of Charles Leclerc's Sauber in 2018. The halo was introduced that year to protect against the kind of accident often seen at La Source. Romain Grosjean was given a one-race ban for causing similar mayhem at La Source in 2012. He had been involved in seven first-lap crashes in 12 races that season.**

Below **Charles Leclerc rounds La Source hairpin his Ferrari SF-23 during the Sprint Shootout ahead of the 2023 Belgian GP.**

before La Source hairpin. There was universal praise for the new layout. It had retained the atmosphere and challenge of the old Spa-Francorchamps, yet provided the safety standards demanded of the 1980s. From 1985 it would be the home of the Belgian Grand Prix... that is, providing the organizers could come up with the race hosting fee.

The new Spa has become the litmus test for F1 talent. In 1991 Mercedes paid for their WEC prodigy Michael Schumacher to replace the temporarily jailed Bertrand Gachot at Jordan for the Belgian Grand Prix. This was long before simulators eased the path into a race debut. Schumacher put the Jordan seventh on the grid, 0.7 seconds quicker, and four places ahead of his vastly experienced team-mate Andrea de Cesaris. No matter that he burned his clutch on the grid, F1 took notice and the next race he was a Benetton driver. Spa would also be the place where he scored his maiden grand prix win in 1992. If you are fast at Spa and Monaco, then you have the right stuff.

Although pole position is the goal for any driver, at Spa P2 can be equally good. With the fearsome Eau Rouge-Raidillon tamed by the immense downforce created by modern F1 machinery, running flat through the sport's most famous corner is now a given. Cars that stay close behind through those two corners get an immense tow up the Kemmel straight to Les Combes. In the 2000 race Mika Häkkinen was closing on leader Michael Schumacher up the straight, when he was edged onto the grass by Schumacher at about 190mph, his

217

Above The grid forms on the old start line for the 1961 grand prix. It turned out to be a clean sweep for the Ferrari team with Phil Hill leading home Wolfgang von Trips, Olivier Gendebien and Richie Ginther all in the 'sharknose' Ferrari 156.

Opposite The run down from La Source to Eau Rouge is not straight, with a notable kink before the old start line. The organizers have embarked on a program of grandstand building, including the one to the left, to ensure the Belgian Grand Prix maintains its place on Liberty Media's calendar.

Right The long Kemmel Straight leading up to Les Combes, one of the sports' best straights for slipstreaming, with or without DRS.

rear tyre damaging Häkkinen's front wing. On the following lap, Schumacher believed he was safe as he took the tow from backmarker Ricardo Zonta up the Kemmel Straight. Schumacher went left of Zonta, Häkkinen went right and pulled off the overtake of the season.

Mika had been a tracheotomy away from dying at the 1995 Australian Grand Prix in Adelaide. He visited Michael in the pits afterwards and made it clear he would not be edging him onto the grass again. Two years earlier it had been Schumacher, chin thrust forward, rushing down the Spa pit lane to confront David Coulthard. In rain and with shocking visibility he had failed to see the McLaren as he came up to lap him and had run into the back of DC, converting his car into a Ferrari three-wheeler – his argument being that Coulthard was dawdling and trying to impede. Given that the full wet tyres shift a lot of water, it was surprising that he hadn't spotted his tyre tracks.

Kimi Räikkönen's moment of epic bravery occurred in 2002. Driving for McLaren the Finn accelerated up the hill through Raidillon only to be confronted by an impenetrable wall of white smoke across the track. Commentator James Allen predicted that Kimi would need to lift, but Räikkönen kept his foot to the floor and hurtled through what turned out to be smoke from Olivier Panis's blown Honda engine. Asked afterwards about the risks he was taking – it could have been an accident – Kimi simply said, "No, I saw the trail of oil..."

Though Eau Rouge-Raidillon is no longer the challenge it once was, making the corner safer hasn't necessarily eliminated the risk. By creating generous asphalt run-offs, drivers have been emboldened to follow closely up the hill through Raidillon in order to get a tow onto the Kemmel Straight. Should a car have problems and hit the barriers, then the following drivers struggle to take avoiding action, as happened to Giuliano Alesi (Jean Alesi's son) in a 2019 F2 race. An undiagnosed puncture sent Alesi into the barriers on Lap 2, the first of the following pack slowed down but Antoine Hubert clipped a slowing car, which ricocheted him off the barriers out on track to be struck fatally by two cars. The dilemma about Raidillon remains.

As does the finances of the circuit. It has dropped off the F1 calendar in the past thanks to over-aggressive local police and the perennial lack of investment by the organizers. A massive new grandstand above Eau Rouge and other facilities were built in 2022 to address some of the concerns, but F1 boss Stefano Domenicali insists venues need to buy into F1's vision of what a grand prix should look like. No matter if it is the best racing circuit in the world.

SUZUKA, MIE PREFECTURE, JAPAN

Suzuka International Race Course

HONDA FIRST BUILT A TEST AND RACING TRACK TO SUPPORT THEIR BURGEONING MOTORCYCLE BUSINESS

Soichiro Honda was one of the great post-war industrialists, helping lead Japan out of the economic misery that followed World War II. Originally he had formed a company to make piston rings for Toyota and the Nakajima Aircraft Company, but in 1946 set up the Honda Technical Research Institute making a motorized bicycle and then a true motorcycle with a 98cc two-stroke engine.

Honda saw racing as a means to promote his engineering, and with the success of Honda motorcycles through the 1950s both nationally and internationally – his first American dealership was established in 1959 – he had the idea to create a test and racing track for motorcycles near his factory in Mie Prefecture. Honda was the engineer, his business partner Takeo Fujisawa, who had joined the company in 1949, encouraged him to make the new test track more like an automotive Disneyland which had been packing visitors in at Anaheim since 1955.

After its opening in 1962 the amusement park rides, such as the big wheel – visible as a backdrop to much of the racing photography – were added for the 'motorcycle sports land' which carried various names over the years: Motor Sportland, Suzuka Circuitland, Techniland and eventually Motopia. Nestled inside the 2.48 million square metres of standard resort attractions was one of the world's stand-out race tracks.

Honda had chosen a wooded hillside location near Suzuka for his race circuit, and when he contacted John Hugenholtz, the man responsible for designing Jarama, the outline of the figure-of-eight track was already in place. As design consultant, Hugenholtz was in charge of adapting the Honda plan to be more race-appropriate and so he changed the opening section of slow corners to create the driver-favourite esses in their place.

The first races in September 1962 were for motorcycles and the East German rider Ernst Degner, riding for Suzuki, was badly injured when he crashed at the long sweeping corner before the crossover. He recovered and a grateful Honda renamed the corner as 'Degner' in thanks. When F1 came to town, the limited run-off at Degner was tackled by making two slower, sharper bends connected by a short straight, thus Degner 1 and Degner 2.

Despite Honda entering the F1 World Championship as early as 1964 there would be no Japanese F1 Grand Prix at Suzuka until

Opposite Nelson Piquet wins the 1990 Japanese Grand Prix for Benetton.

Top Unusually, one of Suzuka's entertainment park rides has replaced a spectator grandstand by the finish line. Red Bull Racing's Max Verstappen pockets another grand prix victory in 2023 as he roars to the unmatchable total of 19 wins in a season.

Above right The 1988 race: Nigel Mansell collides with Nelson Piquet while trying to lap the Lotus-Honda driver, who complained of being unwell and retired. Having taken Williams' supply of Honda engines to Lotus in 1988, Lotus and Piquet found themselves with Judd engines in 1989.

Right Alain Prost exits his notorious 1989 crash with Ayrton Senna at the chicane while the Brazilian driver remains in the car exhorting marshals to push him off the racing line and into the escape road.

221

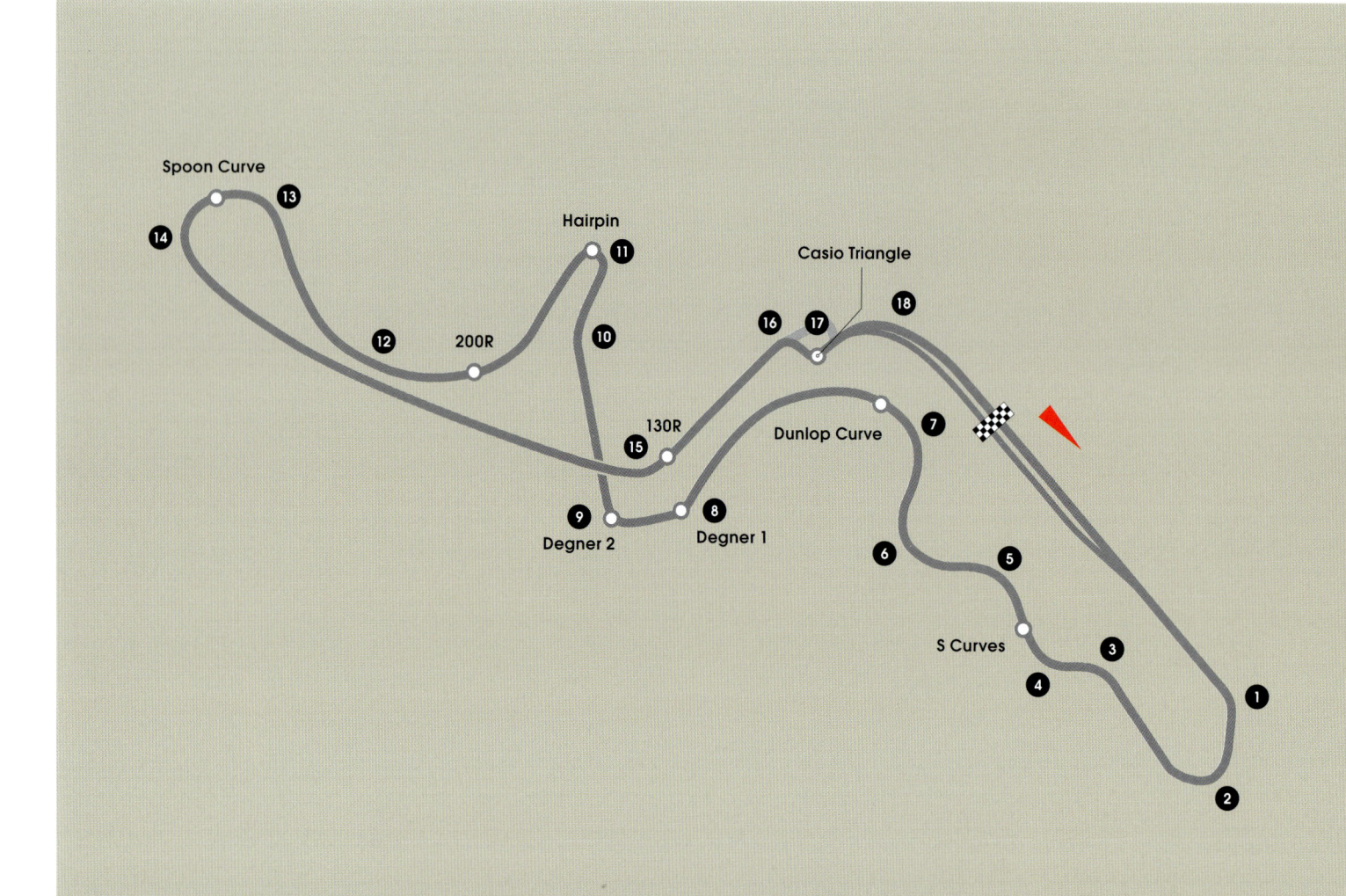

SUZUKA INTERNATIONAL RACE COURSE

Length: 5.807 km (3.608 miles)
Lap Record: 1:30.983 (Lewis Hamilton, Mercedes W10, 2019)
Opened: 1962
First F1 Grand Prix: 1987
Number of F1 Grands Prix hosted: 34
Number of laps: 53
Designer: Honda Corp, John Hugenholtz
Race winning fact: Damon Hill won the 1996 title-deciding race at Suzuka beating team-mate Jacques Villeneuve who lost a wheel after a faulty pit-stop.

The collaboration between Soichiro Honda and John Hugenholtz has been much admired over the years with very little change to the grand prix circuit since 1987. Spoon has been tightened to allow more run-off on the outside and 130R was modified after Allan McNish's somersault over the barriers. The hairpin is unofficially named 'Kobayashi Corner' after Japanese driver Kamui Kobayashi passed five drivers there during the 2010 Japanese Grand Prix.

1987. After their exit from the sport in 1968 following Jo Schlesser's fatal crash at Rouen, they returned as an engine manufacturer in late 1983, winning races in 1984 and 1985 and powering Williams and McLaren to constructors' titles between 1986 and 1991.

Toyota's brief dalliance with the Japanese Grand Prix at Mount Fuji in 1976 and 1977 had not been a success. However, with Honda powering the two cars fighting out the 1987 drivers' title, Mansell vs Piquet, ticket demand was strong. In fact so strong that grandstand places were allocated on a lottery basis and fans queued overnight for general admission.

The race was an immediate success, coming as it did towards the end of the grand prix calendar when championships were on the line. The first was decided in Nelson Piquet's favour when Williams team-mate Nigel Mansell crashed out in practice, badly injuring his back. The following year the wily Ron Dennis had secured for McLaren both Ayrton Senna and a supply of Honda engines and Ayrton delivered a then-record eighth win of the year at Suzuka to become World Champion.

In 1989 it should have been Senna again, but Alain Prost crashed into him at the Suzuka chicane in an incident which under today's racing protocols would see the Frenchman penalized. A DNF for both cars would have handed the World Championship to Prost who abandoned his McLaren. Senna, whose car was on the entrance to the escape road, gestured for the marshals to push him, and using the momentum fired up the car. He needed a pit-stop to replace his front wing, rejoined in

Left The 1990 sequel to 1989's chicane incident: Ayrton Senna in the Marlboro McLaren is about to dive for the inside line with no intention of lifting off when Alain Prost's Ferrari moves across. It was a premeditated move of great danger with the rest of the grid following at full tilt.

Below The smoking remains of Allan McNish's Toyota lie the other side of the barrier at 130R – the Scot having walked away from a monster accident in 2002.

second place and chased down Nannini's Benetton for the win. He was disqualified for cutting the chicane and the acrimonious legal ramifications rumbled on unsuccessfully till year's end.

The following year it was Senna's turn to crash into Prost at Suzuka, the Brazilian clattering his McLaren-Honda into the Frenchman's Ferrari when Prost moved across to take the line for Turn 1. The twin retirements made Ayrton World Champion, but there were those who thought he never intended to try and pass the Ferrari. 'Sure you go for gaps,' said Mario Andretti. 'The trick is finding one wide enough for your car.'

A year later, Ayrton secured his third World Championship at Suzuka, but this time the drama was in the pressroom afterwards. Instead of celebrating a significant milestone he launched into an astonishing tirade about the sport's governing body and effectively admitted that the 1990 accident had been premeditated from the moment that Prost had got a better start.

Tirades at Suzuka became a regular thing for Ayrton. In 1993 *Autosport* journalist Adam Cooper recorded Senna lambasting the attitude of rookie Eddie Irvine, who knew the circuit from competing in Japanese F3000 and had cheekily unlapped himself in the grand prix. Senna confronted him afterwards to administer a stern warning against the chipper Ulsterman and ended up throwing a punch after Eddie's perceived lack of respect.

In addition to Piquet, Senna and Prost – World Championships were determined for Damon Hill, Mika Häkkinen, Michael Schumacher and in 2022, Max Verstappen, in the most anti-

Right Having endured monsoon-like conditions for many of its late-season races, the Japanese Grand Prix benefited from F1's push for a more sustainable race calendar that didn't require excess flying from race to race. Thus in 2024 the Japanese GP moved to spring – and with spring in Japan there is cherry blossom.

Below Suzuka is currently the only F1 track in a figure of eight. The crossover comes just after Degner 2 on the lower level and approaching 130R on the upper level.

Right and below Italian fans are passionate, British fans turn out in all weathers, Dutch fans will follow Max Verstappen across continental Europe, but the Japanese fans have a special respect from the drivers. Their reserved but intense love for F1 manifests itself with the most intricate of hats and models brought along to the races. And with Yuki Tsunoda they have a star driver who has survived the typical 3-season guillotine wielded by the Red Bull organization.

climactic of circumstances. The scheduling of the Japanese GP had always tempted fate, coming at a time when monsoon-like rains were a regular occurrence and races in the past had seen team members float paper boats along the pit lane during the sheer boredom of waiting for the rain to stop.

Indeed, it was the torrential conditions brought on by Typhoon Phanfone in 2014 that caused the accident which cost Jules Bianchi his life. Race director Charlie Whiting had tried to move the race earlier, but the organizers refused. Conditions worsened through the race, with poor visibility and fading light. On Lap 42 Adrian Sutil's Force India aquaplaned off the road at the Dunlop Curve, an incident covered by double waved yellow flags which in F1 parlance means 'slow down be prepared to stop'. Bianchi's Marussia approached the spot where a tractor was removing Sutil's car in excess of 100mph, aquaplaned off the road and struck the recovery vehicle.

The 2022 race was similar in that it was started and stopped after two laps because of torrential rain which caused Carlos Sainz to lose control at the hairpin and put his Ferrari into the barriers. Pierre Gasly and Sergio Pérez were both furious to encounter a recovery vehicle on track in the low-visibility conditions, a situation that surely had been consigned to the past with Bianchi's accident...

The race resumed behind the Safety Car, but only 28 laps were possible before the grand prix ran out of time. It gave Verstappen his twelfth victory of the season, but with everyone assuming that it would be reduced points, his second drivers' title would have

to wait. Except the rules had been changed for 2022 and now a resumed race that had completed less than 75% of the laps could be awarded full points. Although his second title had been a bolted on certainty, it was still a surprise to Max as he waited in the 'cool down' room.

Suzuka is a highlight for the drivers, not least because of the reverence of the Japanese fans. There is still a surge for autographs and selfies, but it is a respectful clamour by fans who often come dressed with their favourite car on a hat. Most of all it is admired because it is 'old school' with an off-track excursion ending in the gravel or the barriers at Degner 1 and 2. Culturally, the Japanese do not like to lose face, but there are plenty of opportunities for drivers to do that in practice around Suzuka.

One corner that has lost its edge, though, is 130R, now taken routinely flat when once it was mentioned in the same breath as Spa's Eau Rouge and Blanchimont. Alan McNish survived a chassis-destroying 170mph accident in his Toyota there in 2002 when he lost control and vaulted the barriers. The Le Mans-winning Scot was disappointed when they reprofiled the corner afterwards. 'I know it tried to make me 1m20cm instead of 1m65cm but it wasn't the corner's fault. The lack of aero from the Toyota and me not catching it quickly enough were the problems, not the corner itself.'

McNish loved going there. 'It was purely Japanese, the writing everywhere, so to even make your way to go to Suzuka was a bit of a challenge,' he says. 'It brought this romantic sort of adventure side of it out and the circuit itself was a bit of an adventure.'

225

WATKINS GLEN, NEW YORK, USA

Watkins Glen International

THE FORMER 'SPIRITUAL HOME' OF THE USGP WAS HIGHLY RATED BY DRIVERS BUT NEEDED MORE THAN SENTIMENT TO KEEP IT ON THE F1 CALENDAR

Watkins Glen lies at the southern end of Seneca Lake, one of several finger lakes all pointing north towards Lake Ontario in upstate New York. It's a place of hiking trails and summer camps and starting in 1948 the Watkins Glen Grand Prix. Run on a 6.6-mile (10.6-kms) course in and around town, the organizers had to reach agreement with the local railroad to stop trains for the event, seeing as the course passed over it.

It was a tremendous success and for five years sports cars roared around town, including the Buick-Mercedes or 'Bu-Merc' of Briggs Cunningham, one of Le Mans' most storied American competitors. Injuries to competitors were viewed a part of the sport, but in 1952 future F1 driver Fred Wacker Jr. was involved in a fatal accident in his Allard. Swerving to avoid running into a Cunningham car driven by John Fitch, he clipped spectators at the edge of the track, injuring ten and killing a seven-year-old boy. Wacker was unhurt, but the meeting was abandoned never to be re-run.

A new, closed course was found to the southwest of Watkins Glen using farm roads and no state highways. Drivers didn't like it. And so when land bordering the second course became available, it was purchased to create a permanent facility, with input from Bugatti racer Bill Milliken and engineering staff from Cornell University in nearby Ithaca. The 2.3-mile (3.7-km) circuit opened in 1956 to popular acclaim. It was fast, with a long front straight, curving round The Loop and then returning down Back Straight to the self-describing Fast Bend.

Formula 1 arrived in 1961 and Innes Ireland scored his only career victory for Lotus at what was the final race of the season. Lotus boss Colin Chapman then sacked him and replaced him with Trevor Taylor. In the 1960s it was a British-dominated podium with wins for Jim Clark, Graham Hill and Jackie Stewart. Jochen Rindt broke the sequence in 1969 for Gold Leaf Team Lotus, and a year later it was Emerson Fittipaldi's maiden victory for the same factory team, now using a Lotus 72C. Up until 1970 it needed 108 laps of The Glen to cover an F1 race distance – for 1971 that would all change.

In 1971 Formula 1 got 'The Boot', a new four-corner section in the shape of a right-facing boot (although some preferred to call it 'The Anvil'), with an 180-degree Toe and a not-quite-90-degree Heel. In addition, the start/finish straight had been redrafted and moved back a corner. The Ninety had been the penultimate turn on the pre-1971 track, now it was the first. The circuit was widened, resurfaced and came in at a length of 3.37 miles (5.43 km), making it a grand prix of 59 laps. It had cost the considerable sum of $2.3 million, but with minor adjustments remains the same course today.

With $267,000 up for grabs in prize money – easily the biggest prize fund in F1 that year – competition was intense for the first race on the new track. US stars Mario Andretti and Mark Donohue were obliged to race in New Jersey that Sunday, but still qualified their cars on the Saturday just in case the Garden State race was called off and they could head north. Mario qualified his Ferrari in sixth place on the provisional grid, but to the dismay of the crowd

Opposite Innes Ireland in a Lotus leads Graham Hill's BRM and Jo Bonnier's Porsche through the Esses in the 1961 USGP.

Top After leaving Alfa Romeo, Kimi Räikkönen tried his hand at NASCAR, in 2022. Here Kimi competes at Watkins Glen driving the No.91 Recogni Chevrolet, during the 220-mile 'Go Bowling at The Glen' race.

Above Graham Hill (6) and Jim Clark (5) start from the front row of the 1967 USGP, shadowed by Dan Gurney (11) in the Eagle-Weslake. Clark built a substantial lead in the race but on Lap 106 of 108 part of the Lotus's suspension broke. Hill was 45 seconds behind with two laps to run as Clark trundled carefully home. Graham was 23 seconds back on the final lap and six seconds behind at the line. It was Jim Clark's final win in America.

WATKINS GLEN INTERNATIONAL

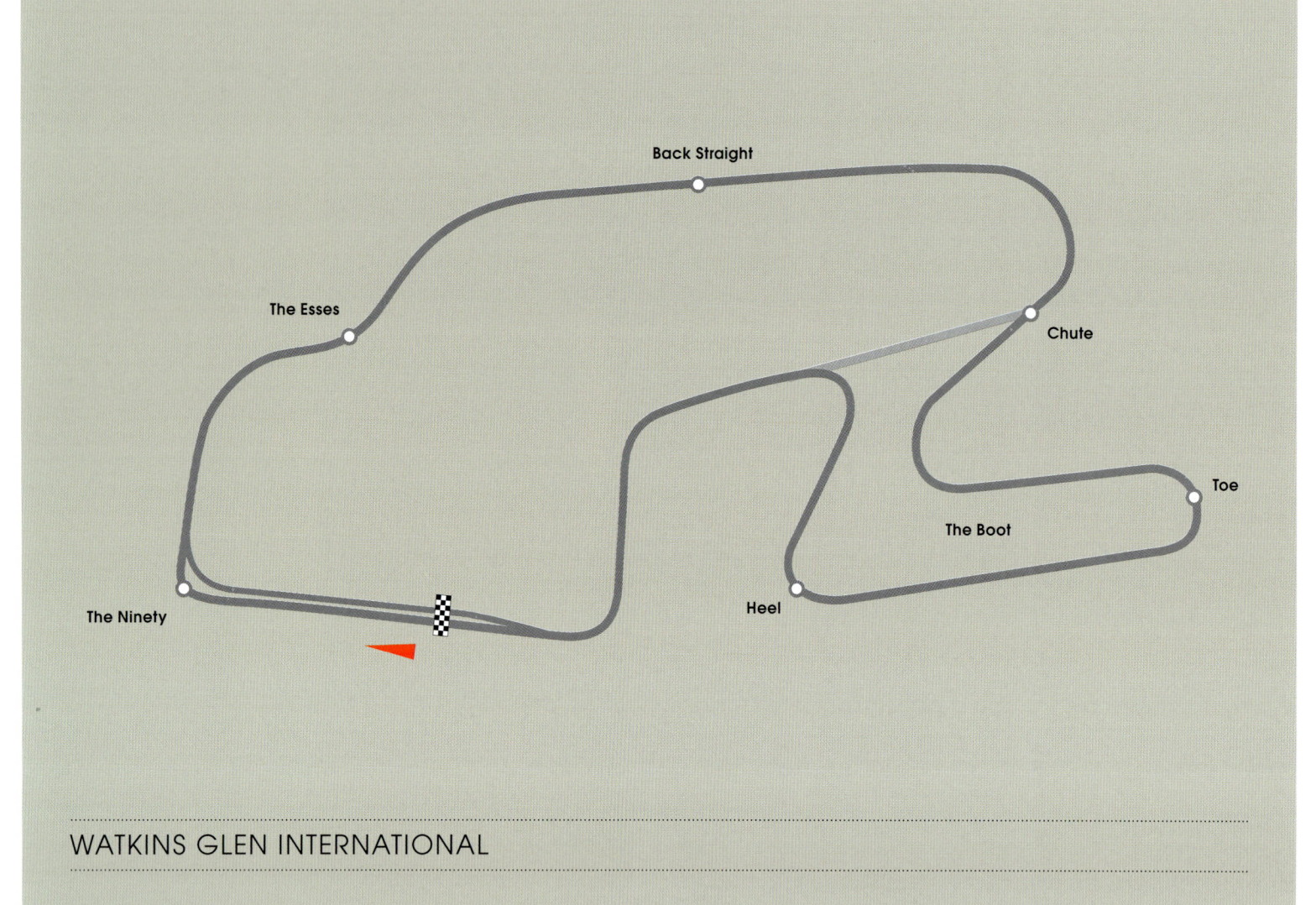

Length: 5.435 km (3.377 miles)
Lap Record: 1:34.068 (Alan Jones, Williams FW07B, 1980)
Opened: 1956
First F1 Grand Prix: 1961
Last F1 Grand Prix: 1980
Number of F1 Grands Prix hosted: 20
Number of laps: 59
Race winning fact: In 1968 it was an all-British podium with Jackie Stewart (Matra) winning from Graham Hill (Lotus) and John Surtees (Honda).

Watkins Glen International hosted 20 grands prix, the first in 1961 and the last in 1980. Having won the 1961 driver and constructor titles, Enzo Ferrari declined to send his cars for the opening race, denying America's first World Champion, Phil Hill, the opportunity to take part in his home race. However in 1968, America's next F1 World Champion, Mario Andretti, put his car on pole at Watkins Glen in his first grand prix start.

---

and the organizers, it was dry in New Jersey on Sunday morning.

Jackie Stewart's Tyrrell team-mate François Cevert took the win in 1971 and a year later the Tyrrell team took a 1–2, Stewart leading home Cevert by half a minute. The 1973 race was going to be Stewart's 100th and last. Unbeknownst to François Cevert, he was about to become Tyrrell's No.1 driver. Stewart, already the World Champion that year, planned to announce his retirement after the race. Team boss Ken Tyrrell knew his decision, but Jackie's wife Helen did not.

However, tragedy intervened during the last few minutes of Saturday morning qualifying as Cevert pushed to take pole from Lotus driver Ronnie Peterson. Going through the uphill Esses, Cevert ran wide on the kerbs, slid into one barrier at 150mph and bounced across the track into the other, penetrating the top layer of Armco which broke the car in two. Cevert was exposed to injuries of shell-exploding ferocity, his body ripped apart. Stewart was one of the last drivers to stop at the scene, noting afterwards that the marshals had left him in the car, "because he was so clearly dead".

So long a campaigner for safety, Stewart retired on the spot, his career tally of 27 wins from 99 races the greatest in F1 history up to that point. Tyrrell withdrew from the race, handing the constructors' title to Lotus.

F1 visited throughout the 1970s, but the far-flung nature of the circuit made it a place where fans would bring camping trailers, bring out the barbecue and drink. Some took it to extremes.

Left The flamboyant, lavender suit-wearing, cigar-smoking Ted Hopkins gets the 1961 Unites States Grand Prix underway with one of his trademark leaping flag drops. He was similarly airborn when it came to waving the chequered flag.

Below A contemplative Lorenzo Bandini waits to go out in his Ferrari 1512 in practice for the 1965 US Grand Prix. A larger and longer pit lane was part of the circuit changes for 1971.

Before the tales of Talladega nights, there was 'The Bog', a mud bowl outside of the circuit where 'Bogladytes' or 'Boggers' would drag old vehicles and set them on fire. In 1974, Emerson Fittipaldi was attempting to become a two-time World Champion and was locked in a title fight with Ferrari's Clay Regazzoni, which would go down to the wire at Watkins Glen.

A party of Brazilian fans chartered a Greyhound Bus to take them to upstate New York. But while the bus was unattended, it was stolen and set on fire. Organizers moved in and bulldozed The Bog, but the reputation lingered.

With speeds increasing through the 1970s, The Glen was in need of change – greater run-offs and a better track surface. Attendances had been dwindling, in contrast to the USGP West, which was thriving so close to a major metropolis. Public money was not forthcoming. Even a month before the final grand prix of 1980, the race was in doubt, so Bernie Ecclestone put his hand in his pocket and loaned the organizers $750,000 from the FOCA account. It proved to be another fine win for World Champion Alan Jones and the Williams team, handing Frank Williams his first constructors' title after 11 years of trying.

When the FOCA debt was not repaid in 1981 Watkins Glen disappeared off the F1 race calendar. No amount of nostalgia about the 'glorious high-speed road course' could counter the fact that it was off the beaten track and unable to withstand the influx of 400,000 over a weekend, as Austin, the USGP's new spiritual home, has so readily accomplished.

Opposite top Carlos Reutemann (7) in a Brabham heads Mario Andretti in the Parnelli-Ford during the 1975 grand prix. Mario qualified in P5, but his race would last just nine laps until his suspension failed.

Opposite centre The charismatic François Cevert was due to take over from Jackie Stewart as Tyrrell team leader in 1974 and his tragic death came just two months after the loss of Roger Williamson at Zandvoort.

Opposite bottom Brazilian fans flocked to upstate New York in 1974 to see Emerson Fittipaldi win his second drivers' title.

Above Scott Dixon leads an IndyCar race at Watkins Glen during the 2016 season. The series introduced their own version of F1's halo, the aeroscreen, during the 2020 season.

Right Patrick Head and Frank Williams, both with headsets, stand over the FW07 of Alan Jones, who would win the 1980 race and the drivers' title. To the left of the frame is the bearded figure of F1 journalist and Stirling Moss's Mille Miglia co-driver, Denis Jenkinson.

ZANDVOORT, NETHERLANDS

Circuit Zandvoort

THE 1985 DUTCH GRAND PRIX LOOKED TO BE THE LAST F1 EVENT AT THE SEASIDE CIRCUIT, BUT THEN ALONG CAME MAX VERSTAPPEN…

The German invasion of the Netherlands in 1940 was devastating for the nation – it also put on hold Zandvoort mayor Henri van Alphen's plans to create a permanent race circuit in the dunes near the seaside resort. The town had organized a successful street race in 1939, but World War II brought an immediate halt to any further plans, although local councillors had already dismissed the idea of a separate circuit as being too expensive.

By 1942, with the tide of war turning against the Germans, the occupiers started to pull down beachside hotels and resorts to create the Atlantic/North Sea Wall which would deter the Allies from using the North Dutch coast as an invasion point. Ever alive to an opportunity, Mayor van Alphen suggested to the Germans that the rubble from the hotels could be used as hardcore for a *paradesstrasse*, a lovely straight road on which the soon-to-be-victorious Germans could parade their troops. And the Germans agreed.

Instead of being shipped off to work in armament factories, a section of Dutch workers were employed to create what would become (and what was intended) as the main straight of the Zandvoort circuit.

When the country was liberated on 5 May 1945, a large part of the circuit had been built by the occupiers. The Dutch Automobile Racing Club took on the task of fulfilling van Alphen's vision to create a national race circuit. They brought in 1927 Le Mans winner and former sports editor of *Autocar*

Opposite James Hunt (1) in the McLaren gets the jump on polesitter Mario Andretti (5) in the JPS Lotus at the start of the 1977 grand prix. The two would later collide, putting Hunt out on the spot. Niki Lauda (11) won the race and tightened his grip on the World Championship.

Left Packed grandstands for the start of the 2023 Dutch Grand Prix. Max Verstappen leads, but the order is about to be turned on its head by a sudden rain shower, rewarding those who gambled and stopped for wet tyres early.

S.C.H. 'Sammy' Davis to create the circuit, with John Hugenholtz appointed as circuit director.

In 1949 the fledgling circuit organized their first *Grote Prijs van Nederland,* and in 1952 the Dutch Grand Prix became the penultimate round of the F1 World Championship. It was won by Alberto Ascari, as were all the races in 1952, and was one of his nine consecutive wins, a record equalled in 2023 by Max Verstappen at Zandvoort.

Further F1 grands prix were run in 1955 and 1958 after which it became a regular fixture on the F1 calendar until 1985. It was a challenging circuit, liked by the drivers for the fast-but-twisty nature of the course snaking through sand dunes, which gave spectators perfect vantage points, unlike many of the flat, airfield sites. And for overtaking there was always the long start/finish *paradesstrasse.*

But as speeds ramped up in the late 1960s and early 1970s, so cars fell victim to the failings of both the circuit and marshalling. Piers Courage, heir to the brewing dynasty, was driving a mid-grid De Tomaso in the 1970 race when the front suspension broke on the bump at the Tunnel Oost kink. The car went straight on, up an embankment which dislodged the engine from the monocoque it was bolted onto and the car burst into flames. The overweight De Tomaso had been fitted with magnesium chassis elements which burnt fiercely (as they had with Jo Schlesser's Honda at Rouen), though it was assumed the driver was had been killed from a wheel which had come loose, impacting Courage's helmet.

Given this warning of the intensity of F1 fires, it was inexcusable when British F1 driver Roger Williamson crashed in virtually the same spot in 1973. The track marshals were poorly equipped and failed to act when his car flipped over on track, the driver conscious but trapped in his cockpit as it burst into flames. It was left to fellow driver David Purley to seize a fire extinguisher from a marshal and try and douse the flames. Despite his urging the marshals to help, without flame retardant overalls, as worn by the drivers, they were hesitant to approach the blazing car. All the while, the race continued, the horrifying accident covered live on television. Purley could not turn the car over on his own, but by the time the circuit fire engine had arrived, Williamson was dead from asphyxiation.

Changes had to be made. The Tunnel Oost kink was slowed by making the following Bos corner into an esses, the Panoramabocht, which also provided a good overtaking spot. But as the 1970s rolled into the 1980s, the alterations needed to slow it down, the safety requirements and less-than-expected race attendance put the Dutch Grand Prix under financial strain. There was no home star to bank the race. Huub Rothengatter made his F1 debut in 1984 with the back-of-the-grid Spirit team, and Jos Verstappen was still racing karts. Raymond Vermeulen, Max Verstappen's manager, puts the modern-day success of the race down to one thing: "The Dutch as a nation only become fully engaged when there's success."

The circuit was owned by the local authorities who could not afford to keep running the race at a loss and so they agreed

CIRCUIT ZANDVOORT

Length: 4.259 km (2.646 miles)
Lap Record: 1:11.097 (Lewis Hamilton, Mercedes W12, 2021)
Opened: 1948
First F1 Grand Prix: 1952
Number of F1 Grands Prix hosted: 34
Number of laps: 72
Designer: Sammy Davis, John Hugenholtz
Redesign: Hermann Tilke (1999 and 2020)
Race winning fact: Lando Norris broke Max Verstappen's 3-year winning streak in 2024 when he recovered from a poor start to take a dominant win for McLaren

Zandvoort has been modified many times over the years, with an F1 lap record holder for each iteration of the circuit. The Dutch track has some prominent names for each layout: Jacky Ickx in a Ferrari 312B, 1948-1971; Gilles Villeneuve in a Ferrari 312T4, 1972-1979; Alain Prost in a McLaren MP4/2B, 1980-1989; Lewis Hamilton in a Mercedes W12, 2020-Present. And as for saloon cars from 1948-1971, that would be Helmut Marko in a Ford Capri RS 2600.

to a plan that would shorten the circuit considerably, selling off some of the land to be used as a golf course and holiday resort. With typical Dutch financial propriety, this measure drastically reduced the circuit length, but was intended as a temporary measure until the budget allowed expansion into the land they had retained for a larger track.

By 1999 they had resurrected a new, challenging Zandvoort through the dunes with a compact layout that was even twistier than the old. The first turn, the 180-degree Tarzanbocht, was still there as was the Hugenholtzbocht at Turn 3. There were still concerns over noise levels and limits to the number of days the circuit could be used, and the classic F3 Masters race (won by both Jos and Max Verstappen) had to be run at Zolder for a

Left A side view of the first corner at Zandvoort, 'Tarzan'. This is the first race that Ferrari had run their second car after Gilles Villeneuve's death at Zolder in 1982. They had entered a single car for Monaco, Detroit and Canada. Gilles' great friend, Patrick Tambay is substituting in the no.27 car.

Below The runoff at Tarzan has been lengthened considerably since Zandvoort disappeared off the calendar in 1985. In addition, the pit lane now wraps round the bend rather than feeding out into the braking zone.

Opposite The Tom Wheatcroft-entered March of Roger Willamson in front of Carlos Reutemann's Brabham in the 1973 Dutch Grand Prix. Tragedy would unfold on Lap 7.

couple of years before returning to its true home. A switch to a new track at Julianadorp proved to be a non-starter.

With the rise of Max Verstappen from his F1 debut with Toro Rosso in 2015, and Red Bull from 2016, organizers started to mull the possibility of a reinstated F1 Dutch Grand Prix. Such was the strength of Verstappen's 'Oranj Army' that whole grandstands at Austria's Red Bull Ring would be filled with Max supporters, yet there was no home race.

To bring Zandvoort into line with F1 speeds and obtain an FIA Grade 1 certificate a variety of improvements were made at key corners, including banking some of the turns. The final turn, named for Dutch Indianapolis winner Arie Luyendyk, was widened and banked for a slingshot onto the main straight.

Other banked turns have provided fantastic racing in F1 events where drivers can take the low line or the outside karting line. Fernando Alonso has made overtaking moves using both in the grands prix that have taken place since 2021.

The initial Dutch Grand Prix on the new track in 2020 was cancelled because of Covid, but a full house of expectant Verstappen fans were on hand to witness his victory in the 2021, 2022 and 2023 races, along what has now become a Max Verstappen *paradestrasse*.

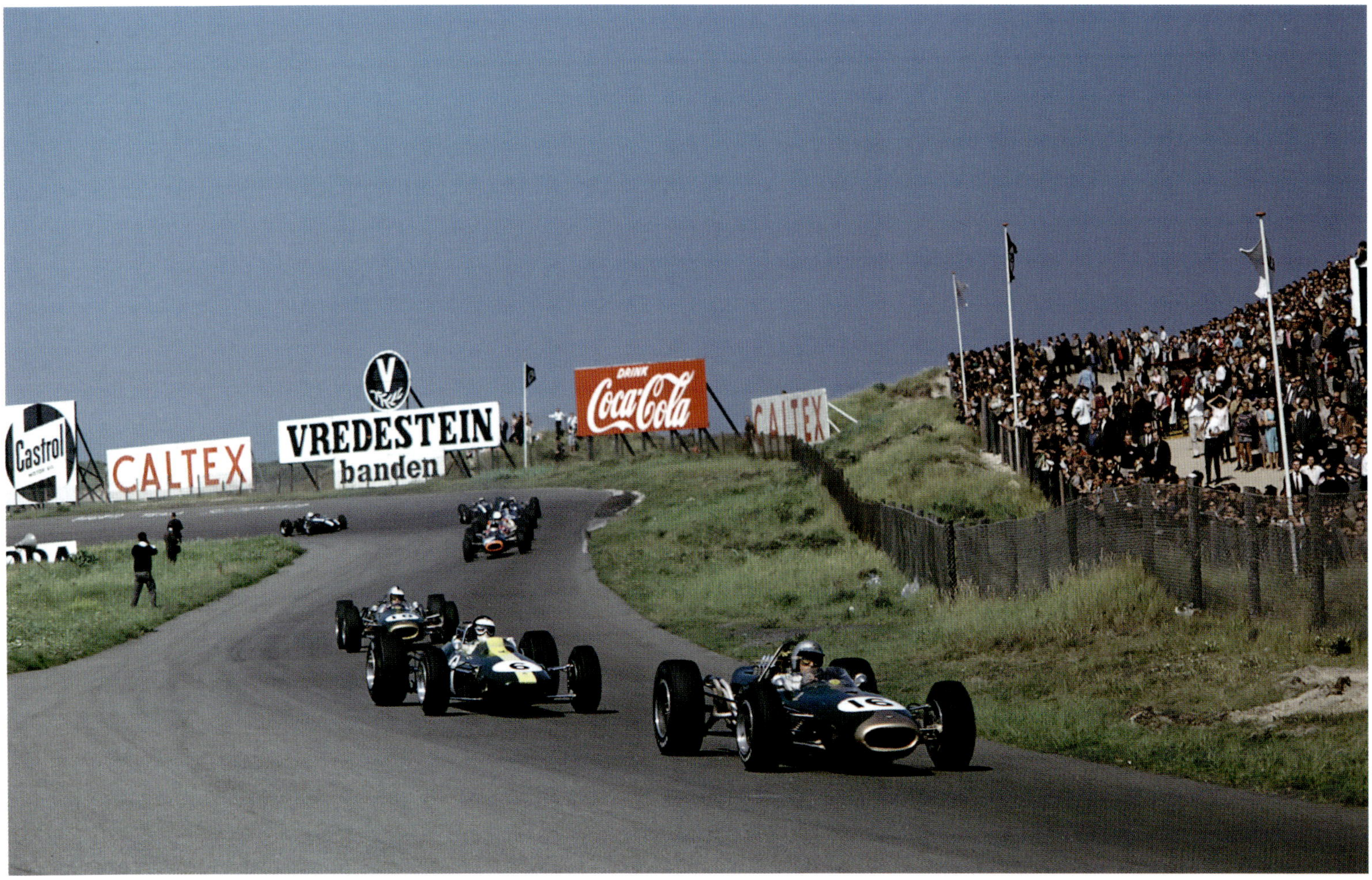
Castrol
CALTEX
VREDESTEIN
banden
DRINK
Coca-Cola
CALTEX

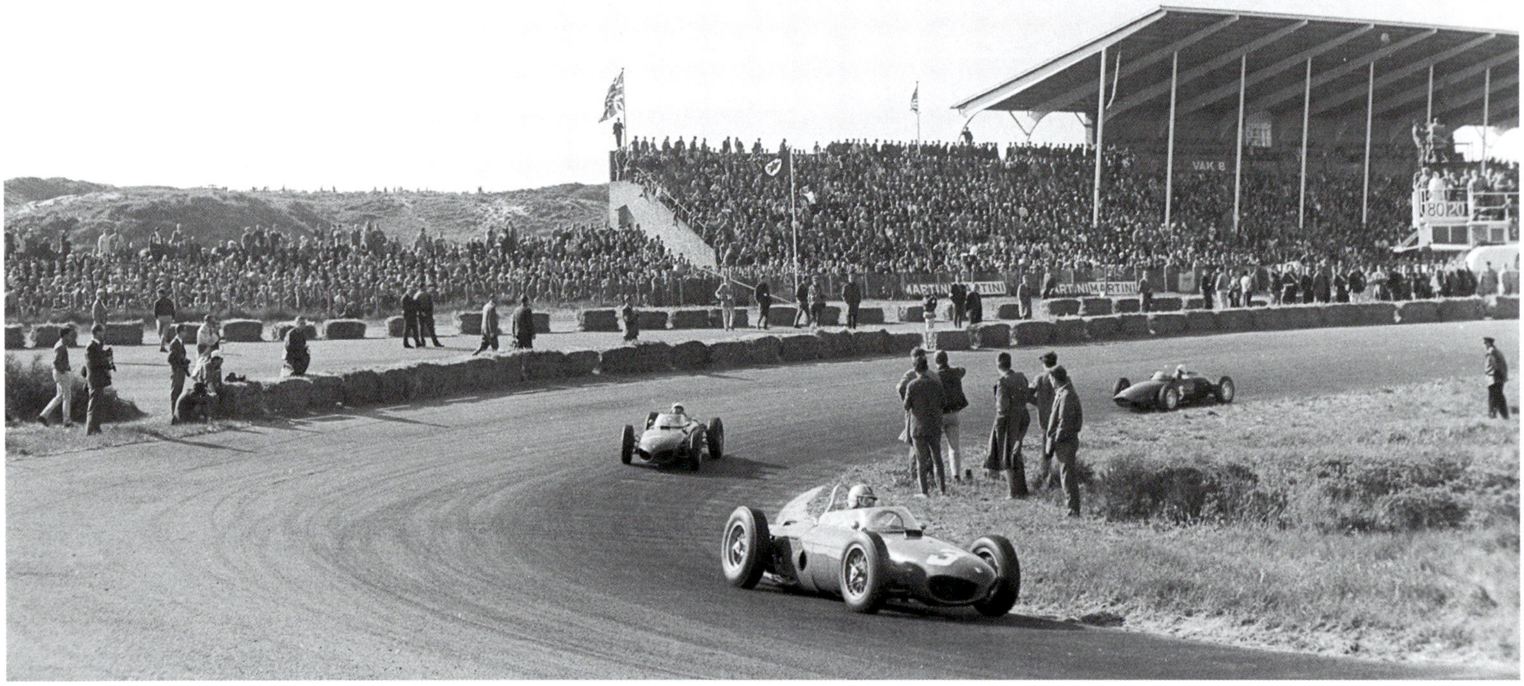

Opposite top **Jack Brabham (16) ahead of Jim Clark (6) and trailed by Denny Hulme, weave through Gerlachbocht at the start of the 1966 Dutch Grand Prix.**

Above **Max Verstappen leads Lando Norris (4) and George Russell (63) through Gerlachbocht in 2023. After a stellar qualifying performance Alex Albon (23) in the Williams maintains his fourth place.**

Opposite bottom **Wolfgang von Trips leads fellow Ferrari 156 'Sharknose' driver Phil Hill through the Hugenholtz corner in 1961.**

Left **To solve the problem of limited run-off, the circuit has banked some of the Zandvoort corners allowing cars to take completely different lines – a perfect overtaking opportunity which Fernando Alonso seizes (100 metres beyond the top photo) at the start of the 2023 race.**

Index

Numbers in italics refer to picture captions

A
A1-Ring 8
Adamich, Andrea de 203
Adenauer, Konrad 158
Agostini, Giacomo 44
Aida 96
Aintree 10–15, *11*, 203
Albon, Alex 89, *175*, *237*
Alboreto, Michele *78*, 99, 100, 153, *155*
Alesi, Giuliano 219
Alesi, Jean *77*, 174, 219
Alfa Romeo 60, 68, *70*, 122, 126, 132, 134, 146, 149, *159*, 160, 161, *181*, *182*, 185, 186, 202, *227*
Allen, James 219
Alonso, Fernando *8*, *9*, *27*, 94, 128, *129*, *204*, *217*, 235, *237*
Alphen, Henri van 232
Alpine *121*, *155*
Amersfoot, Fritz van 157
Amon, Chris *43*, *45*, 46, *47*, *129*, *147*
Anderstorp Raceway 16–19, 177
Andretti, Mario 21, 22, 52, 96, *103*, 104, 137, *176*, 223, *227*, *231*, *233*
Angelis, Elio de 178
Arnoux, René *51*, 52, *68*, *72*, *103*, 126, 174
Arrivabene, Mauricio 148
Arrows 129
Asberg, Sven 'Smoky' *17*, 19
Ascari, Alberto *8*, 72, 124, 125, *130*, *145*, 149, 151, 155, 161–2, *161*, 174, *175*, 187, 194, 233
Aston Martin *8*, *9*, 63, *94*, *204*
ATS 68
Auchatraire, Jean 42, 44
Audetto, Daniele 165
Auto Union 35, 55, *55*, *57*, 58, 122, 160, 161, *185*
Autocar 232–3
Autopolis 56
Autosport 223
Avus 28–35, *190*

B
Bahrain 198
Bailey, Julian 40
Baku 104
Balestre, Jean-Marie 98, 100, *100*
Bandini, Lorenzo *45*, 125, *127*, 130, *182*, 185, *187*, *191*, *229*
BAR *143*
Barrichello, Rubens 77, 82, 84, 171
Behra, Jean *11*, *34*, 35, *173*, 174, *185*, *190*, *195*, *197*, 212
Bell, Derek 55
Bellof, Stefan 126
Beltoise, Jean-Pierre 48, *51*, 52, *110*, 126, *175*, 177
Benetton *76*, 79, 217, *221*, *222*, 223
Bennett, Gordon 42
Benoist, Robert 123
Benson, Andrew 102
Berger, Gerhard 77, 111, 153
Bernoldi, Enrique 129
Bianchi, Jules 225
Bira, Prince 55
Birrel, Gerry 196–8
BMW 68
Bondurant, Bob 213
Bonnier, Jo 17, *31*, 130, *227*
Bottas, Valtteri 65, *117*
Bousquet, Annie 188, *188*, 192
Brabham *17*, 18, *19*, *39*, 53, 68, *68*, 74, 89, 98, *103*, 126, 137, *141*, 178, *187*, *191*, *192*, *197*, 207, *231*, 235, *237*
Brabham, Jack 12, *39*, 47, *47*, 94, 125, 130, 134, *185*, *187*, *191*, 192, *193*
Brambilla, Vittorio *17*, *53*, 137, *137*, 168, *169*
Brands Hatch 10, 15, 36–41, 56, 58, 203
Brasier, Henri 42
Brauchitsch, Manfred von 35, 54–5, *55*, *114*, 123, 161, *187*
Brise, Tony 135
Bristow, Chris *190*, 212
Brito, Jayme 58
BRM 12, *31*, 38, 62, 92, *92*, 108, *118*, 126, *130*, 150, *151*, *193*, 213, *227*
Brooklands 54
Brooks, Tony 12, *13*, 15, *31*, *34*, 112, *117*, *182*, *191*, *193*, *204*, 212
Brown, David 76
Brundle, Martin *145*, 170
Bugatti *114*, 122, *122*, 146, 160
Burti, Luciano 69
Button, Jenson *25*, *27*, 40, 83, 171, 208

C
Caesars Palace 96–101
Cahler, Bernard *190*
Campari, Giuseppe 181
Caracciola, Rudolph 29–30, *31*, 35, *114*, 122, 123, *173*, 181, *185*, *187*
Carlin 174
Castellotti, Eugenio 148
Cesaris, Andrea de 126, 217
Cevert, François 48, *51*, 52, *151*, 174, *175*, 228, *231*
Chambelland, François 48, 50
Chapman, Colin *85*, *137*, 199, 227
Cheever, Eddie 96, 170
Chevron 196, 198
Chilton, Max *121*
Chinetti, Luigi 107
Chiron, Louis 122, 123, 124, 127
Christ, Ernst 64
Circuit of the Americas 20–27, 206
Clark, Jim 12, 38, *45*, 46, 62, *63*, 66, *66*, 71, 74, 81, *81*, 90, 92, *106*, 108, *109*, *123*, 134, 150, *153*, *159*, *163*, 165, 174, *227*, *227*, *237*
Clermont-Ferrand 42–7, 48, 50, 177
Codognato, Plinio *147*
Collins, Peter 125, 162, 164, 196, *197*, 198
Comas, Érik 71
Cooper 12, 36, 44, *106*, *123*, 124–5, 150, 185, *191*, 212
Cooper, Adam 223
Cosworth 175
Coulthard, David 22, *25*, 129, *163*, 203, *217*, 219
Courage, Piers 7, *8*, *41*, 64, *175*, 233
Craner, Fred 54
Creutz, Dr Otto 158
Cunningham, Briggs 226
Czaykowski, Count Stanislas 146

D
Daimler 160
Daly, Derek 40, 126
Davidson, Anthony 40
Davis Jr, Sammy 99
Davis, S.C.H. 'Sammy' 233
De Tomaso 233
Degner, Ernst 221
Delage 122
Dennis, Ron 222
Depailler, Patrick *17*, 18, 52, 68, *70*, 94, *103*, *105*, 137, 174
Dijon-Prenois 40, 48–53, 177
Dixon, Scott *231*
Domenicali, Stefano 172, 174, 219
Donington Park 54–9, 208
Donnelly, Martin 76
Donohue, Mark *133*, 168–70, 227
Doodson, Mike 98
Drive to Survive 25

E
Eagle 39, *227*
Ecclestone, Bernie 18, *19*, 22, 56, 71, 82, 83, 96, 102, 105, *153*, 165, 171, 178–9, 201, 206–8, 230
Edwards, Guy 165
Epstein, Bobby 22, 26
ERA 32, 58, 160
Ertl, Harold 165
Èrundina, Luiza 85
Evening Standard 212

F
Fagioli, Luigi 35, *114*, 123, 124, 134, 181, 182, 185
Fangio, Juan Manuel 7, 8, 10, *11*, 12, 22, 35, *43*, 47, 84, *121*, 123, 124, *148*, 149, 162, *163*, *174*, 182, *182*, 185, *185*, *187*, *192*, 194–6, *195*, *197*, *204*, 212, *215*
Farina, Giuseppe
Farina, Giuseppe (Nino) 54, 60, *121*, 123, 149, *173*, *185*, 194, 202, *203*, 212, *217*
Farman, Maurice 6
Ferrari 7, 12, *14*, 15, *14*, *17*, 25, *31*, *34*, 35, 38, *39*, *41*, 45, 47, 49, 52, 68, 72, 74, 77, *78*, 82, 92, 93, 94, *94*, 104, 107, 111, *112*, *117*, 118, 126, *127*, 129, 130, 131, *133*, 134, 137, 138, *139*, *145*, 148, 149, 150, 153, *153*, 155, *155*, 156–7, 161–2, *161*, 165, *165*, *167*, 168, *170*, 171, *171*, 178, 182, *187*, *187*, 188, *191*, *195*, 206, *210*, *217*, *218*, 219, *227*, 229, 230, *237*
Ferrari, 'Alfredino' 72
Ferrari, Enzo 72, 130, 131, 153, 160, 161, 180, 181, *181*
Ferrari, Laura *14*
Fisher, Carl G. 80
Fitch, John 226
Fittipaldi, Emerson 84, 85, *105*, *136*, 227, 230, *231*
Florio, Vincenzo 146
Follmer, George 136
Force India 225
Foresti, Giulio 144
Forghieri, Mauro *139*
Frankenberg, Richard von 35
Frankenheimer, John 18, 46, 125, 130–31, *130*, *147*, 150, 212
Frentzen, Heinz-Harald 77
Fujisawa, Takeo 220

G
Gachot, Bertrand 217
Ganley, Howden *151*
Garner, James 46, 130, *130*, *147*
Gasly, Pierre *155*, 225
Gaze, Tony 60
Gendebien, Olivier *218*
George, Tony 81, 83
Gethin, Peter 150–51, *151*, 174
Gilbert, Mitch *173*
Ginther, Richie 12, 130, *218*
Giocometti, Bruno *103*
Glock, Timo 88
González, Froilán 84, 187, *193*, *204*
Goodwood 9, 60–63
Gordini 175
Grand Prix 18, 46, 125, 130–31, *130*, *147*, 150, 212–3
Gregory, Masten *193*
Gresini, Fausto *78*
Griffith 63
Grosjean, Romain *41*, *71*, 87, 198, *217*
Grover-Williams, William *114*, 122, \\123
Gugelmin, Mauricio *178*
Gurney, Dan 7, *34*, *39*, 130, *130*, 198, *227*
Gutiérrez, Esteban 111

H
Haas *71*
Hailwood, Mike 44, *151*
Häkkinen, Mika 206, 217–9, 223
Hall, Jim *213*
Hamilton, Lewis 25, 26, *27*, 65, *87*, 88, 128, 152, 208
Hammel, Georges 122, *124*
Hanses, Julian 174
Hardy, Françoise 46
Hartley, Steve *41*
Hasse, Rudolph 58
Hawkins, Paul 125, *130*
Hawthorn, Mike 125, *161*, 162, *173*, *175*, 187–8, 196
Head, Patrick *231*
Heidfeld, Nick 83
Hellmund, Tavo 20, 22
Herbert, Johnny 40, 165
Hesketh 137
Hill 137
Hill, Damon *55*, *76*, *77*, 143, 223
Hill, Graham 7, 38, 46, 61–2, *81*, *106*, *118*, *123*, 126, 130, 134, 135, *136*, *164*, 165, 199, 213, 227, *227*
Hill, Phil 12, *14*, 15, *34*, *39*, 107, 130, *130*, 131, 150, *191*, *193*, 218, *237*
Hockenheimring *23*, 64–71, *75*, 165
Honda 171, 196, 220, 221
Honda, Soichiro 220, 221
Hopkins, Ted *229*
Horner, Christian 208
Howard, Ron 165
Howe, Earl 58
Hubert, Antoine 219
Hugenholtz, John 8, 64, 90, 220–21, 233
Hulme, Denny 18, *43*, 46, *91*, *187*, 202, *237*
Hungaroring 171
Hunt, James 19, *37*, 52, *105*, 137, 152, 153, *167*, *176*, 207, 233

I
Ickx, Jacky 7, *66*, 92–4, *93*, *110*, 126, *164*, *167*, 196
Imola 72–9
Indianapolis 20, 35, 80–83
Interlagos 84–9
Ireland, Innes 227, *227*
Irvine, Eddie 40, 203, 206, *217*, 223

J
Jabouille, Jean-Pierre 52, *72*
Jacarepaguá 85
Jarama 90–95, 220
Jarier, Jean-Pierre *17*, 52, 85, *87*, *103*, 139
Jenkinson, Denis 164–5, 216, *231*
Jones, Alan 98–100, *103*, *105*, *141*, *167*, 168, 230, *231*
Jordan 77, 217

K
Klien, Christian 83
Kling, Karl *11*, 35

L

Laffite, Jacques 38–40, 52, *94*
Lammers, Jan *103*
Lamy, Pedro 79
Lancia 124
Lang, Hermann 35, 55, *55*
Lauda, Niki *8*, 18, *49*, 52, 66, 74, *94*, 104–5, *105*, 137, *141*, 152–3, *164*, 165, *165*, *167*, 168, *233*
Lawson, Liam 174
Le Mans 6, 12, 146
Leclerc, Charles *25*, 26, *78*, *96*, *129*, *139*, 155, *155*, *170*, 171, *178*, *217*
Lehto, JJ 79
Levegh, Henri 42–4
Lewis-Evans, Stewart *153*, 155, *181*, *182*, 185
Liberty Media 25, 53, 71, *96*, *129*, 165, 179, *218*
Ligier *71*, *94*
Ligier, Guy 48–50, 192
Lombardi, Lella 137
Long Beach *96*, 102–5
Lotus 12, 18, *19*, 21, 22, 38, *41*, 46, 50, 52, 61, 66, *66*, 76, 81, *81*, 84, 85, *103*, 104, *106*, 107, *109*, *123*, 135, *136*, 136, *137*, *139*, 150, *151*, *153*, *163*, 166, *175*, 199, 212, *221*, *221*, 227, *227*, 228, *233*
Louis II, Prince 112, 115, 123
Lunger, Brett 165
Luyendyk, Arie 235

M

Magnussen, Jan 40
Magnussen, Kevin *71*, *89*
Magny-Cours 25, 50, 53, 177
Mairesse, Willy 212
Maldonado, Pastor *41*, *121*
Mansell, Nigel *37*, 40, *77*, 111, 126, *129*, 170, *170*, *178*, 203, 206, *207*, 208, *221*, 222
March *17*, 18, *91*, 150, *151*, 168, *178*
March, Earl of 10, 62
Marimon, Onofre *204*
Marko, Helmut 9, *43*, 47, 153, 157
Martin, Charles *32*
Marussia 225
Maserati *11*, *32*, 55, *121*, 122, *124*, 124, 146, 149, *155*, 160, 162, *163*, *182*, 185, *185*, 187, *191*, *195*, 196, 201, *210*
Mass, Jochen *49*, 137
Massa, Felipe *27*, 84, 87–8
Materassi, Emilio 144
Mateschitz, Dieter 171
Matra *43*, 45, 47, 165
Mays Raymond *58*
McCombs, Red 20, 22
McLaren 18, *25*, *37*, *41*, *43*, 52, 62, 83, 85, *87*, *91*, 92, *94*, 100, 104, 111, *117*, *129*, *141*, *141*, 152, *152*, 153, 155, *167*, *170*, *176*, 202, 203, 217, *217*, 219, 222, 223, *233*
McLaren, Bruce 62, *91*, *106*, *123*, 130
McNish, Alan 225
Mercedes *11*, 12, *25*, 27, 29–30, *31*, 35, 42, 44, 54, 55, *55*, 64, 65, 71, *114*, 122, 123, 128, 134, *148*, 152, 157, 160, 161, *173*, *185*, 192, 212, 217
Merz, Otto 160
Merzario, Arturo 136, 165
Mexico City 106–111, *157*
Milliken, Bill 226
Minardi 153, 155
Mitterand, François 50, 178
Monaco 6, 7, 8, *8*, 112–31, *151*, 201, 217
Monger, Billy 174
Montand, Yves 46, 125, 130, *130*
Montezemolo, Luca di *165*
Montjuïc Park 92, 132–7
Montlhéry 80, 83, 186
Montoya, Juan Pablo 83, 174
Montréal 20, 138–41
Monza 6, 7, 19, 35, 124, 144–55, 168, 201
Moreno, Roberto 40
Mosley, Max 56, 83, *137*, 168, 206–8
Moss, Stirling 8, 10. *11*, 12, 15, 36, 44–6, 47, 61–2, *61*, 124, 125, 149, *153*, 155, 158, 180, 185, *185*, *193*, 210, 212, *231*
Motor Sport 194
Müller, Herbert 156
Murray, Gordon 18, *53*
Musso, Luigi 182, 185, 188, *195*, 196, 197
My Twenty Years of Racing 162–4, 185

N

Nannini, Alessandro 223
NART 107
Neileman, Jac 19
Neubauer, Alfred *11*, 12, 65, 192
Nilsson, Gunnar 19, 52, *103*
Noghés, Antony 115, 125
Norisring 9, 108, 156–7
Norris, Lando *25*, *89*, *117*, *141*, 155, *237*
Nürburgring 6, 7, 30, 56, 64–6, *66*, 152, 158–65, 168, 181, 212
Nuvolari, Tazio 55, *57*, 122, 124, 132, 134, *159*, 160–61, 162, 181, 185, 186

O

Ocon, Esteban 9, *121*, 157, *173*
Öfner, Karl Heinz 68
Oliver, Jackie 92–4, *93*
Osella 140
Österreichring 8, see also A-Ring, Red Bull Ring

P

Pace, Carlos *17*, 85, *89*, 137
Paletti, Ricardo 140
Palmer, Jolyon *41*
Palmer, Jonathan 40, 58
Panis, Olivier 219
Parkes, Mike 130
Parnelli *231*
Patrese, Riccardo 19, *105*, 126, 153, 170
Pau 172–5
Paul Ricard 50, *51*, 52, 53, 176–9
Pedralbes 90, 134
Penske *133*, 168
Penske, Roger *109*
Pérez, Sergio *100*, 111, *111*, 225
Pescara 180–85
Pescarolo, Henri *47*, 52, 177
Peterson, Barbro 85
Peterson, Ronnie 8, 18, 19, *19*, 50, 84–5, *85*, 137, 150, *151*, 153, *176*, 228
Phillips, Ian 208
Piastri, Oscar 79, 155
Piquet Jr, Nelson 172–4
Piquet, Nelson *37*, 40, *53*, 68, *68*, 71, 77, 85, 98, *103*, 203, *221*, *221*, 222
Pironi, Didier *41*, 52, *75*, 99, 100, 126, 138–40
Plëch, Anton 30
Pook, Chris 96, 98, 102, 105
Porsche 30, 35, *34*, 107, *143*, 188, *188*, *198*, 227
Porsche, Ferdinand 30
Portago, Alfonso de *14*, 181
Prost 69
Prost, Alain 52, *55*, 58, 65, 68, 126, 153, 169, *170*, *221*, 222, 223
Purley, David 233

R

Räikkönen, Kimi *27*, *81*, 83, 87, 143, *148*, 219, *227*
Rainier II, Prince *118*, 124
Ratzenberger, Roland 40, 77, 79, 140
Read, Phil 44
Red Bull 7, 20, *27*, *23*, *25*, 47, *100*, 129, 152, *153*, *163*, 171, *221*
Red Bull Ring 166–71, 235

Regazzoni, Clay *8*, 66, 104, 110, *133*, 137, *165*, *167*, 230
Reims-Gueux 7, *7*, 9, 48, 150, *161*, 186–93
Remarkable Motor Races 102
Renault *51*, 52, 65, 68, *72*, 126, 169, 172
Reutemann, Carlos 17, *72*, 98, *167*, *231*, 235
Ricard, Paul 177
Ricciardo, Daniel 7, *27*, 129
Richard-Brasier 42
Richard, Georges 42
Richmond, Duke of 60, 62, *63*
Rindt, Jochen 66, 130, 135, *136*, 150, *151*, 155, 166–8, 174, *175*, 197, 227
Rindt, Nina 151
Rodríguez, Pedro 9, 92, 107, 108, 156–7, *157*
Rodríguez, Pedro Natalio 107
Rodríguez, Ricardo 107, 108, *109*
Roebuck, Nigel 7
Rosberg, Keke 40, 100, 128, 206, *207*
Rosberg, Nico 25, 128
Rosemeyer, Bernd 35, 55, *55*, 123, 181
Rosenberger, Adolf 30
Rosier, Louis 42, *43*, 44, *173*, 182, 185
Rothengatter, Huub 233
Rouen-les-Essarts 7, *8*, 48, 177, 186, 194–9, 222, 233
Rush 165, \
Russell, George *237*

S

Saint, Eva Marie 125
Sainz, Carlos *139*, *152*, *153*, 155, *170*, *178*, *210*, 225
Salazar, Eliseo 68, *71*
Salvadori, Roy 15, *195*
Salzer, Eugen 30
Sauber 83, 111, *217*
Saward, Joe 88, 144
Scarlatti, Giorgio *182*, 185
Scheckter, Jody 18, *103*, 104, 138, 202–3
Schell, Harry *173*, *175*, *204*
Schlesser, Jean-Louis 152, *152*
Schlesser, Jo 7, 130, 192, 196, *197*, 222, 233
Schumacher, Michael *25*, 30, 56, *57*, 68, *76*, 77, 82, 87, 128, 143, 165, 171, 178, 206, 217–9, 223
Schumacher, Ralf 83
Schwantz, Kevin 20
Seaman, Richard 55, *55*, 212
Sefton, Lord *13*
Senna, Ayrton 56, *57*, *58*, *76*, *77*, 79, *79*, 84, 86, *87*, *117*, 126, 129, 140, 152, *152*, 153, 169, 206, *207*, *221*, 222–3
Servoz-Gervin, Johnny *129*
Shadow Ford 85, *87*, 136, *167*, 168
Shelby, Carroll 130
Shields, John Gillies 54
Siffert, Jo 38, *41*, *151*, 199
Silverstone 6, 9, 10, 38, 56, 58, 200–209
Simtek 77
Sinatra, Frank 99
Small, Steve 85
Spa-Francorchamps 6, *114*, 150, 194, 196, *197*, 201, 210–19
Spence, Mike *163*
Stacey, Alan 212
Stewart, Jackie *43*, *47*, 46, *61*, 62, 64–6, *81*, 85, *91*, *93*, 108, *110*, 125, *129*, 134, *136*, 158, 164–5, *164*, 174, *178*, 213, 216, 227, 228, *231*
Stewart, Paul 165
Stommelen, Rolf 92, 137, *137*
Stuck, Hans Joachim *105*, 161
Surtees *49*, *53*, *151*
Surtees, Henry 38
Surtees, John 38, 44, *49*, 53, *118*, *129*
Sutil, Adrian 225
Suzuka 220–25
Suzuki 220, *221*
Suzuki, Aguri 77
Szisz, Ferenc 6, 172

T

Talbot *32*, *43*, 185
Tambay, Patrick 52, *68*, *72*, *170*, 235
Taruffi, Piero *148*, 194
Taylor, Trevor 108, *109*, 227
Théry, Léon 42
Tilke, Hermann 8, 20, 22, 23, 25, 58, 66, 71, 111, *163*, 171
Todt, Jean *165*
Toleman *41*, 126
Tomaini, Antonio 139
Topham, Mirabel 139
Toro Rosso 153, 155, 157, 171, *173*, 235
Toyota 225
Trintignant, Maurice 44, 125, *173*, 174
Trips, Wolfgang von 12, *14*, 107, 150, *153*, *218*, *237*
Tsunoda, Yuki 174, 225
Tyrrell 17, 18, *43*, *94*, 100, *103*, 126, 136, *151*, *178*, 198, 216, 228, *231*
Tyrrell, Ken 228

V

Vandervell, Tony *13*, *181*, *195*
Vanwall 12, *13*, *153*, *181*, *182*, 185, *195*, *204*
Varzi, Achille *114*, 122, 134, 181
Vasseur, Fred 155
Vermeulen, Raymond 233
Verstappen, Jos 233, 234
Verstappen, Max *8*, 9, 26, *27*, 79, *87*, 88, *96*, 100, *100*, *117*, 129, 152, *153*, 155, *155*, 157, *167*, 171, *173*, 174, *178*, 208, *221*, *223*, *225*, *225*, 232, *233*, *233*, 234, 235, *237*
Vettel, Sebastian 23, *27*, 71, 129, *148*, 153, 155, *163*, 165, 171
Villeneuve, Gilles *51*, 52, *72*, 74, *75*, *94*, *94*, *94*, *96*, 99, 138, *139*, 140, *237*
Villeneuve, Jacques 143, *143*
Villoresi, Luigi 72, 201, *210*

W

Wacker Jr, Fred 226
Warwick, Derek *41*
Watkins Glen 81, 96, 108, 226–31
Watkins, Sid 76, 77
Watson John *94*, 100, 102, 104–5, *105*, 168, *207*
Webb, John 38
Webber, Mark 40, 83, *209*
Weidenbrück, Hans 159
Wendlinger, Karl *57*
Werner, Christian 160
Wheatcroft, Tom 54, 55, 56, 58, *235*
Whiting, Charlie 225
Williams *37*, *55*, *72*, *76*, 77, 87–8, 98, *100*, *103*, 126, 129, 136, *141*, 152, *152*, 170, *170*, *207*, *221*, 222, 230
Williams, Frank 230, *231*
Williams, Richard *181*
Williamson, Roger 55, 196, *231*, 233, *235*
Wimille, Jean-Pierre 123
Wolf 138
Wolf, Toto 88

Y

Yeongam 96

Z

Zakspeed 170
Zandvoort 8–9, 64, 196, *231*, 232–7
Zeltweg 166
Zolder 138
Zonta, Ricardo 219

Picture Credits

Alamy: Pages 23 (bottom), 33, 36, 37 (top), 39 (bottom), 41 (top), 41 (bottom right), 49 (top), 53 (top), 57 (top right), 57 (bottom), 61 (top), 69 (bottom), 72 (bottom), 88 (top), 103 (bottom), 118, 119 (bottom), 121 (bottom), 156, 157 (top), 159 (top), 174 (top), 175 (top), 177, 201, 224 (bottom), 225 (top)

AudiSport: Page 55 (bottom)

Dreamstime: Page 29

FFSA: Page 43 (bottom)

Frank Hopkinson: Pages 7, 9 (left), 133 (top), 133 (bottom right), 135 (bottom), 136 (bottom), 137 (bottom), 189 (bottom right), 190 bottom, 191 (top right) 192 (bottom), 193 (centre), 193 (bottom right), 195 (top), 197 (bottom right), 198 (centre)

Getty Images: Pages 4, 6, 10, 11, 13 (top), 14, 15, 20, 21, 23 (top), 24, 26 (top), 26 (left), 28, 31 (top right), 32, 34, 37 (bottom), 39 (top), 43 (top), 45, 46, 47 (top), 48, 54, 55 (top), 57 (top left), 58 (top), 59, 60, 61 (bottom left), 63 (top), 65 (top), 67 (centre left), 67 (bottom), 68, 69 (top), 70 (centre), 72 (top), 73, 75 (centre), 75 (bottom), 77 (top), 78 (bottom), 79, 80, 81 (bottom), 83 (bottom), 84, 85 (top), 87, 88 (bottom), 89 (top), 91 (bottom), 95, 97, 99 (top right), 101, 102, 103 (top left), 103 (top right), 105 (bottom), 106 (bottom), 109 (top left), 109 (top right), 110, 111 (top), 112, 113, 114, 115, 116, 117, 119 (top), 120, 121 (top), 123, 125, 128 (bottom), 129 (bottom), 130 (top), 131 (bottom), 136 (top), 137 (top), 139 (top), 139 (bottom left), 141, 142, 143 (bottom), 145 (top), 147 (top left), 151 (top), 152 (bottom), 153, 154 (bottom left), 154 (bottom right), 157 (bottom), 159 (bottom), 161, 162, 164 (bottom), 166, 167, 170 (bottom), 171, 172, 173, 174 (bottom), 175 (bottom), 176, 179 (top), 183 (bottom left), 184 (bottom), 186, 187 (bottom), 189 (top), 189 (bottom left), 190 (top), 191 (top left), 191 (bottom), 192 (top), 193 (top), 193 (bottom left), 197 (top), 197 (bottom right), 198 (top), 198 (bottom), 199, 200, 203, 204, 205, 207, 209, 209, 210, 211, 213 (top), 214 (bottom), 215 (bottom), 216 (top left), 216 (bottom), 217, 218 (bottom), 220, 221 (top), 223 (top), 224 (top), 225 (centre left), 226, 227 (top), 230 (top), 231 (top), 233, 236, 237 (top)

Grand Prix Photo.com: Pages 2, 8, 9 (right), 16, 19, 25, 26 (right), 27, 31 (bottom), 35, 40, 41 (bottom left), 42, 47 (bottom), 49 (bottom), 51, 52, 53 (bottom), 57 (top right), 58 (bottom), 64, 65 (bottom), 67 (top left), 70 (top), 71, 75 (top), 76, 77 (bottom), 78 (top), 81 (top), 83 (top), 85 (bottom), 89 (bottom), 90, 91 (top), 93, 94, 96, 99 (top left), 99 (bottom), 100, 103 (top), 106 (top), 107, 109 (bottom), 111 (bottom), 122, 126, 127, 128 (top), 129 (top), 130 (bottom), 131 (top), 132, 133 (bottom left), 135 (top), 139 (bottom right), 143 (top), 144, 145 (bottom), 147 (bottom), 148 (top), 149, 151 (bottom), 152 (top), 154 (top), 155, 158, 163 (top), 164 (top), 164 (centre), 165, 169 (top left), 169 (top right), 169 (bottom), 170 (top), 170 (centre), 178, 179 (bottom left), 179 (bottom right), 180, 183 (top), 183 (bottom right), 185, 187 (top), 195 (bottom), 206, 213 (bottom), 214 (top), 215 (top), 216 (top right), 218 (top), 219, 221 (centre right), 227 (bottom), 229, 230 (centre), 230 (bottom), 231 (bottom), 232, 234, 235, 237 (bottom)

LAT/Motorsport Images.com: Pages 150, 184 (top)

Red Bull Images: Pages 163 (bottom), 169 (centre)

Shutterstock: Pages 61 (bottom right), 63 (bottom)

Quarto

First published in 2025 by Ivy Press,
an imprint of The Quarto Group.
One Triptych Place, London, SE1 9SH,
United Kingdom
T (0)20 7700 9000
www.Quarto.com

EEA Representation, WTS Tax d.o.o., Žanova ulica 3, 4000 Kranj, Slovenia

Copyright © 2025 Quarto Publishing plc

All rights reserved. No part of this book may be reproduced or utilised in any form or by any means, electronic or mechanical, including photocopying, recording or by any information storage and retrieval system, without permission in writing from Ivy Press.

Every effort has been made to trace the copyright holders of material quoted in this book. If application is made in writing to the publisher, any omissions will be included in future editions.

A catalogue record for this book is available from the British Library.

ISBN 978-0-71129-848-4
Ebook ISBN 978-0-71129-849-1

10 9 8 7 6 5 4 3 2 1

Design concept by Glenn Howard
Design by Cara Rogers
Senior Designer Renata Latipova
Publisher Richard Green
Production Controller Rohana Yusof

Printed in China

MIX
Paper | Supporting responsible forestry
FSC® C016973